Patronage, Brokerage, Entrepreneurship
and the
Chinese Community of New York

Immigrant Communities & Ethnic Minorities
in the United States & Canada: 30

Series Editor: Robert J. Theodoratus
                  Department of Anthropology
                  Colorado State University
                  Fort Collins, Colorado 80523

[ISSN 0749-5951]

Patronage, Brokerage, Entrepreneurship
and the
Chinese Community of New York

Bernard Wong

AMS Press
New York

Library of Congress-in Publication Data

Wong, Bernard P.
  Patronage, brokerage, entrepreneurship, and the Chinese community of New York.

(Immigrant communities & ethnic minorities in the United States & Canada, ISSN 0749-5951; 30)
Bibliography: p.
Includes index.
  1. Chinatown (New York, N.Y.)—Economic conditions. 2. Chinatown (New York, N.Y.)—Social conditions. 3. Chinese Americans—New York (N.Y.)—Social conditions. 5. New York (N.Y.)—Economic conditions. 6. New York (N.Y.)—Social conditions.

  I. Title. II. Series
  F128.68.c47W66 1988   974.7'1   83-45363
  ISBN 0-404-19416-8

All AMS books are printed on acid-free paper that meets the guidelines for performance and durability of the Committee on Production Guidelines for Book Longevity of the Council on Library Resources.

AMS PRESS
56 East 13th Street
New York, N.Y. 10003, U.S.A.

Manufactured in the United States of America

TABLE OF CONTENTS

TABLE OF CONTENTS (Continued),

LIST OF TABLES

LIST OF TABLES (continued)

LIST OF FIGURES

LIST OF DIAGRAMS

LIST OF MAPS

ACKNOWLEDGEMENTS

The fieldwork research and the actual writing of the present dissertation have benefited from the generous help of many organizations and people. It would be impossible to thank all of them individually. A few, however, necessitate special mention. My gratitudes first to the National Science Foundation and the Ford Foundation for supporting the fieldwork research and the preparation of the manuscript.

I am indebted particularly to Professor Arnold Strickon of the Department of Anthropology who generously gave much of his time directing both the fieldwork research and the writing of this dissertation. I am grateful also to Professor Robert J. Miller and Professor Herbert S. Lewis of the Department of Anthropology for their valuable comments; to Professor Solomon B. Levine of the Department of Economics and Professor Charles Cell of the Department of Sociology for reading over the manuscript.

CHAPTER I

INTRODUCTION

The Problem

The main purpose of the present study is a descriptive analysis
of the formation and maintenance of patronage and brokerage and the role
they play in the economic adaptation of the Chinese community of New
York City.[1] Using the 1965 Immigration Law as a point of reference and
the year 1965 as a dividing point, I tentatively segment the history of
the Chinese community into two periods: 1870-1964 and 1965-present. I
shall examine, describe and compare:

1) the nature, formation and functions of various interpersonal
relationships, with special emphasis on patron-client and broker-client
relations;

2) the manipulation of these interpersonal relations, under the reinforcements and constraints inherent in both the Chinese community and
the larger society, for individual and collective adaptation; and

3) the resultant social arrangements, structural characteristics
and effect on the Chinese ethnic boundary in these two periods. The
focus of analysis is on the decision-making activities of the Chinese
and their manipulation of patronage and brokerage for entrepreneurial
pursuits.

---

[1]The term, Chinese community of New York, unless otherwise indicated,
is used throughout this study to refer to the Chinese Community on the
Lower East Side of Manhattan, New York City.

Patronage and Brokerage and the Overseas Chinese Communities

Studies on the overseas Chinese are characterized by their concern with the structural studies of kinship and clanship (Freedman 1957; Tien 1953; Amyot 1960), voluntary associations and elite groups (Tien 1953; W. Willmott 1970; Heyer 1953; Freedman 1960, 1961; Topley 1961; Tsien 1961; Skinner 1968), and acculturation and assimilation (Cheng 1948; Willmott 1960; Hsu 1971; Skinner 1967, 1968; Lee 1960). Although these studies are conducted from a structural-functional perspective and are weak in elucidating the decision-making process of the actors, they have, nevertheless, the following contributions to offer to the present study: 1) the delineation of the interrelationship between social structure and economic activities of the Chinese; 2) the perspective of viewing the overseas Chinese in relation to the larger society and their homeland; 3) they all point out the existence of some mediation mechan-isms between the Chinese and their host country and the existence of patrons and brokers in overseas Chinese communities.

1) Anthropological studies of the overseas Chinese communities are interested mainly in social structure. Thus, Tien's study of the Chinese in Sarawak (1953) is concerned with the description of the various cor-porate associations which constitute the social structure of the Chinese community. Tien then goes on to show the interrelationships between clan associations and rubber plantations of the Chinese in Sarawak. Following the framework of Tien, Jacques Amyot (1960) studies the Chinese community of Manila. He concentrates on the adaptation of Chinese kin-ship and clanship in the urban environment. The method used is structur-al comparison between Manila's Chinese kinship and clanship structures

with those in their home communities in China. Processes involved in the structural change were not dealt with. Like Tien, Amyot (1960) also examined how the various Chinese associations, family kinship and clan-ship contributed to the entrepreneurial pursuit of the Chinese by pro-viding credit, efficient price control, collective boycotting and effective mediation of conflicts. Thus, there are built-in structural features in the overseas Chinese communities favorable for entrepren-eurial activities. These pre-existing structural features can also be looked at as reinforcement and constraint factors for decision-making activities.

2) Structural studies on the overseas Chinese communities also offer us a larger perspective by which we can understand the inter-relationships between the Chinese as an ethnic group, the larger society, and the mother country as well. Methodologically, the nature of over-seas Chinese communities is such that it prevents the employment of the traditional anthropological techniques of isolating a community and describing it in its entirety as suggested by Radcliffe-Brown and Malin-owski (cf. Freedman 1963), for the study of Chinese villages. Chinese communities overseas are not Chinese villages but ethnic groups which are encapsulated in the cities. As observed by both Gluckman and Epstein (cf. Gluckman 1964), the anthropological study of social relations in complex societies should circumscribe its field in relation to specific problems and incorporate all relative facts rather than by limited by the physical boundary of a locality. Writing in "A Chinese Phase in Social Anthropology" (1963), Maurice Freedman specifically pointed out the necessity of seeing the overseas Chinese communities from a wider

perspective:

> Social relationships among overseas Chinese do not round themselves
> off neatly in suitable localities, and it is at once apparent that
> to delimit a 'community' and confine one's attention to it would
> miss the very characteristic of the society which makes it interest-
> ing: its scale and its scatter. . . . He must be mobile. . . . He
> must adjust his vision so that he may see behavior and ideas within
> the framework not only of the immediate locality but also of the
> society from which the migrants have come, of the largest territorial
> settlement within which they find themselves, and of the non-Chinese
> society in which they are embedded (Freedman 1963: 3).

Both the mother country and the host country indeed are important for the

understanding of an immigrant community. Tien (1953), Amyot (1960),

Heyer (1953), Cheng (1948) and various overseas Chinese community studies

have indicated that the traditions in their homeland shape the social

organizations of an overseas Chinese community. Thus, the various

associations which constitute the Chinese social structure in any over-

seas Chinese community appeared to be organized along traditional prin-

ciples of locality, clanship and dialect (Tien 1953; Hsu 1971; Willmott

1967, 1970; Ng 1968). To an extent, Chinese overseas communities reflect

Chinese culture, and many anthropologists (Freedman 1964; Heyer 1953;

Willmott 1970) are convinced that overseas Chinese communities could be

avenues for the understanding of Chinese culture.

Similarly, social economic, political and ecological factors of

the larger society could influence the social structure as well as the

activities of the encapsulated ethnic group. Rose Hum Lee (1960) argued

that the proliferation of Tongs in the 1930's was related to the limited

economic opportunity offered to the Chinese by the larger society.

Loewen's (1971) study on the Chinese in Mississippi demonstrated how the

elaborate caste, class and etiquette systems of Mississippi racism left

open the grocery business niche for the Chinese without substantial
white or black competition. Through the exploitation of this niche, the
Chinese in Mississippi have been able to rise to the middle class stratum.
Thus, the administrative policy, economic environment and social structure
of the larger society could provide economic opportunity for entrepreneurial response.

Glade (1967) also pointed out that entrepreneurial activities of
an ethnic group must be examined in relation to the opportunity structure
of the larger society and to the ethnic group's social structure and
ability of members of the ethnic group to respond to the need of the
larger society. It is obvious, then, that even the Schumpeterian entrepreneur needs a proper economic environment to make his creative response.
Elements in the social structure of the larger society could also affect
the social organization of the ethnic group. Willmott (1970) and Tsien
(1961) demonstrated how the political system of the larger society set
limits on the proliferation of Chinese voluntary associations in the
Chinese communities of Cambodia and Madagascar. The former also significantly pointed out that the presence of other ethnic groups in Cambodian
society could account for the lack of anti-Chinese sentiment in that
country. According to Willmott (1971), the main reason for the relative
harmony between the Chinese ethnic group and the majority of the population is the presence of a sizeable Vietnamese minority which historically
has adverse relations with Cambodians. Thus, the economic adaptive
activities of the Chinese in New York should be viewed in relation to
the larger society and to the mother country. Both do have inputs in
the maximizing activities of the Chinese in New York City. The former

could offer economic opportunities and incentives; the latter could
provide assets and act as constraint factors as well.

3) Most studies on the overseas Chinese directly or indirectly
touch upon mediating mechanisms between the Chinese community and the
host society. Thus, for instance, Jacques Amyot (1960) mentions the
Federation of the Chinese Chamber of Commerce as the overall community
organization among Chinese in the Philippines which negotiates on behalf
of the Chinese with the Philippine government. The Chinese Chambers of
Commerce in Bangkok (Skinner 1958), Singapore (Freedman 1960), and Java
(D. Willmott 1960), all have important mediation roles. In South and
North America, the mediation role falls on the Chinese Benevolent Associations. In effect, it is the leaders or officials of these associations
who shoulder all responsibilities in negotiating with the host country.
These leaders or officials are brokers, who are usually the rich Chinese
in the community.

Not only do these rich Chinese play the brokerage or mediating
functions on behalf of the Chinese communities in dealing with the host
countries, but they are also often the patrons of the community. Un-
fortunately, no anthropologists have focused their attention on patronage and brokerage in the Chinese communities. However, the existence of
patronage and brokerage in the Chinese communities has been recognized.
For instance, Tien (1957), devotes three pages to the discussion of the
patronage system of Chinese in Sarawak. At the top of the social ladder
there are the "leaders," known locally as the "back mountain" who are
the big money lenders. These leaders are the channels through which
contacts between the British Colonial Administration and the Chinese

community are made. These rich Chinese are the mediators or bridges.
Tien (1957) also pointed out that these leaders are not only the links
between the local community and the British authorities, they are also
the indispensable patrons of the community (Tien 1953). Without these
"back mountain" or leaders, no one in the Chinese community of Sarawak
can advance economically or socially. The professional advancement of
a teacher, businessman or coolie depends on the continued support of a
patron. The size of a patron's "clientele," in turn, is a gauge of
social and economic power (Tien 1953:   70).

In colonial situations, many of these influential Chinese are appointed by the colonial governments as official "leaders" of the Chinese.
Thus, in colonial times D. Willmott (1960) noted that the Dutch set up
the Chinese Captaincy in Java through which the affairs of the Chinese
were administered. During the last century in French-ruled Cambodia,
the appointed chief (by the French government) of the various Chinese
communities collected revenues and kept order as well as mediated on
behalf of the Chinese communities (D. Willmott (1970). Up until 1961
in Madagascar, these heads (appointed by the government) still performed
their mediation functions (Tsien 1961). They handle the civil affairs
and administrative documents of the Chinese, act as interpreters,
vouch for members of the community and represent the Chinese community
at official ceremonies (Tien 1961). All these appointed posts are unpaid. However, performances of these functions are rewarded with high
prestige, a reward for which many overseas Chinese compete. Thus, there
is the de facto existence of patrons who are mediators. These Chinese
are known by different names in different places as: "Captain," "President"

of the Chinese Chamber of Commerce, Captain of a captaincy, head of the community, leader or <u>Kiu Ling</u> (<u>Chiao Ling</u> 僑領 in Mandarin).

As mentioned earlier, most of the anthropological studies of overseas Chinese mention the importance of these mediators, but none studies the roles of these mediators and their activity systems. The processes involved in the formation and maintenance of these mediator positions cannot be handled by the static structural model which is followed by anthropologists who study overseas Chinese communities. The present study will pay special attention to these patrons and brokers who undertake the mediation role for the Chinese community in New York City.

Patrons and Brokers in New York's Chinatown

There is extensive patronage in the Chinese community of New York. Phrases used in the community indicate patron-client relations are numerous. The commonly known phrases are:

<u>Chu Hak Kwang Hei</u>[1] (主客關係) - "host-guest relation,"

<u>Chu Ku Kwang Hei</u>[2] (主顧關係) - "host-client relation,"

<u>Bun Chu Kwang Hei</u>[3] (賓主關係) - "guest-host relation."

The patrons in the community are referred to as "back mountain," "back stage," "big person," "big shot," and "Kiu Ling" (leaders of the overseas Chinese). The patrons are usually leaders of the various Chinese Associations, Tongs, Churches. They are rich men and businessmen

---

[1] This is a Cantonese pronunciation. In Mandarin, it is pronounced as <u>Chu Ka Kuang Hsi</u>.

[2] This is a Cantonese pronunciation. In Mandarin, it is pronounced as <u>Chu Ku Kuang Hsi</u>.

[3] It is pronounced as <u>Pin Chu Kuang Hsi</u> in Mandarin.

who dispense favors, protection, connections, service, material resources
and perform the mediation function. These patrons control both wealth
and political power and are linked horizontally and vertically to members
of the community. Thus, they can reach the lowest social stratum of the
community as well as the underground elements of the community.

Rose Lee (1960) and Virginia Heyer (1954) both reported the existence of patrons and brokers in the United States Chinese communities.
Stuart H. Cattell (1962) specifically mentioned the existence of a power
elite and their control of political power and wealth in New York's
Chinatown. Of interest is the "big shot" which Cattell described. "Big
shots" are the association and Tong leaders (Cattell 1962). Being a
social service oriented study, Cattell's Health, Welfare and Social
Organization in Chinatown, New York (1962), is interested in elucidating
attitudes toward and the use and non-use of health facilities by the
Chinese in relation to the social structure of the Chinese community.
However, in one of his concluding remarks, Cattell does mention that the
ineffective use of health services and the lack of success in the various
health programs organized by the larger society are due to the lack of
support by the power elite, which include the "big shots."

Theoretical Orientation

Three groups of relevant concepts and theories are selected for this
study. First is the group of concepts and theories related to patronage,
brokerage and their operationalization. The second group of concepts is
related to the use of patron-client and broker-client relations for goal-
seeking activities. The third group of concepts is selected for the
analysis of the effects of patronage and brokerage on the social rela-

tions between the Chinese and the larger society.

1) Patronage, Brokerage as Concepts:

Patronage and brokerage studies have been conducted in different parts of the world: Latin America (Mintz and Wolf 1950; Forster 1961, 1963; Wolf 1956, 1966; Leeds 1964; Anderson 1964; Strickon and Greenfield 1972);Europe (Boissevain 1966, 1968; Silverman 1965; Campbell 1964; Kenny 1960); Asia (Scott 1972; Lande 1964); and North America (Paine 1971). Although the patron-client relationship has not been treated exclusively by scholars of Chinese communities, its existence has been recognized by many social scientists (Tien 1953; Amyot 1960; Cattell 1962; R. Lee 1960; Tsien 1961).

The concepts of patrons and brokers have been defined by different authors (Foster 1963; Wolf 1966; Paine 1971; Mayer 1967; Kenny 1960; Geertz 1960; Silverman 1965). For the present study, the definitions of patrons and brokers are adopted from those defined by Mayer in his "Patrons and Brokers: Rural Leadership in Four Overseas Communities" (1967). According to Mayer (1967: 168), the patron recruits followers by his powers to dispense favors. The broker is a middleman who attracts followers through his ability to influence the person who controls the resources and favor (Mayer 1967). Thus, the patron-client relation implies the asymmetry of status; broker-client relationship does not. The patron-client relation consists of a mutual tacit agreement between two persons of unequal status in which the superior status person dispenses favors, protection, connections, and service. A broker, on the other hand, considers himself a mediator and advisor, instrumental to his client not necessarily because of his status and wealth.

Two essential aspects of the patron-client or broker-client relations are <u>transaction</u> and <u>prestation</u>. The underlying assumptions of these concepts are: 1) human behavior is purposeful and maximizing; 2) human behavior is to be viewed in terms of reciprocal exchange; 3) social forms are the outcome of institutionalized interactions (Homans 1958; Barth 1963, 1966). All these assumptions are to be embraced by the present study of patron-client and broker-client relations.

The concept of transaction as defined by Barth (1966) implies <u>reciprocal prestation</u>. In each transaction, actors consistently try to assure themselves that the value gained is greater than the value lost. The continuation of the reciprocal exchange of <u>prestation</u> (gifts) depends on whether it is mutually beneficial to the participants. If one participant desires to terminate the relationship, he can deliberately fail to reciprocate a prestation and thus signal the termination of the relationship. However, two points have to be made. First, reciprocity does not have to maintain a perfect balance (Sahlins 1965; Paine 1971; Strickon and Greenfield 1972). That is to say, reciprocity does not mean an unconditional one-for-one exchange, since interpersonal exchange is not market exchange and cannot be reduced to a financial common demoninator (Aubey, Kyle and Strickon 1974). Second, the complete balancing of <u>prestation</u> can be perceived as a signal to terminate the relationship (Aubey, Kyle and Strickon 1974).

Several studies which used these concepts of <u>transaction</u> and reciprocal prestation to analyze interpersonal relationships are particularly important to the present study. These include Burton Benedict's "Family Firms and Economic Development;" Fredrik Barth's <u>Models of Social Organ-</u>

izalization. These studies provide analytic techniques in the study of the processes involved in the maintenance and operation of family firms, elite networks, kinship networks, patron-client diads. Procedurally, the present study will attempt to use the concept of transaction and prestation to describe in a general way the operation of various inter-personal relationships, familial networks, kinship networks, friendship networks, patron-client and broker-client relationships. The second step is to focus on the anlysis of the various forms of patron-client and broker-client relationships and their manipulation for economic activities for the establishment and organization of firms, financing, and dispute settlement.

The general framework adopted for the operationalization of patron-age and brokerage as transactions is presented in Structure and Process in Latin America (Strickon and Greenfield 1972: Introduction). Accord-ing to this framework, three interacting variables have to be examined: 1) the cultural tradition - the idiom in which the negotiations and transactions are conducted; 2) the system of formal position within the insitutional system; and 3) the resources available to the specific actors that may be employed in them in the transactional process. Thus, the operation of patronage and brokerage in the Chinese community will be discussed in relation to the following variables. First is the idiom or the content and symbols of the cultural tradition. In the case of the Chinese, Kam Ching[1] (感情) - sentimental warmth, Yee Hey[2] (義氣)-

---

[1] In Mandarin it is pronounced as Kan Ching.

[2] In Mandarin it is pronounced as I Chi.

trusting righteousness, and <u>Yang Ching</u>[1] (人情) - human feelings are
the essential elements of this idiom. These elements provide the basis
for acceptance andcontinuation of transactions between actors. The
second variable is position and the accompanying rights and obligations.
Social positions of the individuals in various community organizations
and agencies could be assets and constraint factors in the making of
decisions as well. The third variable is resource. In the Chinese
community of New York, resource includes capital, manpower, language
ability, information, property, expertise, and connections.

2) The Use of Interpersonal Relationships for Goal Seeking:

The host of literature dealing with the manipulation of interpersonal
relationships for political and economic activities (Davenport 1960;
Gould 1969; Aubey, Kyle and Strickon 1974; Coombs 1973; Dirks 1972; Mayer
1966; Leeds 1964; Barth 1963; Plotinicov 1967; Gulliver 1971; Barnes
1969; Epstein 1969; Wheeldon 1969; Kapferer 1969; Boswell 1969; Mitchel
1969) suggest useful clues for the present study. Among them, works
which concentrate on patrons, elite, brokers, change agents, and entrepreneurs are particularly of relevance. The paper by Aubey, Kyle and
Strickon (1974) on the investment behavior of the elite in Latin America
illustrates the circulation of information within a circle of trusted
insiders and shows that their access to certain exclusive kinds of information is vital for the accumulation of power and wealth. Leeds (1964)
also demonstrates how the Brazilian elite manipulate network relations
to obtain strategic information important for decision-making activities

[1]In Mandarin it is pronounced as <u>Jen Ching</u>.

in the political and economic fields. It is precisely because of the easy access to strategic information that the entrepreneurs, elite, patrons and leaders can implement their "bridging" act. In fact, the word "entrepreneur" in both the economic and anthropological senses implies the function of bridging. Anthropologically, the entrepreneur is a mediator who bridges the gap in communications between the larger and the smaller structure (Stuart 1972: 33). Economically, the entrepreneur fills the gap in economic structures by allocating skill, service and resources through a series of renovative and risk-taking activities (Belshaw 1955; Barth 1963). Ethnographically, entrepreneurs are often found in the persons of elite (Leed 1964; Cochran and Reina 1962; Hoselitz 1963; Skinner 1958; Strickon 1972). My previous fieldwork in the Chinese communities of Manila and Lima indicates that entrepreneurs are brokers, patrons and change agents (Wong 1969, 1971). In the present study of patrons and brokers, particular attention will be paid to their coordination and manipulation of patron-client and broker-client relationships, social claims and other interpersonal relationships for entrepreneurial activities (cf. Barth 1963; Strickon 1972).

The works of Benedict (1969), Bennett and Ishino (1963) provided special direction and methodological procedure for the study of an important aspect of entrepreneurship: establishing and organizing of business firms. Benedict focuses attention on the manipulation of familiar networks for gain-seeking pursuit in the family firm environment. Bennett and Ishino's, Paternalism in Japanese Industry (1963) which delineated in detail the various paternalistic and patron-client arrangements in the organization of the Japanese forestry industry has provided useful guidelines for the examination of the diverse use of patron-client relations in the establishment and management of Chinese firms in New York City.

3) Patronage, Brokerage and Ethnic Boundary:

A corollary of this study, as mentioned earlier, is to explore the interrelationship between patronage (and brokerage) and ethnic boundary. Since both patrons and brokers are links between the community and the larger society, it is therefore likely that their activities have some effect on the ethnic boundary of the Chinese.

Following the usage of Fredrick Barth (1969), the concept of ethnic boundary means the social boundary which defines an ethnic group; it may or may not have territorial counterparts. As suggested by Barth and his colleagues in Ethnic Groups and Boundaries (1969), ethnic boundary maintenance of the Chinese will be viewed in relation to criteria and signals for identification among the Chinese, the rules and strategies adopted in dealing with members and outsiders, and in particular, the organization of behavior and social interaction which allows the persistence of cultural difference. Further, Barth (1969: 33) pointed out that the pursuance of different adaptive strategies will have different effects on the ethnic boundary. Following this approach, the present study will first delineate the differential use of Chinese ethnicity: values, social relations, ethnic identity, ethnic symbols and ethnic associations as resources used by the patrons and brokers for goal-seeking activities. It will then describe their resultant effects on the Chinese ethnic boundary (cf. Chapter 7).

In addition to Barth, the works of Greeley (1971, 1972); Novak (1971);
Ianni (1973); Glazer and Moynihan (1963); Lee (1960); Douglass and Lyman
(1973); and Yin (1973) are revealing in their treatment of the use of
ethnic identity as a resource for decision-making activities and on the
persistence of ethnic groups in the United States. These works provide
many clues for the understanding and analysis of the boundary maintenance
mechanism of Chinese in New York.

Methodology — Fieldwork Techniques

Data on which the present study is based was obtained from fieldwork
conducted from July 1972 to June 1973 in New York City. New York's
Chinatown was selected for study for many reasons.

First, political problems in the Chinese community of Lima where
initial fieldwork was conducted forced a change of fieldwork locality.
The change was suggested by both my major professor and my contact in
Peru.

Second, as a native-born Chinese from Kwangtung province (the province from which must New York Chinese immigrated), a certain familiarity
was already established with the home communities of overseas Chinese in
New York. Personal knowledge of overseas Chinese in New York could
therefore be obtained through classmates, friends, and kinsmen.

Third, previous fieldwork done in Manila and Lima provided first-
hand experience of overseas Chinese communities elsewhere and would
prove beneficial to my understanding of the Chinese community in New
York City.

Fourth, I speak both the Mandarin and the Cantonese dialect. The

latter is the <u>lingua franca</u> of the present day Chinatown, New York.
The necessity of mastering the language of the natives under study has
been noted by anthropologists if one is to undertake fieldwork activity.
Mastery of dialect is particularly important in conducting anthropological fieldwork in overseas Chinese communities. Chinese who cannot speak
the dialect of the Chinese community of New York are excluded from many
social activities in the community such as joining the various Chinese
associations. It also makes it difficult to find employment in the
community. Dialect ability is an aid in asking questions correctly and
idiomatically, giving instructions, understanding, and establishing
rapport with people of the Chinese community. Stories concerning discrimination against non-Cantonese speakers by Cantonese have been abundant. Many Mandarin speaking anthropologists and Mandarin speaking Chinese
diplomats confided that they did not receive equal courtesy and cooperation extended to other Cantonese speakers by Cantonses restaurants,
associations, and even individual Chinese of New York's Chinatown.
These non-Cantonese speakers were and still are ridiculed as not being
able to speak "Chinese."

Fifth, financial support from foundations was available for the
study of New York's Chinatown. Special thanks is offered to the National
Science Foundation and the Ford Foundation for the fieldwork and dissertation grants awarded for this study.

The fieldwork techniques followed include: 1) participant observation; 2) in-depth personal interviews; 3) the use of census, statistical,
historical and biographical data; 4) the use of relevant written sources
including local Chinese newspapers; 5) the use of a group of master

informants to evaluate the accuracy of data.

Participant observation: Copious information regarding social life
and customs of the Chinese in New York was obtained from conversations
with people in Chinese restaurants, observations of people in different
settings such as: the subway station, in churches, on the streets, and
in various Chinese shops of Chinatown. Since my research interests were
on the interrelationships of interpersonal relationships (particularly
patron-client and broker-client relationships), and the economic activities of the Chinese, fieldwork focused on the following distinct but
related activities:

First, all Chinese family regional, dialect, and trade associations
were systematically covered, including the Chinese Benevolent Association.
Interaction patterns of the Chinese in these associations and the way
they used these associations for recreational, ritual and economic
activities was observed.

Second, considerable time was spent participating and observing
the operation of various Chinese garment factories, laundry firms,
restaurants, grocery stores and gift stores. While observing these
establishments, I worked in such varied capacities as voluntary English
tutor, office clerk, and assisted in obtaining immigration and school
information for the employees of these firms.

Third, through the help of friends and the priests of the Transfiguration Church, numerous visits were made to the families of Chinatown.

Fourth, first-hand experience was gained on how Chinese deal with
the United States courts and agencies of the government.

Fifth, visitations were made to most of the social agencies and community service organizations of Chinatown. Due to the limitation of time, I could only participate in some of the community meetings. However, the experience obtained from these meetings is useful both in understanding the community and the analysis of my data as well.

Sixth, I participated with my friends' families in the observance of the traditional Chinese festivals, and I attended numerous engagement, wedding, birthday celebrations. Such participation provided insight into the dynamics of interpersonal interactions in the community. Many intimate accounts about the manipulation of social relations for goal-seeking activities were imparted to me through my personal participation and observation.

In-Depth Personal Interviews: Most of the people given in-depth interviews were friends and friends of friends. Among these interviewees were oldtime family friends who knew me when I was a child in China. They were most willing to talk about their career histories and success stories. Moreover, they provided introductions to many resourceful informants who normally did not give interviews to outsiders.

In order to neutralize biases, an effort was made to select inter-viewees of different social and economic backgrounds. With cooperation from friends, older, middle age, and teenage informants were interviewed. They included members of the Golden Age Club, members of street gangs, restaurant employees, professionals of the community, bankrupt gamblers, and successful entrepreneurs. Whenever possible, the personal histories of these informants were solicited.

Informants from the Golden Age Club and the Senior Citizenship Program of the Community Center of Greater Chinatown turned out to be valuable informants who provided insightful information about the past and present leaders of the Chinese community and the entrepreneurial activities of these leaders. Of course, many of the things they said could be classified as "noise" or "gossip," and interviewing these retired old men was generally time-consuming. Needless to say, the information obtained from them had to be double checked.

Census, Statistical, and Historical Data: The New York Public Library and the Historical Society of New York were consulted for relevant census and historical documents about Chinatown, New York. The Chinese Chamber of Commerce, the Chinese Garment Maker Association, the American-Chinese Restaurant Association, the Chinese Laundry Association, and the International Ladies Garment Workers Union, Local 23-25, graciously permitted use of their journals, and provided relevant statistical information. The Asian Resource Center of the Basement Workshop in Chinatown gave full access to their statistical and documentary collections. Two of the most important reports which I had access to were: the Chinatown Study Group Report (1969) and the Chinatown Health Project (1970). Both of them contained quantitative and qualitative data of Chinatown relating to demography, housing, employment, family and health care.

A copy of Who's Who of the Chinese in New York (1918) which was obtained from a rare book store in New York turned out to provide valuable historical information regarding the community. Another important his-

torical source consulted was <u>Chinatown Inside Out</u> (Leong 1936) which provided insight into the "wheelings and dealings" of the power elite of
early Chinatown, New York.

Old newspaper articles about New York's Chinatown collected for
many years by the staff of the Chatham Street Branch of the New York
Public Library were made available through the courtesy of the senior
librarian of the branch.

<u>The Use of Written Sources</u>: Magazines, dissertation, books, pam-
phlets on the Chinese in America and in New York were consulted. The
constitutions and by-laws of the various Chinese associations, when
available, were duplicated and consulted. The local Chinese newspapers,
invitations, announcements and letters were diligently collected and
read.

<u>The Use of a Group of Master Informants</u>: This group of people con-
tained old-timers and insiders of Chinatown, and I consider them as my
master informants. They helped evaluate and analyze my findings. I am
indeed fortunate to have their cooperation. Since they play an important role in my fieldwork, I feel it necessary to give brief accounts of
their backgrounds. For the sake of anonymity, their names will not be
revealed and some details about their social and economic background will
be omitted.

<u>Informant A</u>: born in Kwangtung Province. He was educated in Canton
and Hong Kong. He has lived in New York for twenty years and is the
owner of a garment factory, a boutique, and a real estate firm. His
knowledge about the operation of garment factories was particularly

helpful in understanding the Chinese in this business.

Informant B: Born in the United States. He was educated both in China and the U.S. He is manager of an American branch bank in China-town.

Informant C: Born in China. He received his bachelor degree in a college in Canton and earned an advanced graduate degree in business in the U.S. He is a secretary of the Chinese Chamber of Commerce.

Informant D: Born and educated in China. He is an official of a labor union who is familiar with the problems of the employers and employees in the Chinese garment factories.

Informant E: A Chinese-American. He was sent back to China during his teenage years by his parents to receive Chinese education. However, his professional degree was obtained from a college in New York. He is the owner of an accounting firm.

Informant F: He is a Catholic priest who is the founder of a well-respected community service organization.

Informant G: Born in China but lived in New York's Chinatown for more than twenty years. He is the owner of a grocery store and has been elected leader of several family, merchant and regional associations at different times.

Informant H: Born and educated in China and came to New York ten years ago. He is the manager of a Chinese restaurant and has been in the Chinese restaurant business since shortly after his arrival in New York. He is active in the community affairs and is a frequent contributor to the editorial page of a well-established Chinese newspaper in New York.

Informant I: Born in China but educated in the U.S. He is the
organizer of a social agency in Chinatown. He is well versed in social
work and is familiar with the workings of the various social agencies in
Chinatown.

This group of master informants not only provided valuable information about their respective trades and professions but also gave their
insider views of the community. They were my consultants for some of
my fieldwork activities and have patiently helped me ascertain the valid-
ity of some of my findings.

Plan of this Study

The present study consists of eight chapters. In addition to this
introductory chapter, the rest of the chapters are as follows:

Chapter 2: The Setting. This chapter will discuss the establishment of New York's Chinatown in the 1870's, its subsequent development,
the Immigration Law of 1965 and its impact on the physical boundary,
demographic composition, and social welfare. Interaction patterns in the
family and the stratification systems of the community are presented as
background information for the various transactional relationships discussed in the future chapters.

Chapter 3: Social Organizations and Economic Activities of Chinatown: 1870-1964. Patterns of social organizations and **economic activ-**
ities of the Chinese are viewed in relation to the traditions of their
homeland and the opportunity structure of the larger society in this
period. The contributions of the various Chinese associations to the
social and economic activities of the Chinese are discussed.

Chapter 4: Transactional Relationship and the Entrepreneurial Pursuit of the Chinese in 1870-1964. This chapter will discuss the operation and manipulation of various transactional relationships (particularly the patron-client relationship) in the establishment of firms, capital formation, employment and dispute settlements in this period.

Chapter 5: New Resources in the Socio-Economic Environment of 1965-1974. Chinatown has undergone changes since its inception. However, major changes took place only after 1965 with the implementation of new immigration policies. This chapter will focus its attention on the new resources and constraints instrumental for goal-seeking activities. These new social and economic resources will be seen as the results brought about by structural changes in community and by new policies toward ethnic groups initiated by the larger society.

Chapter 6: Transactional Relationship and the Entrepreneurial Pursuit of the Chinese in a New Era: 1965-1974. Various transactional relationships, particularly patron-client and broker-client relationships, will be discussed. The operation, formation and manipulation of patron-client and broker-client relationships in the organization and establishment of firms, capital formation, employment, and dispute settlement will be discussed in relation to the changed social and economic environment of this era.

Chapter 7: Patronage, Brokerage and the Ethnic Boundary. This chapter will discuss the effects on the Chinese ethnic boundary brought about by the pursuance of different adaptive strategies and the differential use of ethnicity: identity, values, symbols, ethnic associations, and social relations for goal-seeking activities by the patrons and brokers of the community.

Chapter 8: <u>Conclusion</u>. This concluding chapter will summarize briefly the differences in the manipulation of patronage and brokerage for economic adaptation in the two periods: 1870-1964 and 1965-1974. Major conclusions drawn from the findings are: 1) the continued formation of patronage within the various Chinese institutions and the continued use of patronage for economic activities; 2) the gradual takeover by brokers in the performance of functions traditionally performed within the province of the patrons; 3) patronage and brokerage as vehicles for cultural stability and change. The wider theoretical implications of this study are also presented in this chapter.

CHAPTER 2

THE SETTING - CHINATOWN AND ITS HISTORY

Chinese in America

The earliest Chinese-American contact began in 1784 when the first
American trading vessel landed at Canton. However, the first wave of
Chinese emigration to the United States in noticeable numbers did not
start until the 1850's. Why did the Chinese leave China? Why did the
Chinese come to the United States in particular? To answer these questions, it is necessary to view the Chinese migration in a larger context:
socio-economic conditions in the Old Country, opportunities in the New
Country, and the international colonial movement. In a sense, migration
is an adaptive decision, a considered choice based on dissatisfactions
with present parameters, calculation on available alternatives, and
visions of more desirable possibilities. Thus factors inherent in the
social and economic structure of the Old Country could act as a force
compelling the actors to seek opportunity elsewhere. The information
about specific opportunities in the New Country and activities of the
international labor brokers could act as a force attracting the Chinese
migration movement.

Until the nineteenth century few Chinese went overseas. First,
there was such a strong feeling about the Middle Kingdom and her
superiority that anyone who left it to live among the foreigners over
seas was thought to be degrading himself (Tien 1953; Morse 1918). Second, there were stiff penalties under the Ching Dynasty for Chinese who

left the country (Morse 1918). In fact, until 1894, any Chinese who left China was committing a capital offence (Morse 1918). Third, for a long time the Chinese government did not have any representatives overseas to protect Chinese abroad. Any Chinese who went overseas did so at his own risk and had to rely on other Chinese immigrants for protection (Morse 1918).

In addition to legal difficulties and emotional stress, there was the hardship of travel. Travel by junk or steamboat was a hardship. The traveling conditions for the Chinese contract labor were so abhorent that many Chinese laborers died on their way to their destinations. One such journey to Peru caused the death of more than two hundred Chinese laborers (Tien 1953; Morse 1918). This was a risk which had to be taken into consideration by the Chinese who wanted to go abroad. Living in a strange land without knowing the language and customs was another serious problem.

Despite all these problems and hardships, many Chinese still made the decision to go abroad. The problems encountered by some Chinese in their homeland were far more serious and numerous. These problems can be considered as the impetus which propelled the Chinese to migrate abroad. First among these forces was the economic pressure (T. Cheng 1923; Wu 1958). Poverty and overpopulation were so great in the nineteenth century in China that they need no specific elaboration. Second of the forces was the Taiping Rebellion of 1840 which had a devastating effect on the economy of China (Tien 1953; T. Cheng 1923; Wu 1958). Losses resulting from the plunder of war and natural calamities had also ruined the livelihood of many. This forced many Chinese to look elsewhere to find their fortunes.

Overseas opportunities were known to the Chinese in the nineteenth century, especially to those in the coastal regions of Fukien and Kwangtung. The major areas to which the Chinese migrated were the Pacific Islands, Latin America, and the United States. Traditionally, the South Seas was a favorite place for the Fukienese, Tiochow and the Hakka to migrate (Tien 1953; Amyot 1960). Cantonese from Chung San, and Nam Hoi went to Latin America (Ho 1959, 1967). Most of the Chinese from Sze Yap and Sam Yap districts south of Canton came to the United States (R. Lee 1960; Wu 1958; Heyer 1953). People from the same locality of origin tended to form clusters in overseas Chinese communities. This was due, as shall be seen later, to the tendency of the Chinese to travel and sponsor friends and relatives who spoke the same dialect and were from the same district in China. Once a stream of emigration began in a given location, it tended to continue to flow from the same source. Since the people from the provinces of Kwangtung and Fukien were the first to emigrate, they established the patterns and were the principal constituents of the overseas Chinese communities.

In the case of the United States, the natural outcome of such a migration pattern was the homogeneity of population in the Chinese communities. They were mostly from the provinces of Kwangtung, in particular the Sze Yap and Sam Yap[1] districts south of Canton (D. Cheng 1948; T. Cheng 1923; Heyer 1953; R. Lee 1960; Wu 1958).

There are other factors which activated and facilitated the migration of the Chinese to the United States. One of them was the net-

---

[1]The Sze Yap districts include the counties of Toy-shan, Sun-wui, Hoi-ping and Hok-shan. The Sam Yap districts are the counties of Nam-hoi, Pun-yu and Shun-tak.

work of informal relations which functioned both as a source of information and of assistance. According to Chen's <u>Chinese Migrations</u> (1923),
one of the principal causes of the Chinese emigration was previous connections. Connections included kinship, friendship, patron-client relationships and even classmates. Other causes such as bad conduct, local
disturbances, and family quarrels could act to trigger the decision to
emigrate.

Economic stress at home and the hope of gain abroad does not explain
why the Chinese selected the United States as a destination for migration.
International labor brokers were active in the two coastal regions of
China: Fukien and Kwangtung. Through the intensive activities of these
labor peddlers, many Chinese were recruited to work in Java, Peru, British
Guiana and Cuba. Those who came to the United States were chiefly attracted by the "gold rush" in California and by the advertisements put up by
the American mining and railway companies (Conway 1971; Brownell 1856;
Wu 1958; R. Lee 1960).

The economic needs of the United States in the nineteenth century
acted as a magnet which attracted the Chinese. American and Chinese
transportation agencies also facilitated the Chinese migration to the
United States by providing passage and making special arrangements for
travelling such as advanced payment by relatives in America (Wu 1958;
R. Lee 1960). Many incoming immigrants were paid in advance by their
relatives and/or the employing companies in the United States. Thus,
the Chinese migration to the United States in the nineteenth century was
caused by push and pull, the push of the Old Country and the pull of the
New Country. Between 1850 and 1890 Chinese immigration continued to in-

crease, peaking in 1890.

TABLE 1

CHINESE IMMIGRANTS TO THE UNITED STATES
FROM 1860-1940

Year	Number of Immigrants
1860	34,933
1870	63,199
1880	105,465
1890	107,488
1900	89,863
1910	71,531
1920	61,639
1930	74,954
1940	77,504

Source: U.S. Census of Population, 1940.

Before 1890, most of the Chinese who migrated to the United
States lived mainly in California and other Pacific coastal regions of
the United States.   Only after the 1882 anti-Chinese campaign and the
subsequent passage of the Chinese Exclusion Law, did Chinese immigrants
start to disperse into different parts of the country.   The dispersion
of the Chinese and the resulting Chinese influx into New York City can
also be considered as a collective adaptive device which will be elabor-
ated upon in the following section.

Chinese in New York City

New York City Chinatown before 1965

The history of New York's Chinatown can be traced back to the 1870
The earliest Chinese resident of New York is said to be that of Lee Ah-bo
(Berger 1957; Beck 1898) who came to New York City in 1850 via the S.S.

"Valencia" from San Francisco. He was reported to be a cook, then entered the tea business and died at the age of ninety in the state hospital for the criminally insane (Beck 1898). The second Chinese resident who settled in the Chinatown area of New York, according to Louis Beck (1898), was Loy Hoy Sing who lived on Cherry Street in 1862. The earliest Chinese resident of Mott Street is supposed to have been Ah Ken who started to live there in 1858. However, noticeable numbers of Chinese came to New York only after the 1884 anti-Chinese campaign in California. The Chinese population in New York in 1890 was 2,559. The majority of them seemed to settle around the lower end of Mott Street, Park Street and Doyer Street (see Map 1) (Beck 1898; Berger 1957; Kung 1962). These streets constituted the early Chinatown. From this core area, it slowly increased in size. By 1898 New York's China- town covered the entire triangular space bounded by Mott, Pell and Doyer Streets and Chatham Square and included Bayard and Baxter Streets. (See Map 1.)

Map 1

New York City's Chinatown

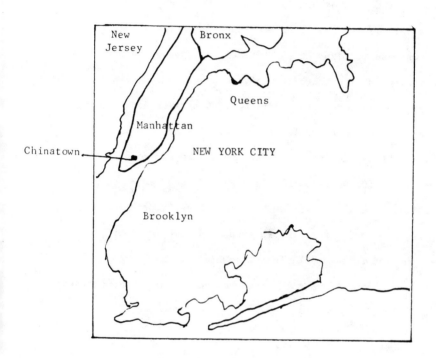

The development of New York's Chinatown from 1879 to 1965 can best be discussed in terms of three major historical events: the Exclusion Law of 1884, the Second World War, and the 1965 immigration law.

From 1870-1884: From its inception, the Chinese community of New York has been described as a racially closed community. Thus, for example, on July 26, 1873, there was an article in the New York Times describing the Chinese as an unassimilated group in New York City, composed exclusively of males who made their earnings either as servants, cooks or stewards in hotels, clubhouses or steamboats, or be selling Chinese candy. The same article also estimated the Chinese population in New York City to be around 500.

From 1884-1965: During this period the Chinese population in New York City steadily increased from 500 in 1873 to 12,753 in 1940. (See Table 2). While the number of Chinese in New York City increased during these years, the number of Chinese in the United States actually decreased. What factors account for such a rapid increase of Chinese population in New York City in 1890? This question can be answered within an adaptation framework, taking into consideration the resources and constraints available to the Chinese in a specific historical context.

TABLE 2

CHINESE POPULATION, 1870-1960

Year	New York City	United States
1870	120	63,199
1880	853	106,465
1890	2,559	107,488
1900	6,321	89,863
1910	4,614	77,531
1920	5,042	61,639
1930	8,414	74,954
1940	12,753	77,504
1950	18,998	117,629
1960	32,831	237,292

Source: U.S. Census of Population 1960.

Unemployment resulting from the completion of the Central Pacific
Railway in 1869 and the closing of many mining companies in this period
created a hot bed for racial unrest. This was reinforced by the fact
that very few Chinese returned to China due to the persistence of poverty and economic stress in China. Many of the Chinese, as well as many
white laborers, had to leave the railroads and mines to look for employment in California. According to various authors (Sandmeyer 1939; Wu
1958), economic competition precipitated the anti-Chinese movement and
the passage of the Exclusion Law. "The Chinese must go!" was a slogan
echoed back and forth in California. This sentiment was so strong that
many white employers were even afraid to employ any Chinese laborers.
White laborers often considered the Chinese potential rivals of employment, for the Chinese worked hard and were willing to accept low wages.
Resentment sometimes vented itself in persecution and even massacre in

some places.[1] Despite the Chinese Exclusion Law, economic difficulties,

and racist sentiments in the population, Chinese immigration continued,

but in an illegal manner. According to Wu (1958), there were three routes

by which Chinese immigrants were smuggled into the United States. These

were the Canadian, Mexican and West Indian routes. It is estimated that

a considerable number of Chinese were smuggled in illegally via these

three routes (Wu 1958).

Due to anti-Chinese resentment in California, the alternatives for

a Chinese were: stay in California; return to China; and leave California.

The majority of Chinese chose to leave California. They devised a new

adaptive strategy, geographical dispersion and occupation adaptation.

Since 1880, Chinese had been departing from the Pacific coastal states

and migrating to other parts of the country, Before 1880 more than 80

percent of the Chinese in the United States were concentrated in the

Pacific coastal area, particularly in the state of California. The Chi-

nese soon realized that the concentration of such a large number of their

kind in an anti-Chinese environment was disadvantageous to their survival

because it accentuated their high "visibility" (Park 1926; Wu 1958).

Geographical adaptation as an adaptive strategy explains why the Chinese

had to scatter themselves around the country, but it does not explain

why the Chinese came to New York City in particular.

New York City was attractive to the Chinese immigrants for many

reasons. First, it is a vast city with many different races. A handful

---

[1]As a result of the anti-Chinese movement and the Exclusion Law, Chinese in the 1890's experienced extreme hardships, even massacre. The infamous Chinese massacre took place at Rock Springs, Wyoming, on September
2, 1885 (Sandmeyer 1869; Calin 1887; Danton 1931; Wu 1958).

of newly arrived immigrants would not be highly visible in such a large
city. Second, New York City, being located on the East Coast, was in-
fluened less by the anti-Chinese sentiment of California. Finally, New
York City offered more economic opportunity for Chinese who did not want
to be laborers.

The adaptive strategy for the Chinese after the Chinese Exclusion
Law was not just geographical dispersion but also included economic improvement and security. Geographical relocation also meant job relocation, and not every state needed oriental laborers. In order to avoid
competition with white laborers in the labor market, the Chinese sought
to find a new niche which was not in direct conflict with the white
laborers. Moreover, the unpleasant memory of the consequences of competition with whites in the labor market in California was still fresh.
All these were factors which induced the Chinese to develop a new survival
technique--occupational specialization.

After 1890, the Chinese in America gradually disengaged themselves
from industries such as mining and started to enter non-competitive
businesses such as laundries and restaurants (Wu 1958). Chinese restaurants and laundries remain today the most important businesses in the
Chinese community of New York.

Not only were occupational choices limited to the Chinese during
the late eighteen nineties, but the scale of the Chinese businesses were
also small. However, most of the Chinese were not interested in large
scale operations. They were content to run small firms. For most of
the Chinese in those days did not consider the United States as their
permanent home. They intended to live a life of elegant retirement in

China as soon as they accumulated enough wealth. Thus, the Chinese in
New York during this period were sojourners who were not interested in
political or social participation in their host country and made no deliberate effort to assimilate (Wu 1958). Their longing for their home
country was so strong that many who could not leave this country while
still living, left the request in their wills that they be buried in
China or that their remains be exhumed after a certain number of years
in the United States and then be shipped back to China to be reburied
at an opportune time (Heyer 1953).

In terms of origin, more than 99 percent of the Chinese were from
Kwangtung Province and the remaining were from Fukien and other parts of
China. Moreover, among the 99 percent of those from the Province of
Kwangtung, 80 percent of those were from the county of Toysan; the remaining were from Sun-wui, Hoi-ping, Hok-san, Nan-hoi, Pun-yu, Shun-tak
counties of the Kwantgung Province (Heyer 1953; Wu 1958). Since most of
the Chinese in New York City are from Toysan, it was natural that Toysanese was the lingua franca of this community. The Toysan dialect is not
the standard Cantonese spoken in the city of Canton but a variation of
the Cantonese dialect. In fact, there was no mutual intelligibility
between Toysanese and standard Cantonese. Thus, in order to be accepted
into the community in those days, a Cantonese had to learn the Toysan
dialect. There was an anecdote related to me by my informants about a
Mandarin-speaking Chinese ordering his food in a Toysanese restaurant
being reprimanded thus, "What a shame, a Chinese who cannot even speak
the Chinese language."

In terms of occupation, the majority of the Chinese during this period were engaged in the operation of small laundries and restaurants. Again it was the Toysanese who dominated these two trades. In terms of education, very few of the Chinese had higher educations. They originally intended to work as laborers in the United States. This explains partially why so few of them could speak good English. After they made their occupational choice by entering the laundry and restaurant businesses, they were not forced by their occupation to improve their English ability, since there was no great demand for English-speaking people in these fields. A minimal command of the English language was enough to enable them to communicate with their customers. Whenever they had leisure time, they came to Chinatown for recreation. To eat a hearty meal in a Chinese restaurant after a week's hard work, to socialize with their friends and relatives at the associations, to play a game of Mahjong at a friend's house, these were the favorite pastimes. Thus, in neither in business nor recreation was there any need to develop skill in the English language.

The population of Chinatown before 1965 was predominently adult male. It was no wonder that there were no juvenile delinquents in those days. On the other hand, the absence of family life and children were considered by many to be the main factors in the non-assimilation of the Chinese in New York City during this period. Schwartz (1948) argued that urban American culture relied heavily upon two institutions: the public school system and the neighborhood settlement houses, as acculturative agents. "Having few women and children in its population," observed Schwartz, "the people toward whom the efforts of these insti-

tutions are primarily directed, the Chinese in New York, have largely
escaped these institutions." This line of reasoning is not without its
merit, but it would not be taken as the only reason for the non-assimilation of the Chinese in New York. There were other factors such as:
social organizations, the systems of patronage and brokerage, education,
attitudes of the larger society toward the Chinese and vice versa. All
these factors had a role to play in the assimilation of the Chinese in
New York City.

New York City's Chinatown after 1965

New York City's Chinatown has changed drastically in many respects
since 1965. Geographically, the boundaries of Chinatown have been en-
larged. The demographic characteristics, occupation, population size,
locality of origin, community organization, and attitudes toward the
larger society have all been altered. One of the most important factors
responsible for these changes in the Immigration Law of 1965.

In the past one hundred years the United States has implemented
several emigration policies affecting the Chinese. First the Chinese
were welcomed to this country. This was between 1870 and 1884; it was
a period of free immigration. However, this period was followed by a
period of exclusion and restriction. In 1884 the Chinese Exclusion
Law was passed by Congress. According to this law, Chinese were excluded from admission to the United States with the exception of relatives of immigrants, ministers, teachers, and their families. Although
numerous changes occured between 1884 and 1964, the significant change
was brought about mainly by the Immigration Law of 1965. This law is

still in effect.

The 1965 Immigration Law abolished the "national origin" quotas and established a system of preferences. Immediate relatives, skilled and unskilled workers, refugees, scientists, and technical personnel were listed under different categories of preferences. For the first time the Chinese immigrants were treated equally with other nationalities by the administration, and thus ended some 83 years of biased immigration laws. directed against the Chinese. With the relaxation of the immigration law, many Chinese once again flocked to this country. As a consequence, the Chinese population of New York City swelled to a record high of 69,000 in 1970.

TABLE 3

CHINESE POPULATION IN NEW YORK CITY, 1940-1970

1940	12,753
1950	18,329
1960	32,831
1970	69,324

Source: U.S. Census of Population, 1970.

According to the estimates of my informants, Chinatown has been receiving between 8,000 and 10,000 newcomers per year since 1970. This would make the number of Chinese in New York City in 1973 in the vicinity of 90,000. Of this number, 50,000 were said to reside in the Chinatown area. Thus, only about fifty to sixty percent of the Chinese in New York City stay in the Chinatown area. Other areas of Chinese concentration are in the vicinities of Columbia University, Flatbush, Jackson Heights and Amherst in Queens. However, our concern here is the Chinatown area.

The increase of the Chinese population in the Chinatown area has a direct effect on the boundaries of Chinatown. Today's Chinese population on the Lower East Side had expanded north to 14th Street, south to the piers, east to Allen Street, west to Broadway (See Map 2). The commercial areas of Chinatown have branched out from Mott, Pell, Bayard, and Doyer Streets to include Mulberry, Canal, Bowery, East Broadway, Catherine, Hester, Elizabeth and Grand Streets. Thus, both the residential and commercial areas of Chinatown have expanded, and other ethnic territories such as Little Italy and the Jewish neighborhoods have been invaded.

The 1965 Immigration Law and the subsequent Chinese migration to New York City has not only changed the geographical boundaries and the population size; it has also changed the social and economic characteristics of the people of Chinatown. Now it is occupied by Chinese who intend to make the United States their permanent home, differing from those sojourners of the past. Chinatown before 1965 was dominated by Toysanese and the lingua franca was the Toysan dialect. Today, although people from Kwangtung still make up more than half of the population, there are people from North China, Shanghai, Hong Kong, and Fukien. The lingua franca is no longer the Toysanese but the standard Cantonese spoken in the cities of Hong Kong, Macao and Canton. Speakers of other dialects such as Mandarin, Fukienese, Shangaiese and Hakka have therefore to learn the Cantonese dialect of Chinatown in order to communicate with the natives. Mandarin speakers are more likely to be understood in Chinatown today due to the fact that many of the young Cantonese also learn the national language, Mandarin.

Map 2   New York's Chinatown (1973)

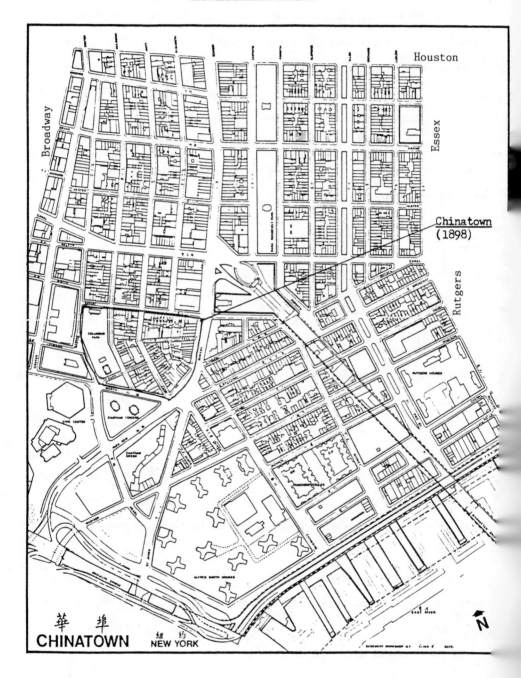

In terms of sex-distribution, the early immigrants were predominant-
ly male. Since 1945, the female population has grown gradually. However, only after 1965 has the male and female ratio narrowed down signif-
icantly. In 1970 the sex ratio became almostly even, $\frac{37,504 \text{ male}}{31,800 \text{ female}}$.
The women of today's Chinatown constitute a solid work force for the
gament factories in the Chinatown area. It is estimated that there are
5,000 Chinese women employed in the 150 Chinese garment factories.[1]

In terms of education, the majority of the Chinese population from
1870 to 1965 had little or no education. After 1965 Chinatown's population became more educated; by 1969 it also had a relatively large number
of college graduates. According to the Chinatown Study Group Report
(1969), 35 percent of the 20-29 age group has had college or post-graduate
education. This figure is higher though very close to the national average for the U.S. population of the same age group living in metropolitan
areas, 33.8 percent with college and post-graduate work. Generally
speaking, the number of educated people in Chinatown is quite large.
According to a survey of the same study group mentioned above, out of
a sample of 1,361 Chinese, 743 have 12 years or less education. This
amounts to 54.7 percent of the sample. Not only there been more educated
people in Chinatown since 1965 (see Table 4), there have also been more
educated people migrating to the United States during this period.

----

[1] The estimate was given by one of the supervisors of ILGW Union,
Local 23-25.

TABLE 4

EDUCATIONAL BACKGROUND OF THE CHINESE IN CHINATOWN, 1969

A. Amount of Education:

12 years or less	6-12 years	more than 12 years	undergraduate college degree	graduate school degree	Total
743	399	138	66	15	1,361
54.7%	29.3%	10.1%	4.8%	1.5%	100%

B. Place of Education:

China	U.S.A.	Both China and U.S.A.	Other	Total
709	535	56	65	1,365
51.9%	39.2%	4.1%	4.8%	100%

Source: Chinatown Study Group Report (1969).

The increase of the population and the diversity of the population were also responsible for the multiplication and specialization of Chinese firms. Of importance were the Chinese restaurants established to serve Chinese customers from different parts of China. Thus, for example, there are many non-Cantonese Chinese restaurants serving Szechuan, Hunan, Peking, and Shanghai cuisine. Due to the availability of large numbers of seamstresses, the Chinese garment industry has become one of the major sources of income for many Chinese. Thus, new alternatives are added to the traditional ones, restaurant and laundry. Further, the size and types of Chinese restaurants and laundries also changed during this period. Partnerships and chain stores have been added to traditional family firms. In the laundry business, in addition to the one man or family laundry, there are washing plants, pressing plants, folding and marketing plants, and self-service laundromats. The new modes of organization and management reflect the new adaptation to the available

technology and modern management techniques. Because of the infusion of

intellectuals, there are more Chinese employed in non-Chinese establish-

ments as professionals. Thus, viewing the changing occupations of the

Chinese from an adaptive perspective, with consideration of the immigra-

tion policies and the resources of the people involved, one can under-

stand more fully why today's Chinatown has become more outwardly oriented

than in the past.

Housing, Health Care, Old Age and Education

New York's Chinatown has one of the oldest housing districts in
the city, as well as in the country. According to a report by the
Department of Buildings, more than 90% of the residential dwelling
units in Chinatown were built before 1901. Many apartments
have problems of pests such as rats and roaches. There are problems with
plumbing and wiring. Some apartments are without heat and
have no refrigerators. The sanitary equipment is far from adequate
and is sub-standard. Some apartments have bathrooms or showers in the
middle of their apartments. Apparently they were added many years after
construction. Into these sub-standard, old tenement buildings is crowded a population of 50,000. Despite the old buildings, the rent in the
Chinatown area is one of the highest in Manhattan. Many Chinese land-
lords have realized that new immigrants need Chinatown as a stepping
stone to the American society and therefore charge exorbitant rent.
In addition to the high rent, there is the practice of charging "key
money" which can vary from $20 to $1,000. Key money is sometimes interpreted as payment for housing information, such as a vacancy or immediate availability. In the past 20 years, despite the rapid population growth, only three buildings were added to Chinatown: Chatham
Towers, Chatham Green and 50 Bayard Street which is a cooperative.
Some Chinese families have been relocated to the Rutgers Houses on the
East River.

Another major problem of the new immigrants is education. Most of the grade school and high school age students went to six crowded, old public school in the greater Chinatown area. There is a great need for a bilingual staff and teachers to help the immigrant students adjust. School officials blame insufficient budgets. The need goes unfulfilled. Inadequate teaching of the history of the Chinese ethnic group has created many stereotypes that are hard to erase; Chinese are still the objects of ridicule by whites and other ethnic groups as well. It is not uncommon to find intense conflicts between Puerto Rican and Chinese students in school.

More than fifty percent of the Chinese families have both parents holding down full time jobs. Thus many school age children are deprived of the care of their parents and thus make themselves easy prey to the evil forces in society. For those who have dropped out of school, street gangs hold the promise of excitement and acceptance; some are forced to join. They become members of street gangs like the White Eagles, the Black Eagles and the Devil Shadows. These gangs are said to be financed by the underground element of Chinatown who tend to use these gangs for their own gains and pursuits.

Chinatown in the seventies is also burdened by the problems of the aged. In the past, Chinatown was a community of adult males.

People then came to New York City usually between the ages of twenty and
forty. After acquiring sufficient savings, many returned to China
to live a life of leisure. Those old men who were sick or homeless were
usually sent back to China by friends or relatives. After World War II
there were many factors which deterred these old people from returning
to home country. First, China experienced an inflationary period after
1945. Next came a political turn-over in the political regime in 1949.
After 1949 there were land reforms and subsequent political movements.
All of these changes were not conducive to overseas Chinese returning
to their homeland. Thus, in the seventies Chinatown accumulated more
old people than in previous periods.

Although quite a few of the older Chinese have their children
in the United States, many of them are acculturated. Like most
young Americans, many young Chinese-Americans prefer independence
and live outside of the Chinatown area. Then there are the recently
immigrated Chinese who migrated with their whole families, including
their parents. Unable to speak the language and unfamiliar with
social security, medical service, and life style of America, many
old people sit and wait for help. Some are particularly in need of
legal aid and the service of translaters.

Thus, Chinatown in the seventies has found that it must depend on
the city, state and federal government to solve many of its problems

whether it be its housing, aged, schools, crime, or unemployment. It
is in these areas that the different associations and social agencies
can bridge the gap between the Chinese community and the larger
society.

To sum up, today's Chinatown is more heterogeneous in terms of
education, social stratification, age,sex distribution, social
organizations, locality of origin, linguistic background, occupational
specialization and political ideology. More Chinese intend to stay in
this country permanently, and the Chinese are becoming more outwardly
oriented to the larger society. Most noticeably of all, Chinatown has
expanded geographically (see Map 2) and in population. However, this
growth has brought about the problems of housing, juvenile delingency,
old age, and welfare which did not exist or were not acute before
1965.

The Chinese Family

Chinese Families before 1965

The Chinese family in New York is a complex subject. A thorough treatment of the subject is not intended here. Since the Chinese family is related to the family firms which will be discussed later, a brief review of the intra-familial relationship in the different types of Chinese families in New York's Chinatown will be sufficient here. Further, a knowledge of Chinese families will also help to understand the social and cultural life of the Chinese in New York.

In the pre-1965 era, there were very few Chinese families in Chinatown. The reasons for having few Chinese families in the population are related to the immigration policy of the larger society and the cultural backgrounds of the immigrants. First, the majority of the early Chinese immigrants who came at the end of the nineteenth century and the beginning of this century wanted to make some quick money and then return to rejoin their families in China (Wu 1958; Cheng 1948). This is true among most of the early Chinese immigrants in different overseas Chinese communities as well (Amyot 1960; Tien 1953; Cheng 1948; Purcell 1951; Wong 1971). However, mention must be made of the early immigrants who did sponsor their children and wives to the United States. The number, however, was not significantly large (R. Lee 1960: 187). The lack of Chinese women and families in Chinatown is also reflected in the male/

female ratio in the population (see Table 5). Second, the Chinese Exclusion Act of 1882 and the Quota Act of 1924 both made entry of the
Chinese wives to the United States very difficult. The Chinese Exclusion
Act excluded all the coolie laborers and made provision for the entry of
Chinese educators, students, officials, business owners, journalists,
etc. (R. Lee 1960: 202; Kung 1962). But few wives of early immigrants
were in the above categories; thus the majority were not admissible to
this country. The 1924's Immigration Act ruled that alien wives were
ineligible for citizenship and therefore were not permitted to enter the
country (Kung 1962; Cheng 1948: 136). Third, many of the early immigrants, as mentioned earlier, were illegal entrants who were smuggled
into the United States; they were insecure about their futures and incapable of sponsoring their wives to the United States (Wu 1968).

According to the Bureau of Census statistics, out of 909 Chinese in
New York State in 1880, there were only 12 Chinese women. In 1890, the
Chinese population in New York State was increased to 2,935. Out of
this number, only 33 were female. This situation of male predominance
persisted till 1965 (see Table 5). Thus, for instance, in 1940 the sex
ratio between Chinese male and female was almost six to one (see Table
6). Up to the end of World War II, New York's Chinatown was composed of
adult, single males. This phenomenon was termed by some authors a
"bachelor society" (Nee 1973; Heyer 1953). Such labelling, if not in-
accurate, is misleading since the majority of this group was married;
their wives, however, were in China (R. Lee 1960; Wu 1958). Cheng Tsu
Wu (1958) demonstrated that the ratio of married Chinese whose wives
were not living in this country to those who were living with a wife

in this country in 1940 was six to one.

TABLE 5

CHINESE IN NEW YORK STATE BY SEX AND SEX RATIO

Year	Male	Female	Total	Males/100 Females
1880	837	12	909	---
1890	2,902	33	2,935	---
1900	7,028	142	7.170	4,949.3
1910	5,065	210	5,266	2,519.9
1920	5,240	553	5,793	947.6
1930	8,649	1,016	9,665	815.3
1940	11,777	1,954	13,731	602.7
1950	14,875	5,296	20,171	280.9
1960	23,406	14,167	37,573	165.2
1970	43,919	37,459	81,375	117.2

Source: U.S. Census of Population, 1970.

The infusion of Chinese women into the population occured only in significant numbers after World War II with the implementation of the War Bride Bill and the G.I. Bill. Many Chinese veterans were able to sponsor their wives from China. Those Chinese veterans who were not already married made use of the opportunity and went to Hong Kong and Canton to look for marriage partners. After their marriage these War Brides came to this country as non-quota immigrants. According to Rose Lee (1960), up to the end of 1950 about 6,000 foreign born Chinese women accompanied by 600 young babies, entered the United States under the War Bride Act. Half of these 3,000 were believed to have settled in New York's Chinatown (Chu 1973). Even with the infusion of the Chinese war brides, however, the female and male ratio today is still far from even (See Table 6). Many informants verified this fact and recalled that there were hardly any Chinese women and children to be seen on the streets of Chinatown till 1965.

TABLE 6

NEW YORK CITY CHINESE POPULATION BY SEX

Year	Male	Female	Total
1940	10,967	1,786	12,753
1950	13,702	4,702	18,404
1960	20,658	12,173	32,831
1970	37,504	31,820	69,324

Source: U.S. Census of Population, 1970.

In discussing Chinese families, many different typologies could be set up.[1] In order to give a succinct yet comprehensive view of the Chinese families in the United States and to also give a brief presentation in a manner related to the present study, four basic types of Chinese families are tentatively distinguished: 1) old immigrant families including families which came in 1924 and war wives' families; 2) Chinese-American families including all second and third generation Chinese-American families; 3) new immigrant families which came to the United States after 1960's. Omitted from discussion here are families

[1]David Cheng (1948) distinguished four types of families: "the mutilated," the "grafted," the "divided" and the "emancipated." In the mutilated family, the husband was in the U.S. while the wife and children were in China. Grafted family was used to indicate the marital union between a Chinese man and an American woman. Divided family was used to designate the natural family composed of father, mother, and children. Emancipated family was the result of the marriage of second generation Chinese (Chen 1948: 135-143). Rose Hum Lee distinguished four basic types: the early immigrant families (which came to the U.S. before 1924); the recent immigrant families (including war wives' families and the reunited families), the stranded families (families of the scholars, intellectuals and officials who could not return to China); the established families (second, third or fourth generation Chinese-American families.

of intellectuals, students and officials who came to the United States before 1949 and were stranded in the United States because of the change of political regime in China. Since this group of families were not and are now not directly connected with Chinatown socially or economically, they will not be discussed here.[1]

Intra-familial Relationships

Among the old immigrant families, both the parent-child and husband-wife relationships reflected the Chinese families in the Old World. First, the husband was the provider and the head of the family. The wife's activity sphere was at home. Although she was expected to assist with the husband's business, she had no transactions with customers or outsiders. Thus, in the laundry firm environment, the husband usually manned the store front and the wife assisted behind the scenes by washing and pressing clothes. Second, there was a double standard regarding sex relations. If a husband had extra marital relations, he was to be tolerated (R. Lee 1960: 199), but the wife was expected to be faithful. Third, having sons, the more the better, was important for these families. Boys were given more family authority than girls. Fourth, both the husband and wife were expected to maximize their savings through frugal living. The wife in particular was expected to be a good housekeeper and spend little money.

What deserves further comment is the value of frugality among these families. Like the Chinese in the Phillipines (Amyot 1960), Peru (Wong

---

[1]For a further discussion of "stranded families," consult Rose Hum Lee's (1960) work.

1971) and elsewhere, frugality was the foundation of many entrepreneurial successes. Many of the older informants who were interviewed constantly used the Chinese saying, "Kan Kim Hey Ka"[2] (frugality is the
beginning of success) to demonstrate the importance of living frugally.
Money saved was used for many purposes: 1) to expand the business;
2) to buy real estate; 3) to buy gold and diamond jewelry which was
believed to have more stability than money and could more readily be
converted to cash; and 4) to send children back to China to receive a
Chinese education and to get married.[1] As mentioned earlier, money saved
was seldom deposited in the bank due to the lack of knowledge about
banking procedures and the English language.

The husband-wife relationship in the Chinese-American families
differed significantly from those mentioned above. First, although
the husband was expected to be the provider and the head of the family,
he was, nevertheless, no longer the disputed decision-maker for the
family. The husband was expected to consult the wife on major decisions
(R. Lee 1960: 245; Liang Yuan 1951). Frank discussions between the
husband and wife were more prevalent than in the old immigrant families.
Further, the wife often had her own employment. Second, the measure
of a successful marriage in the Chinese-American family was the absence
of divorce (Lee 1960: 245). Third, the consumption pattern in the Chinese-American families differed from that of the old immigrant families.
Thrift was not emphasized as much. Chinese-Americans spent more money

---

[1]In Mandarin it is pronounced as "Chin Chien Chi Chia" (勤儉起家).

[2]This practice was discontinued after 1949 when the communists took
over China.

on recreation, furnishings, automobiles, housing, and electrical appliances (Lee 1960). Even if some families had two wage earners and a good income, they did not have much savings or investments like the old immigrants (R. Lee 1960). Rose Lee (1960) even pointed out that although Chinese-American families may have a similar or even greater income than old immigrant Chinese families of similar size, savings and investments of the former are far less than the latter. Fourth, the attitudes toward children differed. Chinese-Americans were not obsessed with having sons. Daughters were equally treated and welcomed.

Parent-child relationships also differed among old immigrant families and Chinese-American families. First, immigrant families retained the values of the Old World. Filial piety was emphasized. Family authority was structured by age, sex, and birth rank. Traditional kinship terminology such as Ko (older brother), Dai (younger brother), Che (older sister) and Muy (younger sister) were used. Boys had more authority than the girls. Among the sons, the eldest was the father's successor. Language used in the family was Chinese. All major traditional festivals such as the Chinese New Year, the Mid-Autumn Festival, and the Dragon Boat Festival were celebrated. The eldest son was usually entrusted with the perpetuation of the family business. In fact, many Chinese sons born on the mainland were sponsored in their late teens by their separated fathers to come to the United States before their mothers were sponsored. The idea was to ensure economic betterment for future generations by learning the family business and perpetuating it through the sons (Lee 1960). Thus, many Chinese fathers wanted to start their sons in the family business while they were still young.

Among the Chinese-American families, traditional Chinese customs were not faithfully followed. They still ate Chinese food and celebrated some Chinese festivals, but they did not speak Chinese in the family. Although the parents might have been relatively interested in retaining some traditional practices such as addressing each other with traditional kinship terminology, the children of these families preferred to follow the American way of addressing one another. There was more spontaneous discussion and communication in the Chinese-American families than in the immigrant families mentioned earlier.

Children of immigrant families also encountered more adjustment problems than children of Chinese-American families. Immigrant children born in China were separated from their fathers for many years. They were brought up in a social environment which differed from that of their fathers. Thus, the generation gap was enormous and the father-son relationship in this kind of family was more strained:

> Teenage children meeting their fathers for the first time, and vice versa, were numerous. Parent-child relations were often strained because each grew up and identified with a different social order-- the fathers with the predominant Chinese-speaking sojouners' group and the children with the republican form of Chinese society. The latter had seen social changes occuring in swift succession, while the fathers had not. Although the fathers were anxious about their families' safety in China, they failed to comprehend children's fears, political leanings, social attitudes, desires for higher education, occupational mobility and relationships (R. Lee 1960:204).

Although this parent-son conflict did not exist among the Chinese-American families, other conflicts did exist. From discussions with the Chinese-Americans, it was learned that second generation Chinese were concerned with transmitting some knowledge about the Chinese cultural heritage to their American born children. Their offspring, however, frequently wanted to be accepted by the larger society and was reluctant to learn the language and culture of China. In order to avoid conflict, an overwhelming majority of these parents compromised with their offspring and tried not to impose their preferences on them.

Absolute obedience was expected from children of old immigrant families. The father was family head and disciplinarian. He made decisions for the family without discussion. Among early Chinese immigrant families, parents frequently selected and arranged marriage partners for their children. They often made decisions about which sons went to school and which stayed home to assist the family business. The eldest son was the head of the family after the death of the father. He usually received more inheritance than the rest because he had the responsibility of taking care of the family household. Daughters received smaller inheritances than the sons. If the father died without a will, the family association also followed the tradition of male dominance, and the eldest was given preferential treatment in the division of the inheritance. However, if there was a will, the inheritance was divided according to its stipulations. In Chinese-American families, the father was not the supreme authority; the mother also played an important role in decision-making. Children could select their own dates and marry partners of their own choice. They had the freedom to select their own careers too.

Children of the immigrant families were expected to take care of their parents in their old age. It was customary, as in China, for the parents to live with the eldest son's family. However, in Chinese-American families, the children had more independence. Some even moved

out of their parents' homes as soon as they became financially independent.

Parents of the immigrant families were not interested in joining
PTA organizations (R. Lee 1960). Chinese-American families, however,
were quite active in the PTA (R. Lee 1960). This does not mean that
the old immigrants were not interested in the education of their children. If they had any children in school, they were concerned that the
children did well. Children were reminded that they could elevate their
family status and glorify their ancestors by being good students. Lack
of time and lack of proficiency in speaking the English language prevented many old immigrants from joining the PTA organizations.

Generally speaking, the immigrant families retained more old world
traditions than the Chinese-American families, especially the Chinese
language and interaction patterns within the family. Children of old
immigrant families had more connections with Chinatown and were more
familiar with the socio-economic life in Chinatown. Children of Chinese-
Americans were oriented toward the larger society. Children of Chinese-
Americans often became professionals and were employed by American establishments.

Chinese Families after 1965

After 1965, the sex ratio among the Chinese in New York leveled
off. Although the infusion of Chinese women began after 1945, only since
1965 has the proportion of male and female become relatively close (See
Table 6). One major reason for the change of the sex ratio is that many
new immigrants came with their families after 1965. New immigrant

families have now joined the old immigrant families and the Chinese-American families in New York's Chinatown. Since the first two kinds of families have been discussed, the discussion here will concentrate mainly on intra-familial relationships of the new immigrant families. The new immigrant families, unlike the old immigrant families, are oriented toward making the United States their permanent home. However, from interviews and observations of new immigrant families, it was found that the majority of the parents intended to instill in their children the traditional values of filial piety and the Chinese language. On the other hand, these parents wanted their children to learn the English language and receive higher educations so that one day they might be accepted by the larger society. That is to say, they hoped that their children would straddle the two cultures: Chinese and American.

Husband-wife relationship: Although the husband was still expected to be the main provider, the wife also contributed to the common purse by working on her own or assisting the husband's business. Unlike the old immigrant families where wives were expected to work at home or within the family firm environment only, the wives of the new immigrants had no such limitations. If the husband had a firm, she usually helped him with it. Otherwise she might seek employment in one of the Chinese garment factories or restaurants. Some even worked as cashiers or secretaries for Chinese firms in Chinatown.

Second, the value of thrift was emphasized in the new immigrant families. Both husband and wife strived to save as much as possible in two ways: by working longer hours to earn extra income and by living frugally. It was quite common among the new immigrants to reside in run-down or sub-standard housing to cut down on rent. However, they were quite generous with their food budgets. They were not stingy about spending money in Chinese restaurants or purchasing food for family consumption. The rationale for this kind of consumption habit was that one must maintain and improve one's health because it was the foundation for all gain-seeking activities. Extravagance in housing was not desirable because they believed that 1) the rent in New York was far too high, especially for good housing; 2) expensive housing was not necessary because they spent most of their waking hours at work and used their apartments only at night to sleep; 3) it is better to save more money for a rainy day or for future investment or expansion of one's business than to use the money "unprofitably" for lodging; and 4) living conditions even in Chinatown, the Bronx or some other inexpensive neighbourhood were no worse than what they had encountered in Hong Kong.

Third, the husband was still the head of the family; the wife was the housekeeper although she may also have had her own employment. The husband, however, was expected to consult his wife on major decisions.

Fourth, children were welcome regardless of sex. Most of the new immigrants, however, preferred to have smaller families.

Fifth, the wife expected the husband to discipline the children. To most Chinese, family education meant discipline by the father. Some mothers blamed the delinquency of their children on the lack of parent supervision, especially the father's conspicuous absence from home due to long working hours. They believed that the father, as a disciplinarian figure, should constantly "watch over" his children, especially the pre-teenagers and teenagers, if they wanted their children to turn out well.

  Parent-child relationships: The new immigrants were generally interested in providing a college education for their children and at the
same time transmitting the Chinese culture and values to them. The
majority of the parents were anxious to find good schools for their
children. On the other hand, they wanted their children to have some
knowledge about Chinese culture and language. Because new immigrants
wanted their children to learn the Chinese language, many churches and
the Chinese Benevolent Association had Chinese language schools which
operated on Saturdays and Sundays and evenings so that Chinese children
might attend both the public schools and the Chinese language schools.
Although not verbalized articulately, most of the new immigrants were
for the establishment of dual cultural identities for their children.
There have been incidents of success in this endeavor; there have also
been failures. Some children had great difficulty in the public schools
because their English was not proficient. They also found it difficult
to attend two schools (Chinese and American) at the same time.

  The new immigrant families differed significantly from the old
immigrant families also in their attitudes toward the larger society.
The old immigrants had always considered the United States a temporary
place to live and wanted to return to China as soon as they had accumulat
some wealth. The new immigrant families chose to emigrate to the United
States of their own volition. They sought two things in the United
States: economic betterment and educational opportunities for their
children. That is to say, the new immigrants came here with the intention of staying here permanently. That is why they were so concerned

that their children have a good education and that they be accepted professionally in the larger society. For this, they worked long hours and lived frugally. It was common to see both parents working six days per week. They made known to their children that the future education of their children depended on the economic well-being of the families. Many children contributed to this goal by assisting in the family firm; they hoped that the prosperity of the family business would enable them to pursue their future careers.

Chinese language was used by the new immigrant families. Chinese kinship terms were used by the children to address each other. Authority in the family was structured along age, sex and birth rank. The parents were also concerned with instilling the sense of filial piety in their children. The parents were quick to point out the evil of the American family system in which the young leave the old. If they did not keep up the Chinese family system, they (the children) would become helpless when they were old,the children were constantly reminded. Within the family, yueng (compromising spirit), yan (tolerance), jen (benevolence), li (porpriety and politeness), wo (peace), were values which the parents constantly tried to instill in their children. Again, this by no means suggests that the enculturation process was successful in all the Chinese immigrant families. New immigrant families which encountered the greatest difficulty in enculturating their children were those which had both parents working full time and had pre-teenagers and young teenagers. These children were known locally as Juk Kaks (Bamboo Joint), meaning hard and unyielding. Most juvenile delinquents[1] were from this group of teenagers who were born on the China mainland, Taiwan or Hong Kong. They came here relatively young and had enormous amounts of difficulty in adjusting to the American system of schooling and living.

Thus, basically, the new immigrant families hoped that their children would achieve two cultural identities. They were expected to speak Chinese and behave like Chinese but be accepted professionally as Americans. The old immigrant families were basically traditional and wanted their children to uphold all Chinese values. Chinese-Americans, especially the third generation Chinese, wanted to be accepted as Americans by the larger society. As Rose Hum Lee said, the third generation Chinese were for integration, meaning the unreserved acceptance of the Chinese by the dominant group (Lee 1960: 409).

One should not get the erroneous impression that all the new immigrant parents were so busy at work that they never socialized with their children. It was customary for many Chinese seamstresses to visit their children in the nearby grade schools, notably, the Transfiguration Church on Mott Street. They could be seen sharing lunch in one of the nearby restaurants. After lunch, the mother accompanied her children back to school. Many Chinese seamstresses accepted work in the Chinese garment factories despite low pay in order to be near their children's schools. Also parents often took their children out to dinner, shopping or recreation. The restaurants of Chinatown on Saturdays and Sundays are full of Chinese families dining together.

---

[1]Although juvenile delinquency occurs in today's Chinatown, its frequency is far less than other ethnic communities in New York and in the larger society in general.

Social Stratification

There are many variations among the Chinese in New York City. In a very general way, the Chinese in New York could be divided into two clusters: the Chinatown-connected Chinese and the non-Chinatown-connected Chinese. The latter is composed of foreign born students, scholars, professionals, government representatives from both Taiwan and the People's Republic of China and visiting merchants. This group of people may or may not have permanent residence status. They live and work in non-Chinatown areas and use New York's Chinatown only as a recreational center (eating in the Chinese restaurants and seeing the Chinese films in Chinatown's movie houses) or shopping center. Since the present study deals with New York's Chinatown, these non-Chinatown-connected Chinese do not concern us here.

Among the Chinatown-connected Chinese, there are major divisions segmented along these self-perceived dimensions: dialects, origins, professions, prestige, time of arrival, life styles, degrees of acculturation, attitudes toward China, income and age. The intention here is not so much to present a sociological model of social stratification, but rather, to present the self-perceived models of social stratification in New York's Chinatown. That is to say, the concern is mainly on how the Chinese classify their own people and make self-assignment of differential social ranking. Thus, these are 'folk classifications' (Strickon 1967), similar to the "conscious model" of Levi-Strauss (1953) and Barbara Ward (1969). These self-perceived, conscious models of stratification are important for the understanding of social structure and social behavior of the Chinese in New York in that: 1) they are potential

guides for social actions (Strickon 1967); 2) they reveal the cognitive
process and subjective dimensions in the differential social ranking
among the natives themselves; and 3) they can "furnish an important contribution to the understanding of the structures either as factual documents or as theoretical contributions similar to those of the anthropologist himself" (Levi-Strauss 1953).

Only the folk-models or self-perceived models of the social stratification of the present day Chinatown are discussed due to the difficulty
in reconstructing accurately all self-perceived models of social stratification for the 1870-1964 period since available data is insufficient.
Whenever relevant, however, available information will be used to point
out similarities and differences between stratification of present day
Chinatown with that of the early period.

The Chinese in the community see themselves divided socially in
many ways. Hence, there are several folk models of stratification.
The first one of these is Lo Wah Kiu (old overseas Chinese), Sun Yee Man
(new immigrants), Wah Yoey (Chinese-Americans) and Hoi Yin (sailors).

Lo Wah Kiu refers to the group of foreign born Chinese who came to
the United States before 1965 and are now quite old. The majority
originated from the rural area of Kwangtung province, principally from
the Sze Yup and Sam Yup districts. Although further subdivisions could
be made among the old immigrants, they do share many things in common,
and for the purpose of this paper, it is possible to discuss them as a
group. Moreover, the Sun Yee Man (new immigrants) and Wah Yoey (Chinese
Americans) tend to lump all old immigrants into one category and are
antagonistic to them as a group. They call them peasants, backward,

and conservative. New immigrants and Chinese-Americans contend that they do not "know how to relax and enjoy life." The old immigrants retaliate by calling the Sun Yee Man (new immigrants) "westernized" and extravagant. They contend that they do not know how to raise children in a "good way" and attribute the increase of juvenile delinquency to the failure of family education among the new immigrants. The old immigrants call the Wah Yoey (Chinese Americans) Juk Sing, meaning useless, unyielding and a group of people who have no roots in either China or in America. The Lo Wah Kiu (old overseas Chinese) consider themselves the "genuine" Chinese who are concerned with preserving Chinese culture which is, according to them, "superior" to the cultures of the "savage" people everywhere. They think that they are more "Chinese" than either the Chinese-Americans or the new immigrants.

Economically, many old immigrants have accumulated some wealth through hard work and frugal living. Generally, they are in the typical Chinese businesses connected with Chinatown: laundries, Chop Suey Restaurants, groceries, and gift stores. In terms of age, they are generally older than new immigrants and Chinese-Americans. Another similarity among the Lo Wah Kiu (old overseas Chinese) is that they are active in all traditional Chinatown associations: family, regional, village association and the Chinese Benevolent Association. They also control all these associations as well. Politically they are anti-communist and pro-Nationalist Taiwan. Stuart Cattell (1962) called these old immigrants who hold leadership positions in the associations (see Chapter 5) the power elite of Chinatown. Not all old immigrants are qualified for leadership positions. Wealth and connections are the prerequisites for the competition of these positions. Holding leadership positions is regarded with prestige. Leaders are called <u>Kiu Ling</u> (leaders of the overseas Chinese); they are the protectors and <u>patrons</u> of the less prosperous Chinese. Those who have not become economically successful are <u>clients</u> of the leaders. The unsuccessful Lo Wah Kiu, for a long time, refused to apply for welfare although they qualified for it. They preferred to live on their savings, take menial jobs such as janitors, or live with their children. Only recently have some of them started to apply for welfare and use facilities provided for the aged by the larger society, such as the Golden Age Club.

As a group of people, the Lo Wah Kiu are known for their proverbial frugality. They dress modestly and live modestly. Even those who have made the grade economically still live in less than comfortable houses. It is for this reason that the Sun Yee Man (new immigrants) and the Wah Yoey (Chinese-Americans) call the Lo Wah Kiu "hill billies" who "do not know how to live." As a group, the old immigrants do not see any need to assimilate into the American society. On the contrary, they are for the maintenance of Chinese customs and the Chinese way of life in America eating Chinese food, speaking Chinese, socializing only with the Chinese-speaking old immigrants, raising their children in the Chinese way (strict discipline with emphasis on filial piety), maintaining connection with Taiwan, celebrating the Double Ten (the National Day of Republic of China), and observing all the major Chinese festivals such as the Chinese New Year, the Dragon Boat Festival, the Sweeping-Grave Festival, and the Mid-Autumn Festival.

The second group of people in this self-perceived model of stratification is the <u>Sun Yee Man</u> which refers to immigrants who came to this
country in or around 1965 after the implementation of new immigration
laws which abolished the national origins quota system. These new immigrants are mostly from the urban area of China and have lived in Hong
Kong for a time. They speak the Cantonese dialect used in Hong Kong or
Canton. They consider themselves more sophisticated, refined, urbanized,
and "more genteel" than the Lo Wah Kiu. One of the reasons why they
came to the United States was because they liked the material affluence
of America. As soon as they found a job and settled down, they wanted
to learn how to drive and purchase used automobiles. They dress better
than the old immigrants, too. However, they are still frugal in their
life style. Maximum savings are attempted through living in low rent
districts. This group of people do not adhere to the pro-Kuomintang
ideology as do the old immigrants. However, they are not for communism
either. This is understandable, since some of these new immigrants fled
communist China some years ago. There is more political apathy among
them. They are not interested in the traditional family or regional
associations in Chinatown. As far as assimilation is concerned, they
want to achieve a double identity. They want to retain the Chinese way
of dealing with one another. They want to be American in that they want
to share the affluent life style and the education of the United States
(see related discussion on the immigrant family).

Economically, the new immigrants are in the garment industries, and
the new Shanghai, Szechuan, and Peking restaurants as well as some
modern Cantonese restaurants (see Chapters 6 and 7). In terms of cash

the new immigrants have less economic power than the Lo Wah Kiu. The
majority of the new immigrants work in restaurants or garment factories.
Some are petty capitalists, owners of small firms. It is possible to
find some new immigrants who can rival the Lo Wah Kiu in economic terms
such as property and income investment. As a group, the Sun Yee Man has
a lower economic status than that of the Lo Wah Kiu.

The term Wah Yoey is used to refer to the Chinese who are born in
the United States. Again, there are some differences among individuals
in this group, since it encompasses first, second, third, and fourth
generation Chinese. However, they have many things in common and are
lumped together by the people in the community. First, the Wah Yoey are
generally professionals employed in U.S. firms. However, some lawyers,
accountants, and doctors who can speak the Chinese language come to Chinatown to practice their professions. Economically, they are more affluent
than the new or old immigrants. Being raised and educated in the United
States, few of them can speak the Chinese language or have Chinese
speaking friends. They socialize mainly with members of the group or
with American peers. This is a fully assimilated group which speaks and
curses in English and usually identifies with Americans. As a group,
they are sympathetic to the People's Republic of China. Naturally, they
dislike Chiang Kai Shek's government. Recently, some members of this
group came to Chinatown to establish a community service with funds from
different government agencies (see Chapter 8). Two of the frequent
criticisms launched both by Low Wah Kiu and Sun Yee Man of this group
are their consumption pattern which is said to be wasteful and extravagant (see discussion on Chinese-American family earlier in this chapter)
and the general lack of knowledge of both the language and culture of

China. The Lo Wah Kiu's utmost dissatisfaction with the Wah Yoey (Chinese-Americans) is that the latter do not behave in a "civilized" (Chinese) way but have been contaminated by the Americans. They generally
leave their parents after they become economically independent or marry.

The fourth group of people is the Hoi Yin (jump ship sailors). They
are China born from Taiwan or Hong Kong. After they jumped ship, they
either got temporary employment from the different family or regional
associations as janitors or from some Chinese restaurant. Prestige-wise,
the group of people is the lowest ranked in the community. They are
threatened with exposure to immigration officials by many employers
if they do not abide by the employers' wishes. In order to get permanent resident status, some get married to Puerto Rican women or other
Spanish speaking Americans. They tend to socialize more with the new
immigrants since they all speak Cantonese. They also share with the new
immigrants their attitudes toward the People's Republic of China and
Taiwan and their consumption patterns.

To sum up briefly, this self-perceived model of stratification is
composed of four layers. The top one is the Lo Wah Kiu, the middle layer
is the Sun Yee Man, the third layer is the Wah Yoey, and the bottom layer
is the Hoi Yin. The cognitive dimensions used in ranking these people
are: life chance, birth place, occupation, life style, consumption
pattern, language, identification with China, attitudes towards the
United States, and prestige.

The second self-perceived or folk model of social stratification is
constructed along dimensions similar to the Marxian model. In this model,
Lo Pan (owners and capitalists of a business enterprise), Chuen Moon Yan

Choy and Da Kun are used to describe three groups of people. Lo Pan is
used to refer to owner-capitalists of business establishments. The bosses
of grocery stores, garment factories, restaurants are called Lo Pan.
Many of the Lo Wah Kiu (old overseas Chinese) are Lo Pan from whom the
new immigrants gained employment. However, the new immigrants strive
for economic independence. As soon as they have accumulated enough
capital, they want to have a firm of their own and thus become Lo Pan
(see Chapters 6 and 7). Obviously, some Lo Pan are richer than others.
To make such a distinction, the adjective Dai (big) and Sai (small) are
added to the term, i.e. Dai Lo Pan and Sai Lo Pan. The term Chuen Mun Yan
is used to refer to professionals such as lawyers, accountants, engineers,
medical doctors, business managers and skilled laborers. The term Da Kun
is a term which refers to people who are employed as blue collar workers,
unskilled laborers, restaurant and laundry firm employees. In this
perceived model the Dai Lo Pan and the Chen Moon Choy are ranked simultaneously on the top layer; the Sai Lo Pan is on the middle; and the Da
Kung is at the bottom. It is obvious that the subjective dimensions
for such a ranking are: 1) control of the means of production or profit-
making; and 2) formalized or specialized training.

Conscious Model 3, as will be shown is constructed along differences
in family income. In this self-perceived model, members of the community
are evaluated within the context of the Chinese community in terms of
income. There are three comonly used terms: Sheung Shing Yap Sig (high
income), Chung Shing Yup Sig (middle income), and Dai Yup Sig (low income). Yup Sig in Cantonese means income. Informants have estimated
that five to ten percent of the Chinese families belong to Sheung Shing

Yip Sig (hihg income); forty percent belong to the Chung Shing Yup Sig
(middle income); and fifty percent belong to the Dai Yup Sig (low invome).
Income of the Sheung Shing Yup Sig family ranges from $15,000 to $20,000.
The range for the Chung Shing Yup Sig family is $10,000 to $15,000 per
year per family. The low income range, Dai Yup Sig, is $10,000 or less
per year per family. Generally, it is presumed that each family has one
or two workers. This is a folk-community model (Strickon 1967). That
is, the frame of reference is the Chinese in Chinatown, not the United
States. When the informants are asked to rank the Chinese in terms of
the United States, the national context, there are significant changes.
These changes will be revealed in Conscious model 4.

The fourth self-perceived model is the national-folk model (cf.
Strickon 1967). When the members of the community evaluate each other
within the context of the United States, the English term "class" is
used. The informants used four terms to describe themselves: upper
middle, middle, lower middle and lower classes. This model is used frequently with other self-perceived models described earlier. Their inter-
relationships can be demonstrated in Figures 1, 2, and 3.

First, Wah Yoey (Chinese-Americans) are generally Cheun Moon Yan Choy
(professionals). This group of people is evaluated to have high
income according to the community's standard but are equated with the
upper middle or middle classes in the context of the United States.
Adhering to the professional group, as indicated in Figure 1, there
are some Sun Yee Man (new immigrants).

Second, a large number of Lo Wah Kiu and some Sun Yee Man are
owner-capitalists of firms. These people are evaluated to be either

high income and middle income people according to the community standard but are seen mostly to belong to the middle and lower middle classes of the United States society.

Third, a considerable number of Sun Yee Man and all the Hoi Yin plus some Lo Wah Kiu are employees or unskilled laborers. These people are considered to be mainly low income wage earners in the context of the Chinese community. They are also equated with the lower class of the larger society by the members of the community.

As indicated in Figure 3, the Chinese see themselves as belonging to the middle and lower classes of American society. No members of the community could be classified as upper class Americans. Are there any Chinese who can be considered as belonging to the upper class in the context of American society? The consensus among all the informants is that there are. But these Chinese are not Chinatown-connected people. One of the frequently cited examples is Chinese shipping magnate, C.Y. Tung.

C.Y. Tung is a China born businessman. He is the head of the C.Y. Tung group of shipping companies, known in New York as Associated Maritime Industries, Inc. According to the New York Magazine (September 27, 1971) Maritime Industry sources consider C.Y. Tung the largest individual ship owner in the world. In 1970, Tung purchased the Queen Elizabeth for $3.2 million to convert it into a floating university (New York Magazine, 1971). Other frequently cited rich Chinese in New York are Gerald Tsai and I.M. Pei. The former is a successful financier. He was the founder and president of Manhattan Fund and the president of Tsai Management and Research Corporation. Pei is a famous architect who has designed many

well-known buildings in New York and other parts of the United States.
In New York City alone, he was commissioned to design the $40 million
National Airlines terminal at Kennedy International Airport, the expansion plans for Columbia University, and the new IBM tower on Madison
Avenue. Although both Pei and Tsai are China born and partially China
educated, they are considered non-Chinatown-connected people since they
do not participate in the social, economic and cultural life of Chinatown.

In conclusion, the Chinese community is categorized by its members
as a four-strata (two models), and three-strata (two models) community.
The patrons and brokers are drawn mainly from two groups of people: the
Lo Wah Kiu (old overseas Chinese) and the Wah Yoey (Chinese-Americans).
The patrons, known locally as Kiu Ling (leaders of the overseas Chinese)
are the old immigrants who are well-off economically and are office
holders in various Chinatown associations. The non-Kiu Ling brokers are
generally Chinese-Americans who are professionals. Some of them perform
their brokerage services for the members of the community for a fee,   .
like the accountants and lawyers. Some are voluntary social workers
who want to get fundings from the government to set up community services
for the disadvantaged Chinese. These two groups of people, as will be
demonstrated in Chapter 7, have an important role to play in the maintenance of the Chinese ethnic boundary in New York City.

Figure 1: Interrelationship of Conscious Models (1 and 2) of Social Stratification

	Professionals	Owner-capitalists	Laborers-employees
Old Overseas Chinese		X	X
New Immigrants	X	X	X
Chinese Americans	X		
Sailors			X

Figure 2: Interrelationship of Conscious Models (2 and 3) of Social Stratification

	Professionals	Owner-captialists	Laborers-employees
High Income	X	X	
Middle Income	X	X	
Low Income			X

Figure 3: Interrelationship of Conscious Models (3 and 4)

Chinese	American
	Upper Class
High income people	Upper Middle
Some high and middle income people	Middle
Majority of the middle income people	Lower Middle
Low income people	Lower

CHAPTER 3

SOCIAL ORGANIZATIONS AND ECONOMIC ACTIVITIES

OF CHINATOWNS: 1870–1964

It was common among overseas Chinese to interact with people who
shared the same speech, locality of origin, and family name (Tien 1953;
Skinner 1958; Ng 1968). The Chinese in New York City were no exceptions.
As mentioned in Chapter 2, the early Chinese immigrant's background was
so homogeneous in terms of locality of origin and dialect that it was
easy to recruit sufficient members to form regional and dialectic associations. People who migrated from the same area were frequently related
or were members of the same clan in a village. Thus, it was understood
that together with the various regional associations in the early days,
there were numerous clan and village associations. It was these regional,
clan and village associations which constituted the basic units of social
structure of the early Chinatown of New York City.

In addition to these regional, clan, and village associations, even
in the early days of New York's Chinatown, there were guilds or trade
associations, secret societies or Tong, political clubs and recreational
associations such as musical and dramatic clubs. There was a hierarchical
order among these associations and an over-all organization which still
exists today. It coordinated all these associations and was called the
Chinese Benevolent Society. Today, it is known as the Consolidated
Chinese Benevolent Association. This is the highest authority of Chinatown. The lowest level of organization is the village association

known locally as <u>Fong</u>. The hierarchical structure of the community's
associations can be shown thus:

Diagram 1:   <u>Chinatown's Community Structure</u>

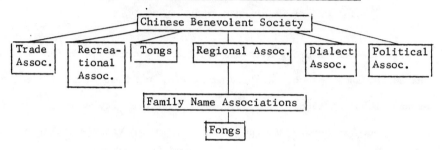

These associations of the Chinese not only gave the community a
structure, they also contributed to the economic activities of the Chinese from 1870-1964.

An outline of the economic opportunities of the Chinese in this era
will be presented. A discussion of the rules, functions, and economic
contributions of the associations will follow.

<u>Economic Opportunities of the Chinese in this Era: 1870-1964</u>

The Chinese who first came to this country in the nineteenth century,
as mentioned in Chapter 2, were mainly laborers who worked in the mining
companies and on the railroads. The majority of them concentrated in
the Pacific states. After 1876, there were significant changes among
the sites of residence and occupations of the Chinese. The immediate
reasons for these changes were: 1) the completion of the Central Pacifi
Railway; 2) the closing of many mining companies; 3) high unemployment
rates for the laborers; 4) the anti-Chinese feelings in the Pacific
states, expecially in California where the Chinese laborers were con-

sidered competitors who posed a threat to the whites' livelihood. Rising
anti-Chinese sentiment and tight markets for laborers induced the Chinese
to use geographical dispersion and change of occupation as adaptive
strategies.

Use of these two strategies is evidenced by the Chinese emmigration
to New York City and their subsequent involvement in non-competitive
businesses. The kinds of businesses which the Chinese involved themselves in during the 1870-1964 era were mainly Chinese hand laundries,
Chinese restaurants and grocery stores. Louis Beck (1898) estimated
the number of Chinese laundry workers in greater New York at three thous-
and. His estimate must have been exaggerated, since according to the
United States Census report there were only 853 Chinese in 1880, 2,559
in 1890, and 6,321 in 1900 who lived in New York City. However, the
number of Chinese laundry men was probably so overwhelming that it con-
veyed such an estimate to Beck.   The number of Chinese restaurants
(including seven restaurant supply shops) recorded in a work by Warner
M. Van Norden in 1918 indicated 67 units in the Manhattan and Brooklyn
areas. In these restaurants alone, there were probably between 600 and
700 employees.[1]

There were about 30 Chinese grocery stores in 1918 in the Chinatown
area (Van Norden 1918: 87). For other businesses in the Chinatown of
1918, see Table 7.

---

[1]This is my personal estimate calculated on the basis of ten employees
per restaurant at the present time.

TABLE 7

BUSINESSES OTHER THAN RESTAURANTS, LAUNDRIES AND GROCERIES

IN NEW YORK CITY IN 1918

Types of Businesses	Units
Bakers	3
Carpenters	3
Cigar Makers	6
Court Interpreters	8 (persons)
Doctors	9
Drug Stores	15
Editors	5
Electrians	2
Fruit Stands	5
Jewelry Stores	3
Laundry Supplies	6
Machine Shops	6
Meat Stores	11
Noodle Stores	4
Novelty Stores	11
Poultry Stores	2
Tailors	6
Typesetters	7
Wagon Peddlers	10

Source: Who's Who of the Chinese in New York (1918).

With the varieties of businesses listed above it is understandable that
Chinatown New York could have been a self-sufficient community. It was
no wonder that many Chinese who lived in New York in those years could
do all their necessary shopping without knowing the English language.

One point requires emphasis, i.e. the laundry and restaurant fields
have long been the important businesses for the Chinese in New York City
Statistics supplied by the United States Census of 1940 showed that 84%
of the gainfully employed Chinese in New York City were in restaurant or
laundry work. This trend in the occupation of the Chinese reamined the
same until the 1960's (see Table 8).

TABLE 8

THE OCCUPATION OF THE CHINESE IN NEW YORK CITY (1940)

(Chinese employed, 14 years old and over)

	Total	Percent
Service workers except domestic	3,558	44.0
Operatives and kindred workers	3,029	37.5
Proprietors, managers and officials	676	8.3
Others	830	10.2
Total employed	8,093	100.0
Total Chinese population in New York City	12,753	

Source: U.S. Census of Population, 1940.

Thus   44% of the work force among the Chinese in New York City were "service workers" which included restaurant employees; 37.5% of the Chinese were in "operatives," which included laundry workers.   The total Chinese population in New York City in 1940 was 12,753.   Thus, more than half of the Chinese population in New York City engaged in these two businesses (laundry and restaurant operation) as late as 1940.

To demonstrate the relationship between the economic life of the Chinese and the various Chinese associations in New York, the contributions of the associations to the laundry and restaurant businesses must be shown.   In the constitutions or by-laws of various associations there were elaborate regulations regarding the conduct and modes of operation.   Thus, the inclusion and creation of various devices for

the smooth operation and well-being of the laundry and restaurant businesses in the community organizations and trade associations were
adaptive techniques and protective devices for the ethnic Chinese in
New York City. Since the laundry and Chinese restaurant businesses had
become the economic niche for the Chinese, efforts were made to protect
these businesses in a formal way through the Chung Hua Kung So (the
highest community organization) and the establishment of the laundry and
trade associations. Although Tongs also contributed to the economic
pursuit of the Chinese, the methods of protection were different. There
were no chartered rules or by-laws specifically directing the conduct
of the Chinese in business; however, the clan and district associations
provided the bases for the dyadic contract and the formation of various
informal relationships such as patron-client, broker-client relationships
which were undoubtedly used for the economic pursuit of the Chinese. The
role of patronage and brokerage in the economic adaptation of the Chinese
during this period will be the subject of Chapter 4. What concerns us
here is the formal roles of those associations in the laundry and restaurant businesses of the Chinese in New York.

The Contributions of the Associations
to the Economic Pursuit of the Chinese

The Over-all Community Organization - The Chinese Consolidated Benevolent
Society (中華公所 or Chung Wah Kung So).

There is only one over-all Chinese community organization. Although
the English name has changed from time to time depending on the administration, the Chinese name remains as Chung Hua Kung So (The Chinese
Public Assembly Hall). It is not a commercial organization. I found

that in both North and South America, the over-all Chinese community
organizations were specially created. They were not an offshoot of a
commercial association. Their duty was to supervise community activity,
regulate the affairs of the community, and facilitate transactions with
the host country and the home country on behalf of the community. In
Latin America these organizations are known as Beneficencia Sociedad de
China, in the United States as Chung Wah Kung So. Another clarification
must be made. Namely, these various over-all community organizations
did not come into existence immediately after the arrival of the Chinese.
Nor did they come into existence under the directives of the host country.
These organizations arose from external pressure and the internal needs
of the community. As mentioned before, in the nineteenth century in
many parts of the world, China had no official representatives.[1] The
overseas Chinese had to rely on their own resources to solve their problems.

In a sense, the establishment of the various Chung Wah Kung So was an
adaptation to a situation where necessary assistance could not be obtained
either from the home country or the host country. The first Chinese
community organization of this kind was the Chinese Six Companies which
were established in 1869 (Hoy 1942: 19-23) in San Francisco. The Chinese

---

[1] According to S.Y. Wu (1954), the Chinese government did not have
any representatives in the United States until 1877.

Six Companies were composed of Chinese from the six major districts in
China: Ning Young, Hop Wo, Kong Chow, Yung Wood, San Yup and Yan Wu.
People from these six districts formed their district associations as
early as 1851 (S.Y. Wu 1954: 14), but called them "companies" in English.
There was a time before the establishment of diplomatic and consular
offices in America, when the Six Companies served as spokesmen for the
Chinese Imperial Government (Kung 1962: 77). Similarly, in New York,
the district associations and family associations existed much earlier
than the Chung Wah Kung So.

The Chung Wah Kung So in New York came into being in 1884 (Leong
1936: 28), after many family and regional associations failed to solve
the problems of the community. It was found that many disputes such as
disputes between members of two associations or two Tongs could not be
settled without a third party. Thus, the situation mandated the birth
of the Chinese Benevolent Association. According to its by-laws, the
association registered with the Peking Imperial Government in 1884 under
the title of Chung Wah Kung So. It was officially incorporated in 1890
under the Societies Act of New York State. The official name of Chung
Wah Kung So was then the Chinese Charitable and Benevolent Association
which was actually a misnomer. It was never merely a charity organization, although the preamble did mention the function of assisting the
poor, the sick and the down-trodden. In 1932, the by-laws were revised;
the preamble says:

> This Association has been functioning for fifty years. In accord-
> ance with out patriotic spirit, its objects are to unify our com-
> patriots, arbitrate any disputes, maintain peace and undertake
> charity and public welfare. It is the supreme organ of the Chinese
> in the Eastern United States (Translated by Leong 1936: 31).

Thus, the Chung Wah Kung So acted as a government for the Chinese in the Eastern United States. According to the by-laws, each Chinese paid a membership fee. There were regulations requiring that all business transactions such as sale and transfer of ownership had to be reported to the association in detail. Business establishments such as laundries and restaurants were required to pay a special fee. Those who failed to comply received no assistance in the form of arbitration in the case of disputes or in the form of transporting bones of the dead after a certain number of years to China. The role of Chung Wah Kung So is the subject matter of Chapter 4 and will be dealt with there.

As for the charitable functions of the Chung Wah Kung So, it was supposed to offer educational and recreational services to its members. It buried the dead and exhumed the bones after a certain number of years to be reburied in China. The Chung Wah Kung So had purchased cemetery plots for the above purpose. Since the old days, Chung Wah Kung So has run a Chinese school. Therefore, it can be called an agent of cultural stability and a conservative force on Chinese culture in the United States. Viewed from outside Chinatown, the Chung Wah Kung So might be seen as an insulator, discouraging contact between the Chinese and the Americans. Nevertheless, the role of brokerage of the Chung Wah Kung So in connecting the Chinese community to the United States society cannot be denied. In the past, the Chung Wah Kung So spoke for the Chinese community quite frequently.

Since Chung Wah Kung So is the supreme organization in the community, the leaders of the association have the highest prestige. Only its four officers are salaried: president, Chinese secretary, English secre-

tary and office boy. In terms of the official salary, the official
monetary reward for the president is by no means attractive. In 1936 it
was reported by Leong (1936: 35) that the salary for the president was
$100 per month, the sum to be used as transportation money. Today, the
transportation money for the president is $200. However, it was never
official transportation money which attracted candidates to the presidency.
In the old days, it was mainly the power and prestige. It was said that
the amount of "kick back" for favors done informally and the usurpation
of public funds was so common that many presidents enriched themselves
enormously. The president was and still is the patron for the community.
He has many friends and connections which he has made through attending
meetings and performing other functions on behalf of the community.

Chinese Consolidated Benevolent Society and the Economic Activities of the Chinese

Being the highest community organization, the Chung Hua Kung So
was supposed to be concerned with the well-being of the Chinese. However, the well-being of the Chinese during this period was so closely
identified with the laundry and restaurant businesses that Chung Wah
Kung So had to devise the means to protect these ethnic enterprises.
Thus ethnicity and the interest of the Chinese ethnic group were conscious phenomena. As a group, the Chinese knew what they should do to
protect their ethnic enclave and the life lines of the Chinese ethnic
group in New York City.

All the Chinese laundry and restaurants were required to register
with the Benevolent Association. All transactions, including the remov

of a store and the reservation of store locations had to be witnessed
and performed by the officers of the Benevolent Association. Otherwise
they were not considered to be "legal" or "official" by the members of
the community. Those who did not comply received no assistance in the
form of arbitration from the association in case of a dispute. In the
1930's, the Benevolent Association had so much power that it could force
a laundry or restaurant out of business if the transaction did not take
place at the association as required by its by-laws. The association
could simply serve a notice on the store and claim that the store owed
the association money. If non-compliance persisted, the association
would send a truck with some musclemen to remove everything and close
the store.

In order to protect the Chinese restaurant and laundry businesses,
specific regulations were promulgated to safeguard autonomy, isolation
and to prevent direct competition. These business regulations devised
by the associations were related to these areas: registration, business
locality, compensation, and transaction and dispute settlement.

According to the by-laws of the association, all Chinese laundries
and restaurants had to register with the association and pay the necessary
registration fees. Each laundry or restaurant which kept its location
had to pay a fee of $2 per year. A one-man laundry had to pay $1; a two-
man laundry paid $2. Chinese restaurants had to pay their annual dues
according to their business volume. For instance, a restaurant which
had a business volume of $240,000 per year paid $16 annual dues, a restaurant having annual business volume of $180,000 paid $12 per year. In
addition to the annual dues, each restaurant or laundry paid the associa-

tion monthly dues according to its business volume. Only those businesses which registered with the associations had the right to a monopoly of the market and the exclusive right to the use of the location for business.

Chung Wah Kung So had specific regulations about business locations. There was only a certain number of restaurants or laundries allowed on a block. The distances between businesses of the same kind were also regulated. If a laundry man invaded the sphere of interest of another laundry, the latter could take the complaint to the Association. If the violaters refused to comply with the decision of the Association, the laundry would be removed by force if necessary.

There were regulations related to the "basic property right." A Chinese who came along to rent a store once occupied by a Chinese paid the former tenant a sum of money for the "basic property right." It was a form of compensation for the former owners of the store. The enforcement of the "basic property right" or p'o tai as it was known in Cantones was thought to be beneficial to the renter as well as to the rentee. The general assumption was that the closing of business due to mismanagement or other factors brought a loss to the owner and the next tenant, who would most likely make money from the location, should compensate at least partially the loss of the former tenant.

All business transactions, including the removal, relocation and sale of Chinese laundries and restaurants had to be registered with the Chinese Benevolent Society. According to the by-laws, "Business transactions of laundries, and restaurants and the like must be reported to the Association by the seller and buyer in person two weeks before the deal, so that the Association can make it known to the public and the deal be made as scheduled; otherwise the deal is not recognized by the Association as legal."[1] The Benevolent Society was glad to enforce this regulation for it collected a fee for such transactions. According to the by-laws, the Association required a fee of $5 for any business transaction. Further, the registration fee for removal of a laundry or a restaurant was based on three months' rent receipts and electric bills as evidence. The registration fee for removal was $10.50. The registration fee for reserving a laundry location was based on a month's rent receipt and took place at the Association's headquarters. The fees collected were divided by the President, the English Secretary, the office boy, and the Association's Treasury. For many years, all the transactions took place in the Association. However, in 1935, the Laundry Alliance took over this function for the Chinese laundry men. A battle against the Laundry Alliance was launched by the Benevolent Association. Due to solidarity among the members and their desire to protect their independence, the Laundry Alliance was able to resist the Benevolent Association.

Thus, the Chinese community of New York City was not always a completely harmonious society without conflicts. It was full of tensions even from early days. However, this does not mean that Chinatown had no solidarity. In fact, Chinatown even in the 1930's had already tried to resist the unnecessary involvement of the white in solving the problems of the community. For every business transaction which took place in the Association's headquarters, only Chinese could act as witnesses to the

---

[1]By-laws of the Chung Wah Kung So.

business deal. The presence of white witnesses was feared by many to weaken the power of the Chinese Benevolent Association. This was evident in the following remark by an older informant, "If we allowed foreigners to act as witness at our business deals, there would be no Chung Wah Kung So."

The Chung Wah Kung So was also the final place for the settlement of disputes. Many disputes which could not be solved by the various Clan or Territorial Associations had to resort to the mediation services of the Chung Wah Kung So. Disputes which involved members from the rival Tongs and rival clan associations were frequently taken to the Chung Wah Kung So for settlement. The decision made by the Chung Wah Kung So was final and had to be abided by. Members of the community also recognized this authority of the Chung Wah Kung So and seldom disobeyed its decisions. A sense of ethnicity certainly played a role in the acceptance of orders or decisions from this over-all community organization. The feeling was, "A Chinese must obey the highest authority of the Chinese Community." Before 1965, most of the disputes were related to laundry and restaurant businesses and were solved within the community. In a sense, the Chinese Benevolent Association did protect the Chinese businesses by legislating rules for the common well-being and efficient settlement of disputes.

It is true that the officials of the CBA profitted from many business deals, but without them many conflicts could not have been resolve since many of the Chinese businessmen in those days could not speak the English language and did not understand American law. There were some states, such as California which did not allow Chinese to testify again whites in the courts (Heyer, 1953: 63). Traditionally, the Chinese preferred to solve their problems in accord with the moral law of the community first before they took their case to the public magistrates. Another factor was "face." The Chinese community used to say that, "Thou shall not expose the ugliness of the family to the outsiders." Unpleasant disputes were thought to be appropriate to solve within the community. This was a moral force which induced the members of the community to solve their problems. Other dispute settlement agents in the community were the various family associations, trade associations, and territorial associations.

Family Associations and Fongs

The various family associations in New York recruited members on the basis of common surname. The bigger family associations in the pre-1965 era were the Lee, Chan and Wong Family Associations. Within the family associations were Fongs which grouped people according to both common surname and common village of origin. Both the family associations and the Fongs had their origins in China. The family name or surname group in China was an exogamous group, and members addressed each other as "clan brothers" (Tien 1953: 22). The surname group was thus a clan group whose members were assumed to be related to one another by descent from a common ancestor (Lang 1968: 20 and Hu 1945: 10). Fong in China was a localized clan group (Tien 1953: 23; Lang 1946; Hu 1948). Members of the Fong in China were patrilineal clansmen by descent from a common ancestor and were associated with a village (Hu 1948; Lang

1946; Tien 1953).[1]

The use of clanship and village relationships to organize and group people among the Chinese communities overseas was an old solution to new problems. In almost all overseas Chinese communities, early immigrants were usually adult males who were married but had left their wives in China. Lack of family life and unfamiliarity with local customs and language created an urgent need for the establishment of Fongs and clan associations in which members could call on one another for help and generate some family feelings or the atmosphere of brotherhood. According to Leong (1936) and some older informants, the Chinese in the early days of New York's Chinatown depended entirely on these Fongs and clan associations to solve the problems they encountered. The most important family name (or clan) associations in those days were Lee, Chan, Wong, Lau Kuan, Chang, Chiu and Ng. Of these the Lees, Wongs, and Chans were the most numerous in New York City. In fact, the Wongs had two family associations in the early days; the Lees had two and the Chans, three. Within each of these family associations, there were smaller groups, Fong. The strength of each Fong of family association in Chinatown depended mainly on the number of followers and the number of well-to-do members. The Chans in New York had some twenty Fongs and were the strongest in Chinatown. Consequently, the rulers of these powerful Fong and family associations had enormous amounts of prestige and power. The

---

[1]I am here giving only the simplest, minimal explanation of both cla and Fong (or Fang in Mandarin) which had been treated in detail by many authors. A Complete exposition of the traditional clan group requires many pages and is beyond the scope of this study. Authors who are autho itative on this matter are Hsien Chin Hu (1948) and Olga Lang (1968).

were called the Kiu Ling (leaders) by the Chinese and were usually the
benefactors and people who had connections within the community and
sometimes with the host society. It is said that some of these Kiu Ling
in the past were "troublemakers" and "hustlers." In the Tong days, they
had incited the members to war in order to save "face" for themselves
and for their respective Fongs or family associations as well. Fongs
varied in size of membership from 20-100. The Fongs were usually associated with one of the family associations.

The Fongs in New York's Chinatown often maintained buildings which
were used as recreation hall or dormitories. Organization of the Fongs
in those days was said to be rather informal. Relationships among the
members were face-to-face, intimate and personal. Since clansmen were
from the same village in China, they addressed each other with such kinship terms as Heng (older brother) and Dai (younger brother). Members
were supposed to come to each other's assistance when the situation
called for it. Thus, the Fongs were actually a mutual aid society in-
stilled with kinship ideology.

In the early days in New York, the headquarters of the Fongs served
as: 1) a place of lodging for the sick, the old, or temporarily jobless
members; 2) a hostel for traveling clansmen; and 3) a recreation hall.

The larger social units above the Fongs were the various clan or
family name associations which were called Kung-sos (Public Assembly) or
Chung Chan Wei (Common Descent Relatives Association). These family
associations were the intermediaries for the Fongs and the regional
associations. As mentioned before, power and prestige of family associations depended chiefly on the number and wealth of the membership.

Thus, the smaller family association was constantly under the shadow of
the big family associations. Due to limited available resources, a
small family association had difficulty fulfilling needs and rendering
sufficient protection of those members who were in need. These smaller
families were able to manipulate the traditional practices to form multi-
surname associations. These practices were the traditional family
alliances of sworn brotherhood, traditional friendship, intermarriage
to remote ancestors; neighboring home districtt or similarity of a radical
in the writing of surnames.

One of the most important multi-family name associations was the
"Four Brothers" Association which was organized by the Liu , Kwan, Chang,
and Chiu families because their forebearers swore brotherhood by the
"Peace-Garden Oath" two thousand years ago for the purpose of saving
the Han Dynasty. Another multi-family name association was the G.H. Oak
Tin Association which was composed of the Chan, Hu and Yuan families who
were traditionally united by friendship. Chee Tuck San Tuck Association
was composed of Wu, Tsai, Chow families who were once neighbors in China.
Similarly, the neighboring families of Loui, Fong and Kwon were united
to form Soo Yuen Association; Gon, Lai and Ho families became the San
Yick Association. Then, the most interesting of all was Chiu Lung
Association which united Tan, Tan, Hsu and Hsieh families because there
was a similarity in the Chinese characters; all of them possessed a
common radical in their names.

Thus, not only was the traditional clanship used but also the
traditional friendship, neighborhood, traditional marriage, and other
traditional principles were social resources used to form the various

family associations. This points to the urgency of group solidarity in the early days of Chinatown. In all the family associations, single family name or the multi-family name, the kinship ideology was deliberately embraced. Kinship terms like Heng (older brother), Dai (younger brother), Shuk (younger uncle), and Bak (older uncle) were commonly used. In a sense, most of the family associations were performing the same functions as the Fongs. They provided recreational facilities such as reading rooms, some Mahjong tables, facilities for temporary lodging, relief services, and means of settling disputes. Solidarity was expressed through various rituals and celebrations. The most common ritual expression was the bi-annual ceremony of visiting the ancestral tombs at the Ching Ming and Chung Yung festivals.[1] The economic significance of the Fongs and family associations will be discussed later. The family associations and the Fongs were indispensable to the survival of the newcomers in the early days.

Due to the important role played by these families and Fongs, the leaders of these associations wielded enormous amounts of power. They became the wheelers and dealers. They were often active outside the formal activities of the associations. These leaders of Kiu Ling, termed by Leong (1936:58) as the "gentlemen," were the most important brokers.

> To get anything done in Chinatown, you have to play politics with them. They cannot only pull the necessary wires in Chinatown, but often in American official circles. The bigger the face of the gentlemen and the bigger the bribe for favor, the surer you are of success. You can rest assured too, as the Charitable Association once said, that 'until all political resources are exhausted, we will not resort to legal procedure'(Leong 1936: 58).

---

[1]This ritual will be discussed in Chapter 5.

The important Fongs and family associations from 1870-1964 are listed
in Table 9.

TABLE 9

CHINESE CLAN ASSOCIATIONS IN NEW YORK

Family or Clan Associations[a]	Family Names Represented[b]
Chee Tuck San Tuck Association	Ng, Tsai, Chow, Ung, Cho
Chew Lun Association	Tam, Tan, Hsu and Hsieh
Chin Shou Kai Fong	Chin
Chin. Wing Chuen Association	Chin (or Chan)[c]
Eng Lung Hing Society	Eng
Eng Suey Sung Association	Eng
Fonn Lung Benevolent Association	Szeto, See[d]
G.H. Oak Tin Association	Chin (or Cahn), Woo, Yin
Gee How Hing Association	Gee (or Chu)[e]
Gee Poykao Association	Gee (or Chu)
Lee King Shou Club	Lee (or Li)[f]
Lee's Family Association	Lee (or Li)
Leung Chung Low Tong	Leung
Lum Sai Ho Association	Lum
Lun Kong Time Yee Association	Lau, Kwan, Cheung, Chiu
Moy's Family Association	Moy
Nam Young Association	Yip, Teng, Yin
Sam Yick Association	Kwong, Lai, Ho
Soo Yuen Tong	Loui, Fong, Kwong
Tseng Sum Sing Association	Tseng
Wong's Family Association	Wong
Wong Shee Bat Suey	Wong
Yee Benevolent Association	Yee
Yee Moo Kai Fong	Yee

Sources: Leong (1936; Van Norden (1918); and interviews.

[a]The Romanizations are in Cantonese. The English titles of these associations are the official ones used by them.

[b]The family names are Romanized the manner which the New York Chine followed.

[c]Chin and Chan are interchangeable. Chin is a Toisanese Romanizati and Chan is a Cantonese Romanization of

[d]The coresponding Chinese character is

[e]Gee is a Cantonese pronunciation and Chu is a Mandarin pronunciation of the same character.

[f]Lee and Li are interchangeable.

Membership in the family associations varied. The nominal membership could range from 500-3,000[1] However, the full-fledged members
(members who paid their dues) in the family association could range
from 500-1,000 (Heyer, 1953: 70). All family associations had a similar
administstrative staff: one president, one Chinese secretary, one English
secretary, one executive secretary, and one treasurer. The leaders of
the Fongs, together with the administrative staff, formed the council of
the family association. Officials of the Fongs or family association
were the important patrons for the members and played an important role
in the decision-making activities of the Chinese (see Chapter 4).

The Formal Contributions of the Fong and Family Associations to the
Economic Pursuit of the Chinese:

In the past, the Fongs and the family associations greatly facilitated the economic activities of the Chinese by way of: 1) providing
credit and financing through operation of informal credit clubs or hui[1];
2) providing temporary lodging for the jobless and job hunters; 3) providing employment services; 4) rendering translation and secretarial
services for the obtainment of business licenses; and 5) settling business
disputes.

Regional or District Associations

Fongs and family name associations could group together many people
of the same surname. However, there were far more surnames than the
family name associations in New York could represent. Out of the 150

---

[1]Processes involved in obtainment of financing, employment, etc.,
will be discusses in Chapter 4.

common surnames among the Chinese, not more than 60 family surnames were represented in the Chinatown of New York's 24 associations. In order to provide a place for every member in a group, many associations had to be created. They had to be organized on a wider base such as the regional associations. Known generally as <u>Wei-kun</u>, these associations grouped members according to the larger district or region from which they had migrated. In a word, these associations were organized on the basis of geography and of people's particular attachment to their common soil or origin. The regional associations in the early days of Chinatown were not as numerous as they are today because the early immigrants were mostly from the provinces of Kwangtung and Fukien. The names of the regional associations were usually taken from the districts, counties or provinces of China. The following were the important regional associations in 1936.

TABLE 10

IMPORTANT REGIONAL OR DISTRICT ASSOCIATIONS IN 1936

Names	District
Ning Young Association[a]	Toisan
Lung Sing Association[b]	Anywhere in China except Toisan
Chung San Association	Chung San
Fay Chow Association	Fay Chow
Hoy Ping Association	Hoy Ping
Hok San Society	Hok San
Nam Shun	Nam Hoy, Shun Tak
Sun Wei Association	Sun Wei
Hainan Association	Hainan Island
Tung Goon Association	Tung On and Po On
Yan Ping Association	Yan Ping
Yee Shan Benevolent Society	Pun Yee
Hoy Yin Association	Hoy Fung
Kwong Hoy Association	Kwong Hoy

Sources: Leong (1936); Van Norden (1918); and interviews.

[a]Romanization of the names of the associations are in Cantonese and are the official English titles used by the associations.

[b]Lung Sing Association is a Federation of Six Regional Associations. A federation was formed to rival Ning Soung Association which has an extremely large number of members since most of the immigrants in New York were from the Toisan District. Even combining six other regional associations, the Lung Sing Association in the early days still could not match Ning Young in membership.

Regional associations recruited members on the basis of wider locality of origin such as shared township or counties. The size of these regional associations, like the family associations, varied. The registered membership in these associations could range from 500-1,000 people (Heyer 1953: 70). In terms of administration, the arrangement was similar to that of the family association. The officials or leaders of the regional associations, however, had more prestige than the family and Fong associations. This was due to two reasons. First, these regional associations were generally bigger, and the leaders had a larger following. Second, the leaders of the regional associations were potential candidates for the offices of the over-all community organization, the Chinese Consolidated Benevolent Society.

Among the regional associations, two were super-regional: Ning Young and Lun Sing Associations. Ning Young Association was composed of members from the Toisan County, Kwangtung Province. Lun Sing Association was a united association composed of all the regional associations listed in Table 10, except Ning Young. Thus, members of the Lun Sing Association came from everywhere in China except Toisan county. Ning Young and Lun Sing Associations were and still are directly responsible for the election of officers to the Chinese Consolidated Benevolent Associations.

The regional associations were the intermediary organizations between the family and the highest community organization in the following senses. First, disputes which could not have been handled satisfactorily by the family associations could go to the regional association for mediation. If the case still was not solved, it went to the Chinese Benevolent Association. Not all the disputes could be handled by the family association. Thus, for instance, if a Lee had a dispute with a Chan, since they belonged to different family associations, the disputes could not be solved within a common family association. However, it was likely that the Lee and the Chan were from Toysan County, and therefore they could use the mediation services of the Toisan Regional Association. The leaders (Kiu Ling) of the regional associations were often bridges between the leaders of the family associations and the leaders of the Chinese Benevolent Association. Thus, for instance, if a leader of the Lee Association wanted to ask for a favor from the president of the Chinese Benevolent Association, it was appropriate for the former through the leaders of the regional association.

The functions of the regional associations were similar to those of the family associations. They were basically mutual aid and mutual protection societies. However, the regional associations were more active in providing special relief to people of their districts in China during the Sino-Japanese War. After the war, the regional associations frequently remitted money for educational purposes to their respective districts in China. As mentioned in Chapter 2, since most of the Chinese were from Kwangtung during the period of 1870-1964, the regional associations were not as numerous as today since heterogeneity in locality of origin increased only recently.

Contributions of the Regional Associations to the Economic Activities of the Chinese

Their contributions are similar to those of the Fongs and family associations, and therefore will not be enumerated here.

Trade Associations

Since most of the Chinese in this period were engaged in laundry and restaurant businesses, the most important trade associations were: 1) the Chinese Hand Laundry Alliance, 2) the Chinese-American Restaurant Association of Greater New York, Inc., 3) the Chamber of Commerce, and 4) the Seamen's Association. They maintained an administrative staff similar to those of the family and regional associations. Members were recruited on the basis of trade or occupation. Among these four associa-

tions, only the Chinese Hand Laundry Alliance and the Chinese-American
Restaurant Association were well-organized. Due to their large memberships, they had considerable economic power. The former was formed in
1933 to provide an efficient organization to regulate prices and to
protect the Chinese laundry trade. The latter, also formed in 1933,
was concerned mainly with the well-being of the Chinese restaurant
owners and employers.

Contributions of the Trade Association to the Economic Pursuits of the Chinese

Except for the laundry association, other occupational associations
such as the Chamber of Commerce and the Seamen's Association were not
well organized in this period. Unlike the overseas Chinese community in
Southeast Asia where the Chinese Chambers of Commerce were the supreme
organizations of the communities, the Chinese Chamber of Commerce in
New York City had very few members; it consisted merely of Chinatown
merchants. The contributions of the Chinese Chamber of Commerce was
limited to the area of fixing prices in accordance with exchange rates.
Only recently has the Chinese Chamber of Commerce started to expand its
membership and become more involved in community affairs. In the past,
it was almost like a social club and not at all influential in Chinatown's
politics.

The Chinese Restaurant Association was established in May of 1933
with the specific purpose of mutual protection and the development of
Chinese restaurant enterprises in New York City. It employed legal
consultants, accountants, and nutritionists to advise the executive

committee. Within the executive committee, there were various sub-
committess in charge of cooking research, equipment installation, regulation, and employment. Since the Chinese-American Restaurant Association was not particularly active until after 1965, a further discussion
of its role will be conducted later in this study.

The contributions of the Chinese occupational associations will
be analyzed in terms of the Laundry Alliance. The Chinese Laundry
Alliance was chosen because of its large membership. It was perhaps
one of the most powerful organizations in Chinatown, and it was considered by many to be the rival of the Chinese Consolidated Benevolent
Society. It rendered great service to the Chinese laundry men by giving
advice, obtaining licenses, and negotiating with the government for a
fairer regulation governing the Chinese laundry businesses. Thus, the
Chinese Laundry Alliance is a prime example of how members of the ethnic
group perceive their economic niches and organize themselves accordingly
to protect this niche.

The Chinese Hand Laundry Alliance was first established in 1933.
The impetus for bringing all the Chinese laundry men together was
pressure from outside sources which impinged on their survival. In
1933 the Chinese laundry trade in New York had already existed for 50
years. Chinese started the hand laundry businesses in New York City
in 1870. The proliferation of the laundries was visible. Economic
competition again aroused the jealousy of many American laundry men
in the eastern United States. According to Leong (1936) there had
been numerous campaigns and systematic attacks directed against Chinese
laundry men in New York. It was not uncommon to find placards and

cartoons showing a filthy Chinese laundry man at work spitting on a
white shirt. In addition to this attack in the printed media, there were
new regulations in New York which discriminated against small laundry
firms, in particular the Chinese hand laundry. According to the new
regulation, every laundry had to pay $25 for licensing and post $1,000
bond. As a result of this requirement, many Chinese hand laundry shops
went bankrupt. These two events made the Chinese feel the importance
of solidarity and the necessity of organizing themselves for mutual protection. In May, the Chinese Hand Laundry Allinace was born. The
leaders of the Alliance immediately explained the financial difficulties
of the Chinese laundry men to the Public Welfare Committee of the Alder-
manic Board. As a result, the license fees for the laundry men were
reduced to $10, and the security bond was reduced to $100. At its inception, the Hand Laundry Alliance had a membership of 2,000. There
were well-organized representations. The greater New York area was
arbitrarily divided into 300 districts which consisted of 10 laundries
per district. Each district sent one delegate to the convention.
From among the 300 delegates, 104 officials were chosen forming the
various supervisory and executive committees. Only two secretaries and
one office worker were salaried. The rest of the officials received no
income except for $10 shoe money (transportation money) per year. It
was said that the leadership was so dedicated and capable that it
alleviated many problems related to the Chinese hand laundry business.
It provided legal aid by way of assisting in the obtaining of
licenses, or transacting with the State Labor Department, and the

police departments. The Hand Laundry Alliance also provided temporary relief to the unemployed and to the family members of the deceased. The Hand Laundry Alliance, realizing the need of English training and recreation for the Chinese laundry men, sponsored English classes and picnics.

The Hand Laundry Alliance in the Chinese community took on many functions which were previously performed by the Chinese Benevolent Society. For a minimal fee, it witnessed the sale of laundries. Financially, due to large contributions derived from the membership, the Hand Laundry Alliance had enormous amounts of money. In addition, the leadership of the alliance was more liberal than the CBA in its outlook and stressed the principles of democracy and self-determination. It attempted to exclude the control of the Chinese laundry men by the CBA. Although the Laundry Alliance continued to use the Benevolent Association's mediation services in its disputes with other associations, its relationship with the CBA was tenuous. Finally in 1950, after the Hand Laundry Alliance refused to participate in an anti-communism campaign organized by the CBA during the Korean War, it was expelled as a participating organization of the Chinese Benevolent Association. From published materials and interviews with older laundry men, the Hand Laundry Alliance was said to have done a great deal to protect the Chinese hand laundry business in New York City.

The Tongs

Of interest to the American public as well as of importance to the discussion of social life in Chinatown are the tongs. The tongs were neither a Chinese nor an American phenomenon; they were a combination of both. Various authors have attempted to ascertain the origin of the tongs. Some have attributed their origin to the various family associations which banded together and hired hatchet men to deal with the bandits who molested the Chinese in San Francisco and to protect family members from the exploitation of major family associations (Mann 1924; Leong 1936). Others believed that the tongs originated in China as secret societies (Culin 1887; 1889). While it is true that there was some resemblence between the secret societies in China and the tongs in America, their natures and functions were quite different. The secret societies in China were mainly political organizations which aimed originally at overthrowing foreign rule of the Yuen and Ching dynasties. The tongs in America were originally fraternal organizations formed to promote the personal gain of their members. This pursuit of gain centered mainly on the illegal businesses and vices. Rose Hum Lee (1962) pointed out that the creation and existence of the tongs was to meet the needs of some individuals who desired prestige and quick money, because these opportunities were denied to them by the larger society. As mentioned earlier, the Chinese were treated as second class citizens for a long time, since the immigration policy and other economic opportunities of the larger society discriminated against them.

The tongs were organized nationally. The three important tongs in New York during this period were: the Gee Kung Tong (the Chinese Free Masons), On Leong Tong and Hip Sing Tong. While the first one was traditionally one of the weakest of the three, this organization still exists in many parts of the world, such as Canada, Peru, and England.

Sometimes it is known as Hung Man Man Chi Tang. The Gee Kung Tong participated frequently in many of the tong wars but was defeated miserably. The vitality of this tong has not been felt since the tong wars of the 1930's.

During the period of 1870-1964, the most powerful tongs were the On Leong and Hip Sing. They were rivals in many respects. They warred against one another frequently. These two tongs divided the territory of New York's Chinatown into two areas. Bayard Street, Mott Street and the north and west of Mott Street were under the influence of On Leong Tong. Pell Street, Doyer Street and the eastern area of those two streets were under the influence of Hip Sing. Members of these rival tongs conducted their business exclusively within the designated territories. If territorial right was violated, war resulted. While it was difficult to prove whether the tongs directly financed and operated various illicit businesses, it was acknowledged by all informants that the tongs had collected and levied tributes from various businesses. As a group, the tongs did not operate gambling houses, houses of prostitution, or opium dens, but some members of these tongs were directly involved in these businesses.

Tongs had some connections with illegal businesses in Chinatown such as the business of smuggling Chinese into the United States, as well as the businesses mentioned above. However, this does not mean that the tongs owned these businesses as a group; they did not. In addition, not all businessmen in the tongs were in illegal businesses. Illegal businesses were owned and operated by individual tong members.

Those businessmen who were in illegal businesses were particularly in need of the tongs and were eager to obtain leadership positions. The tong leaders rose because of their ability to attract a following and from their personal skill in fighting and organizing the tong wars as well. It was said that those tong members who wanted to compete for leadership positions had to spend a handsome amount of money to buy votes. This practice still persists in the tongs of present day China-town. Once a tong was elected, he gained protection money from both legal and illegal businesses. On Leong was wealthier than Hip Sing. The former had more members who were rich businessmen. The latter was composed of laundry men, laborers, and seamen, as well as some businessmen. Both the Hip Sing and On Leong Tongs tried to exert their influence on the CBA and tried to have it located in their territory. From the data available, it seems that the CBA was always situated in the On Leong Tong territory, even at the present time. It i« said that On Leong Tong has more influence in the CBA.

Contributions of the Tong to the Economic Pursuit of the Chinese

The Laundry Alliance protected the Chinese economic niche by guarding the legal rights of the Chinese laundry men; the tongs pro-tected the interests of their members by the threat of force. In the early days, between 1870-1930, the tongs were powerful in Chinatown, and the infamous tong wars led many honest and innocent people into joining the tongs for protection. Since the two tongs, On Leong and Hip Sing divided their sphere of influence in Chinatown, merchants located in their areas of influence usually joined the respective tong. Thus, the merchants in Mott and Bayard Streets became members of On

Leong; merchants in the Pell and Doyer Streets joined the Hip Sing. Those merchants who belonged to Hip Sing but worked in the On Leong area were constantly under the threat of On Leong and vice versa. Merchants who had no Tong connections were at the mercy of both Tongs. Thus, a merchant was practically forced by the Tongs to join them. Business competition and violations of the rules of the Tongs were dealt with by dragging the competitor or violator from his store and vandalizing his place. Disputes between Tong connected businesses had to be resolved by the Tongs first. However, conflict between the rival Tongs, if not settled by themselves, was taken to the CBA. That is why both the On Leong and Hip Sing were interested in supporting the CBA.

Other Organizations

In addition to the Fongs, family, district, trade association, the Chung Wah Kung So, and the Tongs, there were dialectic, political, veteran, athletic, and recreational associations.

In the period of 1870-1949, the pro-Kuomintang sentiment was strong because the Kuomintang had been responsible for the overthrow of the foreign Manchurian rule in China. The early Chinese immigrants who left China had been under the reign of Manchu and were generally dissatisfied with the Imperial Government in China. The anti-Manchurian activities of the enlightened Chinese intellectuals and the personal dynamism of Dr. Sun Yat Sen had enlisted the support of many overseas Chinese to participate in the anti-Manchu movement and the establishment of the Republic of China. In fact, Dr. Sun Yat Sen's Kuomintang party had such a vast membership in the eastern part of the United States that

the party had both its eastern United States regional office and its
branch office located in the Chinatown area of New York City. There
was another political party which was Min Chih Tang (known also as the
Chinese Freemasons Democratic Party) which championed the anti-Manchurian
cause but opposed the **Kuomintang**.

Thus, the politics of Chinatown during this period was more oriented
toward China than toward the United States. Nevertheless, there were
American-oriented political clubs--the Republican and Democratic Clubs
of Chinatown. Between 1870-1964 these two clubs were not influential
and had no official representatives due to small membership to participate in the government of Chinatown, the Consolidated Benevolent Society.

There were also various recreational, musical, cultural, athletic
and dramatic associations and the Veterans of Foreign Wars, Chinatown
Post. Their presence has been felt only in recent years.

One point must be emphasized. All the associations, organizations,
and groups discussed in this section not only divided and segmented the
people of Chinatown, they also united and integrated them. First,
membership in many associations was not mutually exclusive. Thus, for
instance, one could be a member of his family association and regional
association at the same time. Second, all the associations were coordinated under the leadership of the overall community organization,
the Chinese Consolidated Benevolent Association. There were about
sixty important associations participating in the CCBA. The 70 representatives from the associations made up the general assembly of the
CCBA. Out of the general assembly, 19 were selected to serve in a
standing committee. The representatives and the leaders of the various

associations were often referred to as <u>Kiu Ling</u> (literally, leaders of
the overseas Chinese) and informally, as "big persons." Each of them
was concerned with forming a following. They were the patrons and a
complicated patronage system existed from the inception of Chinatown.

Since the membership in different associations was not mutually
exclusive and one could be a member of different associations at the
same time, many social scientists were mistakenly led to think that
class distinctions in Chinatown were not acute (Heyer 1953; Crissman
1972; Willmott 1970). In reality, due to financial, temporal and spatial
limitations, it was almost impossible to be active in more than one
association unless one was rich and could leave his business to be
attended by his assistants. Thus, the fact that there was cross membership in many associations did not necessarily imply social equality.
On the contrary, it was common to find that those who were active in
different associations were a special class of people (see Chapter 4).
Often, they were the same group of people. Furthermore, there was the
practice of according the honorary position upon a former leader or
official of an association. These Kiu Ling are of interest to us not
merely because of the fact that they were the officials of the various
organizations but also because of the fact that they were usually entrepreneurs and patrons of the community. Their influence in the community
and the entrepreneurial pursuit of the Chinese will be discussed in
Chapter 4. The point to be re-emphasized here is that the interlocking
of association's politics and the criss-crossing of membership did not
automatically level off social inequality. Social asymmetry existed
from the very inception of the community. This social asymmetry was

further complicated by the uneven access to social resources. The Kiu

Ling had more connections and made more money which could be converted

to political power and to attract a large following.[1] The economically

deprived and the weak had to seek protection from these Kiu Ling. There

was a saying, "If you want to get ahead in Chinatown, know some Kiu

Ling." The word know in Chinese implies friendship, respectful inter-

action. In order to know the leaders of Kiu Ling, to contract any

dyadic relationship, one had to be a member of an association. Thus,

the structure of the Chinese community provided favorable conditions

for the formation of patron-client relationships and the functioning of

a system of patronage.

In summary, there is a definite relationship between the various

Chinese associations and the businesses of the Chinese. The associa-

tions were essentially protective devices for the Chinese in New York.

Having no protection from the home country nor the host country, the

Chinese had to resort to the various associations and the Tongs. The

consciousness of what constituted the livelihood of the community led

them to devise particular solutions for their protection and for their

self-exploitation as in the case of the Tongs. Hence regulations were

made to safeguard the economic niche of the Chinese; the Chinese hand

laundry, Chinese restaurants, and other Chinese types of businesses.

In this period of 1870-1964, Chinatown was devoid of family life, most

of the Chinese channeled their recreational needs into the gambling,

---

[1]A lengthy discussion of the formation of patron-client relationship
will appear in Chapter 4.

prostitution and opium houses. This in turn gave the Tongs the
opportunity to rise and expand, and it gave those individuals who were
in need of wealth and power a special outlet. The formation of protective associations such as the Hand Laundry Alliance, Restaurant
Association, and Tongs can be seen as an adaptive technique in a particular situation.

To an extent, these associations were organized along traditional
lines. However, the final outcome of the organizational effort was
typically related to the situation. There was no association in China
which could duplicate the Chinese Hand Laundry Alliance in New York.
Similarly, though there was some resemblence between the secret society
(秘密會社) in China and the Tongs in the United States, they differed
in goals, ideology and methods of organization. Finally, the establishment of the CCBA, the government of Chinatown, was an American product.

All these associations, Tongs, and the CCBA were Chinese in that
they had to depend on Chinese people for their continued and prosperous
existence. Thus, if the Chinese in New York were all assimilated or if
the Chinese in New York could speak the English language or if the
Chinese in New York's Chinatown all moved out to the different suburbs
in New York City, there would have been no need of a Chinese government
within the United States; there would have been no need of the Tongs and
the various traditional associations.

CHAPTER 4

TRANSACTIONAL RELATIONSHIP AND THE

ENTREPRENEURIAL PURSUIT OF THE CHINESE IN 1870-1964

Since patron-client relationship could be contracted within institutional set-ups such as family firm (Benedict 1968), clan, regional
and dialect associations (Tien 1953; Amyot 1968), clubs and other tra-
ditionaal organizations (Barth 1955; Leeds 1964; Aubey, Kyle and Strickon
1974; Wheeldon 1969; Mitchell 1969), and since structural features can
often act as factors of constraint or reinforcement of the formation and
manipulation of patron-client relatioship for decision-making activities
(Bailey 1969; Barth 1955; Stuart 1972), it is significant to look into
the structures and functions of the associations which constituted the
structure of the Chinese community. Chapter 3 concentrated on the
social structure and the contributions of the various Chinese Associations to economic activities. What remains to be shown are the mechanisms involved in the formation and manipulation of patron-client relationships within these various Associations for goal-seeking pursuits.[1]
The analysis of patron-client transaction mechanisms will take into
consideration the three major variables as suggested by Strickon and
Greenfield: 1) the cultural tradition (the idiom in which the negotia-

[1]The manipulation of patron-client relationships for goal-seeking
activities within the Tongs will not be discussed in this chapter for
two main reasons: 1) many goal-seeking activities were said to be
illegal, and 2) the information obtained on the activities of the Tongs
in the past cannot be verified.

tions and transactions are conducted); 2) the system of formal positions
within the institutional system; and 3) the resources available to the
specific actors that may be employed by them in the transactional process
(Strickon and Greenfield 1972: 15).

In the Chinese community of New York, Kam Ching[1] (sentiment), Yee
Hay (trusting righteousness)[2], and Min (face)[3] are the three essential
elements of the idiom. These elements, as will be shown , provide the
basis for the initiation, maintenance, acceptance, continuation of transactions between actors in the Chinese community. The second variable
is position and the accompanying rights, obligations, and resources of
the actors. Social positions of the individuals in the clan, regional,
dialect or the overall Chinese associations could be assets or constraining factors of decision-making. The third variable is resource. In
the Chinese community of New York, resource includes capital, manpower,
property, and connections.

The focus of analysis in this chapter is on the formation and manipulation of patron-client relationships within the various Chinese institutions for gain-seeking activities: establishing a firm, obtaining
employment, financing, and settling business disputes.

---

[1]It is pronounced in Mandarin as Kam Chin. The corresponding Chinese characters are 感情 . Cantonese Romanization is used because
the words were given to me in Cantonese during my fieldwork.

[2]It is pronounced in Mandarin as Yee Chi. The corresponding
Chinese characters are 義氣

[3]It is pronounced in Mandarin as Mien Tzu, in Cantonese as Min Tsi.
The corresponding Chinese characters are 面子

Chinese Firms: a General View

Before discussing the processes involved in the establishment of a firm, it is necessary to present a descriptive account of the various types of Chinese firms existing in New York's Chinatown during this period. The organizations of Chinese firms were couched upon traditional relationships: kinship, clanship, ritual brotherhood, common locality of origin and patron-client relationships.

Firms which were organized by brothers or groups of patrilineal male relatives were more numerous. Quite a few were organized by people sharing the locality of origin. Some were organized by people who originated from neighbouring towns in China but spoke the same dialect. For instance, the people from Sam Yap district composed of the three towns of Sun Wei, Ham Hoi, Shung Tak would come together to pool their resources to establish a partnership firm. With the information obtained from the Who's Who of the Chinese in New York (Van Norden 1918), and the oral accounts of some elderly informants from the Golden Age Club and the Senior Citizen Division of the Greater China-town Community Center, the following table was constructed. Table 11 shows the principle types of Chinese firms found in the 1920's. The number of firms in Table 11 is not the totality of all Chinese firms in New York. They were the firms which had more complete histories and were listed in the Who's Who of the Chinese in New York (1918). What concerns us here is not the exact statistics, but the various types of businesses and the various processes involved in the establishment of these firms.

TABLE 11

TYPES OF CHINESE FIRMS

Owned and Managed by	Number of Firms	Percentage
Family (father and sons)	3	3.08%
Brothers	15	15.4
Patrilineal Kinsmen (cousing, uncles, and Nephews)	47	48.4
Members of the larger clan group (members of the clan association)	19	19.4
Friends from the same region in China	4	4.1
Friends from neighbouring towns in China	8	8.2
Other	1	1.0
Total	97	99.5%

Table 11 also indicates that the most common type of business firms were run by patrilineal kinsmen such as classificatory paternal cousins, uncles, and Nephews. Thus, shared blook lines were important in business partnerships. In the order of importance, the various types of interpersonal relationships important for partnership cooperation were:

1. Patrilineal kinsmen
2. Members of the larger clan group
3. Brothers
4. Friends from neighbouring towns in China
5. Friends from the same area in China
6. Family
7. Other friends

Thus, next to blood lines, family name or assumed common ancestry provided the basis for economic cooperation. In a word, it is easier for a Moy to enter partnership with another Moy. However, such a cooperation is not automatic, a dyadic relationship has to be created. As a rule, due to the existence of clan associations, there was more opportunity for a Moy to meet another Moy and become friends. People from

the same locality in China often came together to organize a business,
locality of origin always plays a role in the economic activities of
the overseas Chinese (Tien 1953; Amyot 1960; Skinner 1958). The pri-
ordial feelings attached to these relationships of blood and locality
of origin were recognized by many anthropologists (Geertz 1963; Dewey
1962; Khuri 1965; Weightman 1954; Lewis 1974) as important factors for
organizing many goal-seeking activities. Not only did the hometown
mates (or Heung Lay - 鄉里) enter business partnerships, it was
found that people who migrated from the neighbouring towns in China
frequently organized themselves to start partnership firms. Thus, the
principles of consanguinity, clanship, locality of origin, shared dialect
etc. used for social organization in Chinatown (see Chapter 3) were also
used for organizing economic activities of the Chinese. Ethnicity was
thus a social resource which was used both for social organization and
for structuring economic activities (Barth 1969).

Three constraining factors for the non-development of family firms
were related to the immigration policies of the larger society, the
values of the Chinese, and the social organization of the Chinese community. First, there was the conspicuous absence of Chinese families
between 1870-1945; the community was then composed mainly of middle-aged
males who were married but left their wives in China. Second, very few
Chinese in those days intended to stay in the U.S. permanently. The
United States was a place to make money but to reside in only temporarily. Although some Chinese returned to China to marry, they did not
sponsor their wives to come to the United States. Instead, they made
remittances to China and visited China whenever they accumulated suffi

cient wealth and could afford the time to stay away from their businesses. Investing in China and building brick houses in home villages was more important and prestigeous for the early day immigrants. Third, because of enforcement of the "Chinese Exclusion Law" which inhibited the free flow of Chinese women, many Chinese bachelors in New York could not establish families.[1] However, after World War II many Chinese G.I.s made use of the G.I. war Bride Bill to sponsor their wives to come to New York. Consequently more family firms became established after 1945. The number of Chinese family firms could not be ascertained. What is evident, however, is the seizure of the immigration policy of the larger society for goal-seeking activities.

The absence of Chinese families before World War II did not inhibit the economic activities of the Chinese, it merely restricted the establishment of family firms. Instead of having immediate family members running a firm, many Chinese who were related by blood, by common ancestry or by common origin of locality came together to organize partnership firms. Table 11 indicated that most of the Chinese firms in the 1920's were run by clansmen and kinsmen. A fuller explanation of such a phenomenon can be achieved only if we take into consideration the constraint factors, the alternatives and the social economic resources available to the Chinese in those days. Strategic decision-making activities can be accounted for satisfactory only if these activities are viewed as constrained choice activities undertaken in a situation

---

[1] Interracial marriage was not common in those days. Further, there were miscegenation laws in many parts of the United States which prohibited intermarriage between Chinese and white Americans.

influenced by cultural, economic, and socio-economic variables (Barth
1956, 1959, 1963, 1967, 1969; Howard 1963; Keesing 1967).

Economically, there was the financial restraint. Most Chinese
were originally laborers or small businessmen who had no command over
capital. The very rich Chinese in the old days did not migrate to the
United States (Chan 1940; Coolidge 1969). Thus, due to the limited
available resource for investment, it was difficult for an individual
to start his own firm. Second, the United States Immigration policy
in general and the "Chinese Exclusion" in particular favored the establishment of partnership firms. These immigration laws made special
provision for Chinese businessmen to travel and to re-enter the United
States. Since most of the Chinese in those days wanted to visit China
for business and personal purposes, it was convenient if they were
bonafide businessmen so that they could travel freely and return to the
United States to continue their businesses. Third, Chinatown's social
structure itself gave ample opportunity for the formation of patron-
client networks (賓主關係). The clan associations, the regional
associations and the dialect associations facilitated the interaction
of many clansmen, kinsmen, and village-mates. Friendships with clansmen, kinsmen and village-mates often led to business partnerships. The
fourth factor is the traditional habit of the Chinese to travel and
work together with clansmen, village-mates (Tien 1953; Ng 1968). All
these factors explain why there were so many Chinese business firms
organized along the lines of kinship, clanship, common speech and commo
locality of origin. The processes involved in the establishment of the
firms will be demonstrated in the next few sections.

Family Firms

There were very few Chinese families in the early period of Chinatown (cf. Chapter 2). Chinese firms based on family firms were even
less. This does not mean that family firms were non-existent, however,
the number of family firms during this period was not significant enough
to warrant a detailed description. Further, some of those so-called
father-son firms might not necessarily be run by father and son. Many
of the declared father-son relationships, according to my informants,
were not actually related by real paternity. They may have been just
kinsmen bearing the same surname. To circumvent the immigration laws
of this period which gave preference for admission to this country to
the children of naturalized citizens or permanent residents, some of
the younger kinsmen were sponsored by older kinsmen into the country as
"sons." This phenomenon was known commonly as the "paper-son," i.e.
some one related to someone as father-son on the legal paper only.

The "paper-son," sometimes, was not even related by kinship or
friendship. I was told by some elderly informants that a person in
China willing to pay a handsome amount of money could get the necessary
papers to come to this country as a son of an established Chinese in the
United States.

Family firms, as a form of business organization, became popular
in the community only after the 1950's, especially after the implementation of the 1965 Immigration Law (cf. Chapter 2). The processes involved in the establishment of the Chinese family firm and the transactional relationship within it will be discussed in Chapter 6 in
relation to the social and economic environments of the post 1965 era.

Partnership Firms

Partnership firms were by far the most common type of Chinese firm
during this period. There were several variations in this type of Chinese firm: partnership by brothers, partnership with clansmen, and
partnership with people from the same locality of origin.

In addition to kinship, clanship, common origin, and ritual
brotherhood also played important roles in the formation of partnership
firms. There were many forms of ritual brotherhood in the traditional
Chinese society as well as in the overseas Chinese communities (Amyot
1960; Comber 1957). A further and detailed discussion on this subject
would require many pages. Briefly, there were two common ways of forming ritual brotherhood in New York's Chinatown. One is by using the
traditional family alliance formed by sworn brotherhood. The prototype
of it was the families' alliance of the Lau, Kwan, Chang, and Chiu which
were formed many centuries ago. The bearers of these surnames, sometimes
used this historical anteceedant to bring themselves together and to
pledge their allegiance to each other. The names of the founders of
the families' alliance of the original Lau, Kwan, Chang and Chiu were
invoked. The mutual emotional, economic and political assistances
practiced by these ancestors were served as examples to be imitated.
The second way of forming ritual brotherhood was through a ritual
ceremony in which the participants shed some of their blood (滴血為盟)
and then swore to assist each other with this oath, "My life is your
life."

Friendship and common interests, however, were the pre-conditions
for the formation of ritual brotherhood. Examples of firms run by

ritual brothers were the <u>Sam Kee</u> and <u>Sam Wo Companies</u> (run by ritual brothers Lau, Kwan and Chiu). Thus, business partnership required a closer relationship which had its basis in kinship, clanship, locality or origin, or ritual brotherhood. A relationship per se, however, was not adequate. <u>Kam Ching</u> (sentimental warmth) also had to exist. In the case of partnership between brothers like <u>Quong Wo Chong</u> (run by the Chin brothers), the blood ties between them generated more trust, and if both were willing and had the resources, it was easier for them to expand their partnership firm. In the case of patrilineal kinsmen, clansmen and ritual brothers or hometown-mates, personal relationships had to be formed and cultivated.

Although there was no business monopoly **controlled** by any single Chinese group, there was the concentration of some businesses in some groups. Thus for example, in the pre-1965 era, there were more Toysanese in the Chinese hand laundry and Chop Suey restaurants; more Hok San Chinese in the noodle businesses and the Chinese coffee shops; more Leungs in the grocery businesses; more Lau, Kwan and Chiu in the tailor businesses; and more Lees in gifts, handicraft and transportation businesses. The processes involved in the formation and manipulation of traditional social relationships for the establishment of partnership firms is demonstrated with a concrete example: Long Kee Trading Co.

Long Kee Trading Co.

Long Kee was founded by Mr. Lau who came from Toysan district via Hong Kong in 1950 after Communists had taken over China. The fact that he was both a landlord and a Catholic made his life unpleasant there.

He escaped China with his family to Hong Kong where he was able to get
a visa and the necessary money to pay his fare to the United States.
The visa was obtained for him by his relatives in New York. Thus,
before he had arrived in New York, he was already a debtor to his kinsmen.

After his arrival he worked in his kinsmen's grocery store without
much salary for many years to repay the trip as well as the favor of
bringing his family over to the United States. Mr. Lau told me that
the kinsmen were so greedy that they never raised his salary.

Since he was a Lau, he was able to join the Four-brothers (Lau,
Kwan, Cheung and Chiu) Association which used the traditional ritual
brotherhood between the Lau, Kwan, Cheung and Chiu to recruit the
Chinese who bore those surnames in New Yrok. Within the Four-brothers
Association, Lau met others who had migrated from the same district as
he had--Toysan. These friends in turn introduced him to the Ning Young
Association.[1] According to Mr. Lau and his friends, he was known to
be generous with his friends in both Associations. He had Yee Hey
(trusting righteousness), it was said. He was one of the few who had
a college education from China and could read and write both Chinese
and English. He read and wrote letters for other clansmen or friends
without charge. Soon, he became a patron for many of these illiterate
clansmen. His generosity was considered to have Kam Ching (sentiment).
In order to reciprocate Yee Hay and Kam Ching, these clan brothers made
counter-prestations by giving him gifts, inviting him to tea and

---

[1]This is an association exclusively for the Toysanese.

extending him financial assistance. According to informant Lau, he frequently confided in his clan brothers on the problems he had with his employers and his plan to start a new business with a partner. His plan met the approval of his friends in the clan association, and some clan members lent him money without interest. Others allowed him to order goods on credit, the debt to be repaid after one year. One clansman-friend became his partner. Thus, the problem of financing was solved.

The firm, Long Kee, has been prosperous since its inception. According to informant Lau, if it had not been for the Yee Hay of his friends and clan brothers, he could never have become so prosperous. He said that in those days, traditional kinship, clanship, and other informal relationships were necessary for one's well-being and one's economic activities in Chinatown. In fact, most of the customers in his grocery stores were clansmen, or members of his hometown associations. They all felt that they had to do business with him because they were related to him. If these friends of the associations were seen buying goods from another grocery store, they were reprimanded by fellow clansmen or members and were labelled as not having Yee Hay and the spirit of brotherhood. Sometimes gossip from other clansmen or members brought back the non-conforming kinsmen or clanship. Thus, gossip became a moral force which regulated deviate behavior. (cf. Pain 1967; Morris 1956, 1968). Many clansmen could not afford this kind of gossip and thus returned to Lau's shop to purchase goods.

Knowing the importance of the various associations, Lau ran for the presidency in one Tong and one clan association. It is said that

he had many friends "just because he was president once in both the
Tong and the Four-brothers Association." Informants said that he
realized his obligations to these members who had made him the founder
of a business, the president of the associations and a prosperous businessman. He reciprocated the prestation by donating foods and other
groceries to the Association for the annual festival celebrations. He
said that the amount of groceries he donated every year could amount to
$1,000. If he had not been generous, he would have been gossiped about
or even reprimanded.

Mr. Lau does not want to sever his ties with the associations, and
he will continue to reciprocate the Yee Hay of the members of these
associations. Because of his good deeds and his generosity, he has
been awarded many honorary posts in different community associations.
He is known as Kiu Ling (leader of the community). He is still well-
respected and has a solid following at this date. In the Fifties, when
different clansmen had problems, they all had to see him. He was a protector and patron for them. Thus, if one clansman was bullied by some
rascals, or if one clansman wanted to sponsor his immediate relatives
to the United States, they all came to Lau for solutions.

The story of Mr. Lau reveals that the processes involved in the
establishment of a partnership firm are: 1) active membership in an
association; 2) prestation through the idiom of Yee Hay and contract
compatible dyadic relationships; 3) financing through friends and clansmen; 4) partnership with friends or clansmen; 5) customers recruited
through clanship and friendship; 6) insure business prosperity by establishing oneself as a Kiu Ling, a patron for the community, which attract

a larger following and more customers as well. Thus, successful manipulation of transactional relationships lead to economic success which in
turn brings social prestige and leadership positions. Being a patron and
a Kiu Ling will attract more customers and thus generate more gain. Then
the circle is complete.

Occupational specialization along kinship, clanship and locality of
origin also exist in New York's Chinatown. Thus, a Lee in the wagon
business will attract more Lees in the same business. More Toysanese
hand laundries will attract other Toysanese through the Toysan Association. The tendency of people from the same region or who speak the
same dialect to interact with each other socially leads to business
interaction: exchange of business news, mutual aid in financing, entering partnership together. This explains then the formation of partnership firms along association or clanship lines. Thus, the traditional
social organization in Chinatown provided the bases for the formation
of various transactional relationships which usually lead to various
gain pursuits.

Althoug family, kinship, clanship, membership in the associations
and Tongs were the common bases for business partnerships, other forms
of partnerships did exist. A friend could enter business with another
friend. It was not uncommon to find some Chinese who had been "buddies"
in the Army who entered business partnerships after they were discharged
from service. Many restaurants and laundry firms after 1945 were in
fact established by Chinese veteran-friends. However, cooperation between
Chinese and the non-Chinese Americans during this era was not common.
Cultural and linguistic barriers perhaps prevented the successful

cooperation of such partnerships. Cross cultural cooperation in this era was premature. Economic organization and cooperation in those days presupposed a common base, Chinese ethnicity. To put it differently, the ethnicity of the Chinese (Chinese values, Chinese kinship, membership in various Chinese associations, language.) provided a solid basis for the economic activities of the Chinese in this period.

The social structure of Chinatown in those days also posed constraint factors for some Chinese in their economic activities as well. Thus, a Chinese who was not from the south of China, was unable to speak Toysanese, lacking a surname and therefore without representation of an association, could expect little or no assistance from New York's Chinatown. There was also a limitation on the number of associations a Chinese could join. Usually a person needed two members to introduce him and act as character references before he could join any Chinese associations. Further, a person could join only his clan association, regional association, and dialect association. Thus a Wong from Hoi-ping could join the Wong Clan Association, the Hoi-ping Association and one of the two tongs. If these associations had few members, the influence of the leaders of these associations was limited. A patron with a small following was handicapped. To compensate for this deficiency, there was a tendency of small associations to merge. Traditional neighbourhood, traditional ritual brotherhood, and marriage alliances in China were all manipulated by smaller associations to form larger associations.

Processes Involved in Obtaining Employment

In general, Chinese who came to New York had connections. The connections could have been friendship, kinship, clanship, business partnership or even neighbourhood relationships in China. Some Chinese were contracted with passage paid in advance by prospective employers who were either friends or kinsmen. The fact that the passage was paid was not a requirement of the work contract, but it was simply an act of prestation, a calculated act to solicit future counter-prestation. It was understood that the emigree would place himself completely under the disposition of the sponsor. The sponsor was a protector, guarantor, and employer to the emigrant. In addition to these, there was the tie of kinship or friendship. Because of the involvement of these relationships, the newcomers often stayed to work in the firms for years without demanding much payment because they wanted to show their gratitude, trust, and appreciation to their employer-kinsmen-patrons. The practice of employing kinsmen or friends generated gain for the employers since most of the newcomers knew little about American society, living costs, salary ranges, and they needed security and the protection of their sponsors. Because of ignorance, many newcomers feared deportation if they transferred jobs. Other employees felt they would appear ungrateful or lacking in Yang Ching (human feelings) if they left their jobs. The decision to seek employment elsewhere was taken only after a number of years, after the sponsor had been repaid for passage and his kindness, when the newcomer had become more familiar with the employment situation and had made some good friends in the Chinese community, better still, when he had found a prospective employer-cum-patron.

Changing employers in Chinatwon in those days was a big move which involved gossip and confrontation. The employer always complained that his employee showed ingratitude toward him; the employee complained that he had been treated unfairly for too long. An employee could not con-front his employer unless he had support from his friends, kinsmen, and had found a prospective employer. To help dissociate with the former employer, the friends or clansmen would label the former employer as not having been "fair," not having had Yee Hay (trusting righteousness). If gossip or accusations became an open affair, the employer had three alternatives at his disposal: 1) let the employee go immediately so that things would quickly quiet down; 2) try to retain the employee and increase his salary; or 3) bring the case to the family association for a settlement. Informants said it was customary for the employer to let the employee go.

Although sponsorship was one method of obtaining employees, it was not the only means available. Another method of obtaining employment was through the introduction of some Kiu Lings. A Chinese who was job-less because of lack of funds or his employer's bankruptcy could go to the Fongs or clan associations to get temporary shelter. While he was in the Fong, he came in contact with other clansmen and leaders of the Fong or association. Word was then passed that he was looking for a job. If there was an available job, the prospective employee was intro-duced by two clansmen or one Kiu Ling. Thus, clanship and patron-clien relationships were important in getting employment. After employment was secured, the employee was expected to reciprocate to clansmen or the Kiu Ling. Reciprocation to the Kiu Ling was given by allegiance (a vote was cast for him during election) or a <u>Red Wrapper</u> (money wrapped in a red paper wrapper). The employee was expected to invite those clansmen who had helped him find the job to tea or to a meal. This system of employment thereby insured the functioning of the patron-client relationship.

The third way of getting employment was on the invitation of a friend. In this case Kam Ching and Yee Hay determined the salary to be paid. A friend did not automatically employ his friends unless there was some <u>Kam Ching</u> (trusting sentiment) between them.

Process of Securing Financial Backing

The practice of obtaining finance through informal credit clubs, <u>hui</u>, has been common since 1870 in Chinatown. <u>Hui</u> is basically a financial institution based of informal relationships of kinship, friendship, and patron-client relationships. Since its operation depends on trust, admission into the hui is selective. In most of the family associations during this period, hui was organized informally. Within the association closer relationships were needed to be a member of hui. Normally, kinship and friendship were sufficient. <u>Hui</u> (known as credit clubs or saving societies) provided many new business undertakings with loans. Each member deposited the amount agreed upon by the rest of the members to start a hui. Usually a hui consisted of no more than twenty members who deposited between $50-$100, as required. If a member wanted to start a new business or buy a farm, he could get a substantial amount from the hui.

The procedure for securing a loan from a hui was that, first,each of

the borrowers declared verbally or in written statements the rate of
interest each was willing to pay. The one who declared the highest rate
could have the deposits of all the members at once. He could use his
business as sole security or have two friends or one Kiu Ling as guarantors. The procedure for repayment of the loan was interesting. Its
operation can be demonstrated with an example. If the credit club, hui,
was organized on the basis of $100 depositors, and the borrower declared
a ten percent interest rate, he got $90 from each member. After the
money had been withdrawn   (from a group of 30 he got $90 x 20 =
$1,610), the borrower was call a "ripe" member. Repayment was made to
the hui at $100 per month until every member was paid or the hui went
defunct. Such a credit system has financed many small Chop Suey Restaurants and many hand laundries in the past.

The functioning of such a system undoubtedly needed trust. That
is why not every individual was accepted into a hui. A prospective
member had to show that he was reliable and had friends and clansmen to
vouch for him. Since it was organized within an association, the
leaders of the association sometimes felt responsible if someone left
without repaying his debts. If this occurred, the Fong or family
associationapproached the guarnators for a refund. It is said that if
the "ripe" member or the guarantors refused to repay, all means were
used to recover the monetary loss of the members. An older informant
said that sometimes the association even had to resort to force[1] to
induce the recovery of the money. At any rate, abuses did occur, and

---

[1]Such as hiring "muscle men" to impose some physical harm or proper
damage on the part of the debtors.

some bad members had no means of repaying the loans. Hui are still in use today and seem to function quite well in the Chinese community. However, the present day Chinatown has many other loan institutions now, such as banks and credit unions which will be discussed in Chapter 6 of this study.

Kiu Lings were an important part of the hui since they were often used as quarantors. This added to their prestige. If a Kiu Ling was one's guarantor, people gave him more face. However, it was not always easy to get a Kiu Ling to be one's protector or one's guarantor. A person had to prove himself as a follower. Long before he intended to participate in a hui, he had to make some preparations for knowing some Kiu Ling. The process of prestation should have started long before. If a person could not get a Kiu Ling to be his guarantor, two respectable clansmen or friends could act as guarantors. Participation in the credit clubs thus required the help of friends, kinsmen, clansmen and/or patrons (Kiu Ling).

Other methods of obtaining financing included pooling personal and family members' savings, borrowing from kinsmen and friends, and getting a loan from the loan sharks in Chinatown. These loan sharks charged an interest rate of 50%-100% per year. People had to be desperate before they resorted to borrowing money from the loan sharks after other connections and means were exhausted. Knowing this, loan sharks charged high interest rates. Since loan sharks frequently had connections with the Tongs, borrowers were said to follow the regulations laid down by the loan sharks religiously. Money was returned with high interest. The fear of bodily harm and loss of face made the borrower see to that.

A debtor who did not return the money could be beaten up by an underling
of the Tongs. Further, if vicious rumors went around in the community
that trust was violated by a person, all further business connections
with him were dropped. Loan sharks were not looked on favorably by the
community, but if a person used these loan sharks, they were expected
to keep good faith.

An estimate of the sources of finances of firms established from
1900-1950, compiled from informants, is given in Table 12. Table 12
indicates that the majority of the firms started with capital supplied
mainly by personal savings and hui. There were few families in those
days and the number of family firms was small. Individual kinsmen and
friends sometimes helped financially. When that happened, they normally
were given partnerships. These kinsmen or friends sometimes worked as
partner-cum-workers since management in Chinese firms was rather informal.
Firms were sufficiently small that detailed division of duties was not
necessary.

TABLE 12

SOURCES OF ORIGINAL CAPITAL FOR ENTERPRISES

Supplied Mainly by	Number	Percentage
Personal savings	48	35%
Family of orientation	14	10
Hui	55	40
Kinsmen	12	9
Friends (Chinese)	8	6
Total	137	100%

Table 12 also indicates that the informal financial institutions, **hui, played an important role in the establishment of many Chinese firms.** Presumably, this is due to a variety of reasons. First, hui was a traditional practice, common in the home districts of the overseas Chinese. Up to the present date, many hui are organized in Hong Kong and Macao by friends and kinsmen as savings societies. Second, hui was informal and red tape was not required. Third, between 1870-1950 very few Chinese could write and speak English; fewer still were familiar with loan procedures in American banks. This also explains why hui were particularly common in the past. After 1950, immigrants who came to New York were better educated and could speak English. Many of them used banks for loans. Further discussion of this matter will be carried out in Chapter 6.

The point to be emphasized here is that informal relationships: friendship, kinship, association relationships were the basis for loan practices in Chinatown. Without connections in an association, especially without a patron-guarantor, it was impossible for a person to participate in a hui. Without friends, or clansmen, it was difficult to join any of these Chinese associations in which these hui were usually organized. That is why one Chinatown informant emphatically stated that, "Without connections in New York's Chinatown, you simply do not come here!"

Processes Involved in Dispute Settlement

Disputes in Chinatown were mainly related to business matters such as unpaid debts, laundry or restaurant labor disputes, violation of the

rule of "Basic Property Right,"[1] or intruding in the business sphere of
another laundryman by opening a new laundry next to his. Other disputes
could arise from family quarrels, inheritance, and from daily interaction between clansmen. In the past, the infamous Tong wars created
problems for the various associations' mediation services.

There were three ways to solve disputes. The first involved mediation through a mutual friend. The second employed the mediation services of the various family, regional and dialectic associations, more
specifically by the Kiu Ling of these associations. The third method
called upon the highest authority of Chinatown, the Consolidated Chinese
Benevolent Association. Thus, kinsmen, friends, and Kiu Ling were the
main mediators for the Chinese in this period. However, criminal cases
such as homicide and narcotics were excluded. Problems arising from illegal businesses such as prostitution and gambling dens were mediated by
the Tongs who controlled them. However, disputes which involved members
of rival Tongs were frequently brought to the CCBA for mediation provided that the matters to be mediated were not criminal. However, not
all disputes were accepted by the CCBA's mediation service. First,
the leaders of the board met to decide whether or not they would accept
the responsibility to adjuciate. The case was not accepted if it was
a criminal case[2] or if the disputants did not show their willingness to
have the CCBA mediate. The CCBA solved many cases; they were so successful that some authors (Beck 1898; Leong 1936; C. Lee 1965; Rausbenbush

---

[1]This was discussed in Chapter 3.

[2]Criminal cases were referred to the United States Courts.

1926a, 1926b), labelled it the "supreme court" for the Chinese in Chinatown.

Mediation through Friends

It was quite common for a mutual friend of both disputants to come
forward voluntarily to persuade the two to reconcile their differences.
However, a go-between was often requested to intercede by one of the
parties. Each party explained his grievances to this go-between or
Chung Kan Yan (中間人). It was said that reconciliation could be
achieved only if there was enough Kam Ching (sentimental warmth) between
the two disputants. The go-between usually appealed to the two parties
on the basis of "reason" and, most importantly, on the former bonds of
affection or Kam Ching. A commonly used phrase was "Let us not harm
Kam Ching. If the two were reconciled, it was celebrated with a handshake followed by a meal and tea. If the case was not solved, it usually
went to the associations.

Mediation through Associations

If the two disputants belonged to a common clan, regional or
dialect association, then the mediation service of that association was
used. Their complaints had to be brought to the attention of the
president or the secretary of the association by the parties involved.
Both had to speak the same dialect. For example, if Party A was a Lee
who spoke Hanan, and Party B was a Lee who spoke Toysan, the Lee Association would not accept the case since the Lee Association used the Toysanese dialect for mediation. Solving disputes in the family association was not a completely new institution. It had its roots in the clan

court in traditional China where the elders and leaders of the clan
heard cases and mediated the disputes (Hu 1948; Lang 1948).

If A was a member of one clan association and B a member of another,
they had to find a common association to which both belonged. If both
were from Hainan Island and spoke Hainanese, they could then settle
their dispute in the Hainan Association. If A and B shared no common
association, they brought their case to the CCBA. Normally, CCBA was
the final mediation organization. If the disputants first took their
case to the CCBA, they were usually referred to their respective family,
regional or dialect association. In all these associations, the function
of dispute settling was conceived as a means of maintaining the friendship between members. Thus, the word Kam Ching was frequently used in
dispute settlement. Further, the associations with the exception of
CCBA[1] were not obligated to take any case automatically. The leaders of
family, dialect, and regional associations considered their mediation a
"favor" since these leaders were not usually salaried and had to take
time to hear the cases. If A was seen by the leaders of the family
association as a bad member, they could refuse to help solve the case.
Thus, a certain relationship between the member and his leaders had to
exist. Normally a patron-client bond or merely a leader-follower bond
could warrant the favor.

Matters of no grave importance were often heard by the president
(Kiu Ling) and a secretary at a restaurant or at the family association's

[1]The by-laws of the CCBA stated that it was obligated to resolve the
disputes of its members. Many clan associations had no by-laws. Functions were performed according to tradition rather than written rules.

office over tea. If it was a serious matter, some leaders and former leaders were invited by the secretary and the president to join in and mediate the matter. If the case was not solved or if the parties refused to abide by the decision of the informal court of the association, they could appeal to the CCBA. Generally speaking, the mediation services of the family associations were quite successful. Most of the disputants did not object to the decisions of the association leaders for fear of possible ostracism or destruction of their reputations. For if the word got out that they were trouble makers who disregarded Kam Ching and did not have enough Yee Hey, they sufferred the loss of future economic opportunity and loss of "face." However, unsolved cases existed and were usually taken to the Chinese Benevolent Association for final settlement.

The mediation service of the Chinese Benevolent Association was a relatively formal one. One had to fulfill the following conditions in order to have his case heard. First, he must have had paid his annual membership dues for the three preceeding years. Second, if the matter was related to a business transaction, he must have had paid a fee for the business. Third, he was expected to demonstrate Jang (willingness to compromise) and must have come to the association voluntarily without physical coercion. Both parties were expected to give "face" or respect to the mediators by arriving promptly when summoned. Fourth, both parties had to speak the same dialect as the mediators of the association. In the pre-1965 era, the language used to settle disputes was Toysanese. People who spoke other dialects such as Hakka or Hannan were expected to bring their cases to these dialect associations. Thus structural constraint was evident in the dispute settlement activities.

Not all the people brought their cases to the CCBA for mediation out of self volition. Some came because there was a lack of alternatives. Some came because they expected a favorable ruling. Thus, it was said that On Leong Tong always got favorable rulings whenever it brought its disputes with the rival Hip Sing Tong to the CCBA. The major reason for this, according to informants, was due to the influence of On Leong on the CCBA which was actually situated in the territory of On Leong. The On Leong's leaders had more economic power and political power. For that alone the leaders of the CCBA gave some particular "face" when the leaders of On Leong requested the mediation service of CCBA. Favoritism did exist. However, according to informants, the mediation service of CCBA had been quite successful.

Few cases went to American courts of justice. This did not mean that decisions made by the CCBA were abided by voluntarily by the disputants. Some accepted the decisions because of social pressure, economic pressure and the desire to preserve one's good "face." Those who refused to abide by the decisions of the CCBA were sometimes physically forced to go out of business or to leave the community. Informant T related a case concerning a Chinese laundry man who confronted the CCBA deliberately. The laundry man won his case in the American court, but he felt safer to leave the Chinese community. This is the story informant T related:

> One of my friends rented a store in the 1940's from a white American landlord who previously rented it out to another laundry man. The former laundry man went bankrupt and closed the store. The

landlord, not knowing the rule of the CCBA on "Basic Property Right,"[1] rented it out to my friend. My friend was a self-styled individual. He neither paid money to the previous Chinese tenant nor registered his firm with the CCBA. The previous tenant then demanded the compensation and took his complaint to the CCBA which, as expected, issued a summons to my friend. He went to the CCBA and found that he had to pay a fine of several hundred dollars for not paying the former tenant and not registering with the CCBA. He knew that there was no place for such a practice in American law. He purchased property insurance immediately, anticipating that his store would be vandalized. One day a truck with some muscle-men came with an order from the CCBA to close his store. He refused to close it. The store was completely destroyed. Naturally the insurance agency took the case to court. The vandals were arrested and prosecuted.

In a sense, this story was a unique one. However, it reveals that some cases had to go to American courts for settlement and some disputants refused to abide by the decisions of CCBA. The same informant also said that his friend, after the incident, did not visit Chinatown for fear of reprisals from CCBA. He asked some of his friends to make trips to Chinatown to shop for him. Eventually he left New York City and started a hand laundry in a city in the Midwest. Thus, he was practically ostracized from the community as a consequence of his non-conformity to the rules and customs of the Chinese community of New York.

Since 1945, CCBA's regulations concerning laundry businesses have not been enforced. The nonenforcement is alledgedly due to the fact that very few laundries had been opened.[2]

---

[1]See Chapter 4 for details.

[2]This explanation was given to me by a CCBA spokesman during my fieldwork in 1972-73. Further investigation revealed that the nonenforcement of these rules concerning Chinese laundries had several causes: 1) Hand Laundry Allinace took policing power from the CCBA; 2) practice of charging money for "basic property right" was illegal in American courts; 3) vandalism and assault on non-conforminst was criminal action punishable by American courts.

One point must be emphasized. Despite abuses of authority and the misues of methods, CCBA for many years was the most respected dispute settlement agent in Chinatown. CCBA solved many disputes and facilitated the activities of many Chinese businessmen as well as the members of the community. The leaders or Kiu Ling of CCBA were under social pressure to be fair. Unfair mediators were sometimes subjected to gossip and mockery by the leaders of the various clan, hometown, and regional associations. Thus, the power of the mediators and the Kiu Ling of CCBA was checked and balanced by the force of gossip, criticism and the desire to keep good "face."

Mediation Process in the CCBA

The procedure of mediation was rather complex in the CCBA. First, the case had to be presented to the president and the secretary of the CCBA, then a hearing of the case had to be granted. To initiate these first steps, strings had to be pulled. Former officials of the CCBA or leaders of the various associations could facilitate the presentation and the acceptance of the case. If the matter was simple, after it was presented and accpted, the president and secretary had a meeting with the disputants. Individual differences were heard, and the president and secretary helped reason with the two parties and attempted reconcil-iation. For matters of great significance such as a Chinese landlord who wanted to expel his tenants so he could use the property for commer-cial purposes, or laundrymen's labor disputes, a meeting of the Benevol Association's Board members was called. There were about twenty member on the board. Usually, the twenty members (with the president) worked out satisfactory compromise; for the disputants. If the case was not solved, the whole of the Assembly (approximately 60 members) was called upon to decide and vote on the matter.

The decision was based on fairness, face, Kam Ching, and Yee Hey. Thus, a Chinese could be persuaded not to insist on opening his laundry store next to another Chinese laundry because neither laundry would benefit if they were too close since they had to compete for the same customers. The process of obtaining mediation is demonstrated with a case well known in Chinatown.

Case 1: Dispute between a Cook and his Employer

On a hectic day in the 1950's, the chef of a well-known Chinese restaurant in the Chinatown area came to demand a raise of $30 per week from the owner-manager. The request was refused. The hot-tempered chef walked off his job immediately and stayed at home for four days. After the fourth day, the chef sent a bill to the owner for four days unpaid wages plus $30. The owner sent a bill to the chef charging for $600 damages and the threat of further legal action. Neither party paid. However, the chef felt that he had been underpaid. He was confident that he would win if he could get a proper forum to hear his case. He went to a Kiu Ling who was the president of his family association and asked him to present the case to the CCBA. To show his Yee Hey (trusting righteousness) - prestation, the Kiu Ling of the family association appealed to the CCBA for the chef's wages and denied the owner's rights to claim damages. To show his responsibility and to give face to the Kiu Ling of the family association, the President of the CCBA specifically sent his secretary to investigate the matter. He found out that the restaurant owner still wanted the chef back and was willing to give a weekly

raise of $10. An increase of another $10 was promised if future performance proved satisfactory. Having acquired this information, the secretary invited some relatives and friends of the chef to learn of his character in order to decide how to approach him. The secretary then summoned
the chef to the office and explained the situation. The chef accepted
the offer of a $10 raise. With an understanding of agreement from both
the restaurant owner and the chef, the CCBA formally called for them to
meet with the board members in a formal mediation meeting. A formal
presentation of the case was made. Both parties had their friends state
their differences and their agreement. The president then stood up and
made a traditional speech on the value of harmony and the wisdom of
reconciliation. In his speech, phrases such as "peace and harmony are
supreme," "mutual face giving," "reconciliation is noble" are
abundant. The chef finally apologized with a gesture of handshake and
an offer of tea to the owner. The restaurant owner reciprocated by
pouring a cup of tea and offering it to the chef. Thus, they finalized
the settlement by drinking tea together.

What facilitated the settlement of the case was the mutual giving
of face among the Kiu Lings. If the Kiu Ling of the chef's family
association had not presented the case to the Kiu Ling of CCBA, and if
the Kiu Ling of the CCBA had not given full and rapid attention to the
matter, the case could not have been solved in such a short time.
Thus, it was the patron-client relationship between the Kiu Ling of the
family association and the chef which was instrumental in the presentation of the case. Note also that friendship and kinship also played a
role in the mediation process. They were asked about the circumstances

and were invited to be the spokesmen as well as the witnesses during
the mediation meeting with the Board of CCBA. What do the officers or
the Kiu Ling get for the mediation? As mentioned in Chapter 3, officers
of the associations were paid little or no salary. They did not receive
official financial payment for their services in disupte settlements.
However, the disputants were expected to reciprocate by giving gifts to
them on important Chinese festivals. There was also the reward of social
prestige which could be converted into economic gain. Prestige could
attract more following and more customers, as well as business contracts.
Further, the former disputants were expected to give donations to the
associations, especially during fund-raising campaigns and during the
Chinese New Year celebrations as tokens of gratitude; thus they reinforced their ties with the associations. Frequently, disputants who
had had their problems solved with the aid of the Kiu Lings rewarded them
with money as a token of gratitude, indicating their willingness to
continue the patron-client relationship.

Thus, kinship, friendship, clanship, and patron-client relationships
all played important roles in the economic activities of the Chinese such
as: immigration, capital formation, employment, and dispute settlement.
These relationships were important not only in economic pursuit but also
in the social life of the Chinese. A Chinese newcomer to New York City
had to depend on his clansmen, kinsmen, and friends to help him find a
job, to secure a place to live, to meet other friends, to recreate, and
to learn American customs. The patron-client relationship contracted
within the community (in particular within the various clans and regional
and dialect associations) was of special importance because these Kiu

Lings or patrons acted as guarantors for clansmen to participate in credit clubs, settled disputes, protected clansmen from the attack of their enemies and presented Chinese to a higher association for mediation. The case of the chef who had his family association's president contact the president of CCBA is a perfect illustration of the broker role of the Kiu Ling.

Thus, inter-group and inter-association relationships were mediated by the community's Kiu Lings. They were the pillars of the community. To some cynical Chinese, these Kiu Ling were nothing but "politicians" (Leong 1936). Since the Kiu Ling of the family, regional and dialect associations had larger followings, they were more prestigeous than the Kiu Ling in the Fongs (villages level organizations in Chinatown). Of course, the highest prestige went to the President of the CCBA. Nevertheless, various family, dialect, and regional associations also enjoyed good face. The "big Kiu Lings" were conscious of their power and constantly encouraged the "little Kiu Lings" (leaders of the Fongs) and the ordinary Chinese to curry their favor so that the former could have more following. It was said that the maintenance and operation of the various associations depended solely on the resourcefulness and tact of their Kiu Lings. The influence and political power of the associations depende on the intelligence and shrewdness of these Kiu Lings. Leong (1936) cynically remarked about the power of the Kiu Lings whom he called the "gentlemen:"

> The gentlemen are not only identified with the Association, but
> are the association--except when they need money. Their word is
> law, and like all politicians they prey on the ignorance and pass-
> ivity of their clan by means of eloquence and endless red-tape of
> their creation. It is they who keep the Charitable and Benevolent

Association what it is. They are the envy of every gentleman of little face, and drive these leaders of Fongs and village groups to curry their favor at no small expense to kinsmen and supporters. The gentlemen-in-the-making hope, by careful back-scratching and costly entertainment of the important gentlemen, to become "big shots" themselves (Leong 1936: 62).

The description is of particular interest to us not because of its cynical tone but because it points out three important features of the leadership of Chinatown. First, there was the constant making of prestation and counter-prestation between the Kiu Lings. Second was the role of money in the making of Kiu Lings. The points of Leong could have been exaggerated, however, it was verified by informants that a person had to spend an enormous amount of money to be a Kiu Ling. Third, there was a patron-client relationship even between the Kiu Lings. The leaders of the small village level associations attempted to contract dyadic relationships with the leaders of the higher level associations. The leaders of the higher associations also felt the urge to socialize with the wealthy entrepreneurs. With biographic data from 72 Chinese entrepreneurs, a table was constructed showing their membership associations (Table 13).

TABLE 13

POSITIONS OF 72 ENTREPRENEURS IN DIFFERENT CHINESE ASSOCIATIONS

Positions	Number of Entrepreneurs
Leaders (President and Board members) of CCBA	21
Presidents and officials of various clan (family) associations, regional and dialect associations	39
Presidents and officials of various trade associations	41

The explanation for the active participation of the entrepreneurs

and their cravings for leadership positions was summarized thus by one

informant:

> As you should know, the important things for the Chinese men are money,
> women, and name. If you work very hard and are lucky, sooner or
> later you will save some money. A person may be good with women,
> but where could you find them? Very few could gain the favor of
> American women. A lot of Chinese could not even speak English and
> thus it was not possible for them to socialize with American women.
> There was a constant shortage of Chinese women. You cannot even show
> off your success with women, because polygamy is prohibited by law in
> this country. That is why, after making some money, many Chinese want
> to make a name for themselves. Everyone wants to be a Kiu Ling. Of
> course, Kiu Ling can also help you to make more money. After you have
> a good name, you will have more power and money! (Informant K).

Patrons as a Bridge Between the Community with the Larger Society and Between Members of the Community

The Kiu Lings in the Chinese community of New York were mostly

entrepreneurs and as such they had access to money, connections and in-

formation. It was precisely because of these resources that the entre-

preneurs were able to perform their bridging functions. In performing

the bridging functions for the community, gain was further maximized.

According to some elderly informants, many Kiu Lings pocketed a great

deal of money from the donations given to various educational projects

by the Chinese. One informant even emphasized that the opportunity for

the usurpation of common funds for community projects like erecting

buildings for the CCBA, for the Chinese School, and for the charitable

activities in the home country attracted many Chinese to run for the

office of president in many associations. The more associations a person

belonged to, the more opportunity for him to become a Kiu Ling. This

explains why the Chinese entrepreneurs liked to have membership in various associations (see Table 14). Such behaviour fully demonstrates the strategic character of the entrepreneur's decision-making activities (Barth 1966).

Membership in most of the Chinese Associations was ascriptive, based on one's family name, occupation, locality of origin, and dialect. However, in order to be a full-fledged active member, an entrepreneur had to pay his fees and give donations to community projects as well. He had to "spend some money" before he could receive. After he became a big Kiu Ling, it was said that the money just rolled in from different sources.

TABLE 14

MEMBERSHIP OF THE 72 ENTREPRENEURS
IN DIFFERENT CHINESE ASSOCIATIONS

Types of Chinese Associations	Number of Entrepreneurs
Consolidated Chinese Benevolent Associations	72
Clan Associations	65
Regional Associations	72
Dialect Associations	5
Trade Associations	30

The fact that entrepreneurs held various memberships and positions in various associations and were in charge of public funds is documented in the Who's Who of the Chinese in New York. As an example, here is the story of Mr. Lee Yock Deep, and entrepreneur who held positions of responsibility in various associations and was a patron-cum-broker.

Lee Yock Deep was born in the year 1864, in the district of Hoy San in the province of Kwangtung. At the age of twelve he came to the United States. For many years he was content to live in the West, but New York finally lured him East. In 1891, the enterprise of Quong Yuen Sing was organized under the able hand of Mr. Lee. He had acted in the capacity of business manager for the firm since its doors opened for business. The Chinese School of the colony in New York commenced in 1908. Its organization and supervision has been entirely dependent upon Mr. Lee. He assumed the onerous duties of President, Secretary, and Treasurer of the school board. Mr. Lee was also actively solicitous of the financial welfare of the Canton Christian College, and contributions to its support, through his ingenuity, have totaled more than $11,000. Mr. Lee is Treasurer of the New York depository for such funds. The Chinese Merchant's Association elected Mr. Lee as President for the term of 1914. The Ning Young Railroad of the Hoy San district, Kwangtung Province, delegated the power of New York representation to Mr. Lee. He was also a director of the company (Van Nordon 1918: 56).

While it is unscientific, as well as illegal and immoral to infer that

since he was in charge of various fund raising projects for the hometown

he must have "pocketed" some money, the frequent usurpation of common

funds by the Kiu Lings in the past is acknowledged by the community

leaders of present day Chinatown. Rose Lee (1965: 152-159) attributed

conflict between the Kiu Lings to this practice. What concerns us here

is the bridging function of the Kiu Lings. Like Mr. Lee Yock Deep, Kiu

Lings were the bridge through which the overseas Chinese in New York

could assist the underpriviledged in China and contribute to the welfare

political and educational projects of China. Thus, for instance, funds

were collected from the Chinese community of New York for the establish-

ment of a college in Canton or the building of a railroad in Toysan,

China.

Patron or Kiu Ling as a bridge between the Chinese community and

the larger society has been recognized by students of the community

(Beck 1898; Berger 1957; Kung 1962; R. Lee 1960; K. Lee 1965; Leong 193

and by the American public as well. As mentioned in Chapter 3, the
leaders of the various Chinese trade associations often negotiated with
the United States government of behalf of the Chinese businessmen in
the trade. The Chinese Consolidated Benevolent Association had on
numerous occasions made transactions with the city, state, and federal
governments on behalf of the Chinese on matters affecting the Chinese
such as immigration policy, traffic problems, procedure of licensing,
rules governing business activities on Sundays and crime. To cite a
few examples, the CCBA negotiated with the Social Security Administration to send a Chinese staff member to the association center every Sunday to help the elderly apply for Social Security. It negotiated with
the Hamilton-Madison House, a private foundation, to establish a service
center to help solving the problems of housing, jobs, education and
health of the Chinese. Leaders of the clan and regional associations
showed their Yee Hey (trusting righteousness) to their followers by
helping to translate government documents for them.

Patrons or Kiu Lings also bridged the relationships between various
Chinese Associations. A Chinese in a Fong had no chance to meet other
Chinese unless the Kiu Lings or friends introduced them to other Chinese in the clan association. Similarly, it was the Kiu Lings who introduced their clansmen to the regional associations. They presented
the disputes of the clansmen to the highest authority, the CCBA. In
some clans or regional associations, there was no well-organized struc-
ure and no written charters; inter-relationships between members of
hese associations were particularly in need of the bridging activities
f the leaders. Normally, the twice-a-year visits to the ancestral

graves in Grooklyn's Evergreen Cemetery and the annual celebration
on the birthday of the founder of the clan gave the opportunity of
collective ritual expression of solidarity. On these occasions, leaders
of the clan associations often led the collective ceremony of paying
respect to the ancestors. Later, a buffet dinner in the association's
hall created a friendly atmosphere and the opportunity for clansmen to
meet each other.

These leaders were also sponsors of various Chinese community activities such as: the celebration of the Double Ten (October 10); the Foundation Day of the Republic of China; and the Chinese New Year Celebration. The Kiu Lings were active in the establishment of Chinese schools
which taught Chinese languages and culture. In the past, these Kiu Lings
had expressed their love of China by sending their children to China to
receive a Chinese education. While all these activities of the Kiu Lings
can be seen as prestige enhancing mechanisms, they also constituted a
force for the preservation of the Chinese cultural identity in the
United States. Thus, the patrons were also stabilizers of the Chinese
culture of New York.

Conclusion

The social structure of New York's Chinatown, itself an adaptation
to American society, provided both structural constraints and the opportunity for the entrepreneurial activities of the Chinese. The structural variables were: dialects, clanship, locality of origin, kinship
and friendship. However, it was these associations which were organized
on the above relationships that constituted the social structure of
Chinatown, and it was within these associations that many patron-client

relationships were formed and manipulated for economic activities such as capital formation, employment and dispute settlements.

Given the encapsulated situation and the historical context of China-town, patrons or Kiu Ling were important not only in the entrepreneurial pursuit but in community activities and social life because they connected the community with the outside world (United States). With constraints imposed by the larger society such as limited available economic oppor-tunity, immigration policy, and the language barrier, it was to the advan-tage of the Chinese to have the community structured and run in a manner familiar to them; this created psychological security. The existence of the various associations were advantageous to the entrepreneurs because it was within these associations that valuable dyadic contracts were formed and manipulated for the maximum gain. This illustrates the point made by Barth (1969), Greeley (1972), and Novak (1972) that ethnic boun-dary maintenance is sometimes useful for the members of an ethnic group.

There are many theories and arguments on the non-assmiliation of New York's Chinese in this period of 1870-1964. Some attributed it to the lack of family life (Schwartz 1948). Some contend that Chinatown voluntarily segregated itself from the larger society to avoid racial conflicts (Yuen 1963). Some authors believe that the distinctive Chinese cultural pattern of Chinatown associations is itself American, a part of the growing ideal of culturally pluralistic American society (Leong 1936; R. Lee 1960; Hsu 1971). Then there are those who argue that the Chinese differ so much from other Americans in physical appearance that they can never be assimilated (Gordon 1969).

With the findings at hand, any argument on the non-assimilation of the Chinese in New York which does not take into consideration the community structure and the operation of patron-client relationships in the community will miss a great deal in understanding the nature of the community. As discussed earlier, most of the Chinese in the community in those days did not have any contact with the American society at work, in recreation, in seeking dispute settlement,in securing financial backing, in finding employment, even in dealing with the government. When it was necessary to have contact with the government, it was the Kiu Ling of the CCBA, or the Kiu Lings of the trade associations who negotiated and made transactions on behalf of the Chinese. Thus, the Chinese ethnic boundary was deliberately maintained.

In summary, then, the ethnic identity of the Chinese was preserved during this period because of the continued use of Chinese traditional principles for social organizations and for the formation and manipulation of patron-client relations in economic adaptation; and 2) the psychological security involved in dealing with people who shared similar outlooks, feelings, languages, and traditions.

CHAPTER 5

NEW RESOURCES IN THE SOCIO-ECONOMIC
ENVIRONMENT OF 1965-1974

This chapter will examine the new resources for decision-making
activities of the Chinese brought about by the proliferation of Chinese
Associations, the establishment of numerous social agencies, the changed
immigration policy, the employment policies, the changed attitudes
toward China on the part of the United States government. The changing
community structure and the newly available economic opportunity undoubtedly (as will be shown in this chapter) influenced the formation
of various interpersonal relationships and their manipulation. This
chapter intends first to outline the new structural features of the
community, to identify the policies relevant to the Chinese ethnic
groups implemented by the larger society, and finally to point out the
economic significance resulting from the structural changes and the
attitudinal and policy changes toward the Chinese ethnic group.

Changed Social Structure and the Larger Society

Various students of overseas Chinese communities observed that the
community structure was closely related to the administrative policy,
economic environment and social structure of the larger society (Freedman 1963; R. Lee 1960; Loewen 1971; Willmot 1970; Tsien 1961; Wong
1972). Patterns of migration and structural changes in the Chinese community of New York were likewise related to the socio.-economic environment of the larger society.

To begin with, the patterns of Chinese migration (Table 15) to the United States could be seen as responses to the stimuli of the socio-economic environment of the United States in the past one hundred and twenty four years. The major stimuli during these years were: 1) the Gold rush and the building of the Central Pacific Railroad in the second half of the nineteenth century; 2) the Quota Act of 1924; 3) the War Brides Act of 1945; 4) the Refugee Act of 1953; and 5) the New Immigration Law of 1965. In response to the needs of the mining companies and the railroad construction, many Chinese came to the United States. After the discovery of gold in California at Sutter's Mill in 1848, Chinese rushed into the state. By 1880, there were 106,465 Chinese in the United States,[1] of which eighty three percent were located on the Pacific Coast.[2] After the completion of the railroad and the subsequent anti-Chinese legislation[3], many Chinese left the United States. In 1920, there were only 61,639 Chinese in the United States.[4] The Chinese migration movement got a slight impetus with the passage of the Quota Act of 1924 (Table 15) and by 1930, the Chinese population in the United States was up to 74,594[5]. Thus, there was a gain of 13,000 Chinese in ten years.

---

[1]This statistic was obtained from the census of 1880.

[2]According to the census of 1880, there were 87,828 Chinese on the Pacific Coast. The percentage of the Chinese on the Pacific Coast was computed thus: 87,828/159,468 = .83.

[3]The Chinese Exclusion Action of 1884 is an example of these anti-Chinese legislations.

[4]According to the U.S. census statistics of 1920.

[5]According to the U.S. census statistics of 1930.

Immigration statistics also showed that there was a strong influx
of Chinese immigrants to the United States during 1920-1924 (Table 16).
The main reason for this influx was apparently due to an anticipation
of the passage of the 1924 National Origins Act. According to this
legislation, children and wives of Chinese Americans could not be admitted to the United States after 1924. Thus, to beat the deadline, depen-
dents[1] of the Chinese-Americans rushed to the United States. After the
passage of the 1924 Act, as indicated in Table 16, there was a general
decline in Chinese migration. The War Brides Act of 1945 facilitated
the entrance of Chinese women to the United States. According to the
estimates of informants, there were about 10,000 Chinese women admitted
to the United States as War Brides in the years 1946-1953. In 1950 the
Chinese population swelled to 117,629. This number came very close to
the peak of the Chinese migration movement in the last century.

TABLE 15

CHINESE POPULATION IN NEW YORK CITY AND
IN THE UNITED STATES (1870-1970)

Year	New York City	United States
1870	120	63,199
1880	853	106,465
1890	2,559	107,488
1900	6,321	89,863
1910	4,614	77,531
1920	5,042	61,639
1930	8,414	74,594
1940	12,753	77,504
1950	18,998	117,629
1960	32,831	237,292
1970	69,324	435,062

Source: U.S. Census of Population, 1970

[1]Children of Chinese-Americans born abroad were said to number about
8,894 (Kung 1964: 86).

TABLE 16

CHINESE IMMIGRANTS ADMITTED TO THE
UNITED STATES (1911-1930)

Year	Number Admitted
1911	1,307
1912	1,608
1913	2,022
1914	2,352
1915	2,469
1916	2,239
1917	1,843
1918	1,576
1919	1,697
1920	2,148
1921	4,017
1922	4,465
1923	4,074
1924	4,670
1925	1,721
1926	1,375
1927	1,051
1928	931
1929	1,071
1930	970

Source: Annual Report, of the Immigration and Naturalization Service, 1930.

In the 1950's, some Chinese were able to make use of their refugee status because they fled Communist China, applying for refugee visas under the 1953 Refugee Relief Act. Due to the communist revolution, quite a few Chinese decided to make the United States their home and became naturalized.[1] In turn, they sponsored the entry of many new im-

[1]The extent to which the Chinese Communist Revolution in 1949 influenced the Chinese community of New York City, although difficult to determine, is nevertheless interesting. It would be a fruitful dissertation topic in itself.

159

migrants. In the 1960's, the Chinese population increased from 117,629 in 1950 to 237,292 in 1960 in the United States, double that of the 1950's. However, most rapid changes came about in the 1970's. The major reasons for the rapid increase of Chinese immigrants in the United States and in New York in particular were: 1) greater adjustment of permanent and citizen status among the Chinese which allowed them to sponsor more family members and relatives; 2) President Kennedy's 1962 Refugee Parole Act which permitted many refugees from Hong Kong and Taiwan to enter the United States; and 3) the new immigration act of 1965 which abolished the national origin system and provided equal oppor- tunity for the Chinese to come to the United States. After 1965, Chinese immigrants flocked to the United States in large numbers. In 1970, the Chinese population increased more than two hundred percent in ten years (Table 15). The Chinese population of New York City reflected this trend.

The impact of the sudden increase of Chinese population in New York City affected many changes in New York's Chinatown.[1] Of relevance to the present discussion is that the rapid infusion of large numbers of Chinese from diverse backgrounds made a great impact on the social structure of the Chinese community of New York. As mentioned in Chapter 2, the new immigrants who came to the United States were more hetero- geneous in terms of education, dialects, age-sex distribution and local- ity of origin. First, the various associations established in the pre- vious years (which consisted mainly of adult males from Kwangtung pro- vince) were incapable of absorbing these immigrants from different social

---

[1]Chapter 2 highlighted the major changes in Chinatown after 1965.

economic, geographic, and educational backgrounds in China. As a consequence, there was a proliferation of associations. In addition to the
sixty major associations established in the old days, more than 200 different Chinese family, dialect, regional, political, commercial, alumni,
and religious associations were established (Appendix 1). More family
names were represented due to the increase of family associations. The
number of regional associations was increased similarly. In the past,
Chinatown had been dominated by the people from Kwangtung province. After
1965, people from northern, central, and eastern China were represented
by their regional associations. Thus, for instance, the San Kiang Regional Association was established for the people from Kiang-su, Cheik-Kiang
and Kiang-si provinces; the Wha Pei Association represented people from
Hu-pei, Shantung, Shan-si, Ho-nan, An-wei, and Hu-pei provinces of
northern China. Since there were more educated Chinese among the new
immigrants, many alumni associations were formed such as the Hing Wah
Alumnus Association; the Kwangtung Kou-Min University Alumni Association;
the Lingnam University Alumnus Association; and the Taiwan University
Alumnus Association. The proliferation of the various associations
created an opportunity for the formation of leader-follower relationships
and provided more positions for leadership. Thus, the numbers of Kiu
Lings were so great that in every parade organized in Chinatown, there
was a Kiu Ling corps.

In addition to the large number of Kiu Lings (the traditional patron
of the community), a new group of brokers arose after 1965 in the Chinese
community of New York. Again, the emergence of the new brokers was related to the new resources available to the Chinese in this era. These

resources included manpower, new fundings available through the Economic

Opportunity Act and the consciousness of ethnicity.

The second generation Chinese who were raised and educated in the

United States, among whom were those with an expertise in law, business,

and social work, realized that they could tap resources from the city,

state and federal governments for the betterment of their ethnic group.

They started to organize social agencies and to participate in the organ-

izations established by outsiders such as the Community Service Society.

The more radical, young Chinese-Americans, influenced by the Black and

Puerto Rican movements, and conscious of their cultural heritage and the

power of the People's Republic of China, returned from the suburbs to

Chinatown to organize their people to fight "oppression,"[1] to fight for

equal opportunity, and to fight for more funds for community services

in Chinatown. Thus, they were also brokers for the community.

The important social agencies in this era are: the Community Service

Society, the Chinatown Advisory Council, and the Chinatown Foundation.

The last two agencies are newly established. The Chinatown Advisory

Council was established in 1970 by Percy Sutton, Manhattan Borrough

President. It is composed of representatives from the government and

from the schools, churches and hospitals in the Chinatown area. The

function of this agency is to provide community services in the areas of

housing, employment, education, the aged, youth and health. Thus, the

Chinatown Advisory Council, basically performs all the brokerage functions

---

[1]The radical strategy used by the Chinese-Americans such as the anti-
tourist demonstration of I Wor Kuen gained popular support in Chinatown.
Many radicals found that they had to work with the various agencies to
help the poor of Chinatown.

also performed by the Chinese family, regional, and dialect associations. The second of these agencies is the **Chinatown** Foundation which was established by second generation Chinese-Americans with the intention of securing funds for all long-range service programs. Although these second generation Chinese do not draw salaries for their service, it is obvious that they are interested in political power. Through their services, it is said, they hope to gain the support from the people of Chinatown to compete for offices in the city's future elections.[1]

The Office of Economic Opportunity, according to my informants, has also funded some agencies with full time, paid social workers to serve the people of Chinatown. Thus, for instance, the Chinatown Planning Council was founded in 1970 with funds allotted by the Office of Economic Opportunity. The Chinatown Planning Council, according to its director, has been concerned with the problems of child care, youth, medical care, legal aid, and voter registration. Since the survival of this agency depends on the number of people it serves, efforts have been made by officials to draw a large clientele from the community. These social workers want to be the principal brokers for the community and have made numerous attacks on the Chinese Consolidated Benevolent Association for its incompetence in obtaining the necessary help for the poor in Chinatown. The counter attack of the CCBA was that these social service people actually exploit the Chinese people in their "altruistic service."

---

[1]Chinatown is located in the 19th U.S. Congressional, 60th New York State Assembly, 24th New York State Senatorial and 1st Councilmanic districts. So far, no Chinese has attempted to compete for offices beyond the city's councilmanic level.

In the words of one of the Kiu Lings: "These social workers are for their pockets! But we are different. We help the poor with money from our own pockets." The point here is that some of the social agencies are competing with the traditional associations in recruiting clientele. There is a great deal of disagreement between the agency people and the leaders of the associations over approaches to social problems. The leaders of the associations are for the use of peaceful means such as writing letters to the proper authorities asking for assistance. The agency people are prone to use demonstrations and strikes.

There are also various youth groups, church groups, and newspaper agencies who are eager to assist immigrants and to bridge them with the larger society. From my fieldwork, I observed that the Health Clinic and the Basement Workshop (organized by young Chinese-Americans) and the day care centers organized by the churches are active in seeking funds from the larger society to assist the poor and the disadvantaged. Thus, the clergymen and youth volunteers have become brokers for the community as well. The relatively high literacy rate among the new immigrants has caused newspapers to flourish. In New York Chinatown, there are five major daily newspapers and two weeklies. The editors and publishers of these papers often consider themselves as the bridges between members of the community and between the community and the larger society because of their command of information.

Another source of brokers are the labor unions, law, accounting, travel and employment firms organized to fulfill the bridging functions. Travel agencies handle more than just travel. Because of their possession of bilingual staffs, these travel agencies in Chinatown often file

income tax, pay gas, electric and phone bills, and obtain licenses for
clients. All these services require the payment of fees.

To summarize then, the influx of immigrants caused by the 1965
Immigration Law and the availability of funds from the larger society
have caused structural changes in the community: the proliferation of
associations and the establishment of numerous social agencies, churches
and brokerage firms which in turn produce a large number of patrons and
brokers. The distinction between the Kiu Ling-patrons and the agency-
brokers is important, because the former are patrons who control both
wealth and political power and are linked horizontally and vertically
with members of the community through the various traditional associations. Brokers from the labor unions, agencies, religious organizations
or newspaper agencies are middlemen who attract followers through their
ability to influence those who control the resources and favor. These
brokers themselves are strictly middlemen who consider themselves instrumental to their clients not so much because of their wealth per se
but becasue of their functions and their ability to mediate (Mayer 1967;
Stuart 1972; Paine 1971). Thus, the structural changes in the Chinese
community brought forth a new kind of interpersonal relationship, the
broker-client relationship.

Economic Opportunity of the Chinese and the Larger Society

The economic behavior of members of an encapsulated ethnic group
should be viewed in their relationship to the larger society. It is
toward the macro-economic environment, the opportunity structure of the
larger society, that entrepreneurs of an ethnic group have to make thei
creative response (Aubey 1969; Glade 1967). Fredrik Barth (1963, 1969)

and Clifford Geertz (1963) both emphasized that the "niche" of an ethnic group or the economic opportunity of a minority group have intimate relationships with the resources available in the larger society. The task in this section is to demonstrate the interrelationship between the economic pursuit of the Chinese and the changes of policies concerning part of the larger society.

First, the 1965 Immigration Act which brought numerous structural changes in the Chinese community also brought changes in the economic niche of the Chinese. The new immigrants brought with them entrepreneurial assets such as families and expertise which is instrumental for many changes in the business establishment of the Chinese. Due to the availability of family members, many firms were organized and run by family members. The fact that these firms have to be incorporated does not alter the nature of a family firm. Thus, on paper, family members are considered share holders. Incorporation cannot prevent the operation of the firm in a family firm fashion. That is to say, the father or the head of the family could still be the sole decision maker. Other family members who are share holders could still work as employees under the supervision of the family head in the firm.

In the pre-1965 era, due to the shortage of families, very few family firms were organized. In the present day Chinatown, special preference is given the family firm by the new immigrants. Everyone dreams of having a family firm himself. It is not uncommon to find that many firms which were started and run by a group of partners sooner or later split. One of the partners stayed with the firm, and the rest of them, if possible, went out to establish their own businesses. The process of fusion and fission involved in the partnership firm will be discussed later. The family is an asset and the avilability of family members was made possibly by the New Immigration Law of 1965.

The niche for the Chinese traditionally was composed of the Chinese hand laundry, Chinese **restaurant,** Chinese grocery and the various Chinese novelty stores. As a consequence of the changes in the larger society such as the immigration policy, U.S. relations with the People's Republic of China and innovation in management and technology in the larger society, the niche of the Chinese also underwent changes. The niche of the Chinese today includes the Chinese restaurants, Chinese laundries, garment factories, gift shops, and grocery stores; but within each of these trades, there are numerous re-organizations and renovations.

Re-organization and renovations within the Chinese ethnic niche are the necessary adaptation demanded by the social and economic environment of this period, 1965-1974. Since there are more educated Chinese in the community and since many of the second generation Chinese have finished their **college/professional** training, there are more Chinese employed in non-Chinese establishments. The increased number of Chinese professionals employed in American business firms or government is in part related to new hiring policies in the larger society. The Equal Opportunity Program and Affirmative Action have definitely contributed to the hiring of the Chinese in Con Edison, New York Telephone and other American firms as well. The following shows how the larger society effected five major Chinese businesses: restaurants, laundries, garment factories, novelty and handicraft shops, and grocery stores.

Chinese Restaurants: The influx of immigrants from different parts of China and Nixon's visit to China in 1972 played an important role in the development of the Chinese restaurant trade. The Chinese responded to the demand of American customers in several ways: 1) increased numbers of restaurants; 2) increased range of food served and the addition of Chinese cuisine from different regions of China; and 3) renovated restaurants with emphasis on Chinese ethnicity - Chinese decor and symbols.

The number of Chinese restaurants in recent years has multiplied. According to the Overseas Chinese Economy Year Book (1972), there were about 25,000 Chinese restaurants in the United employing more than 200,000 restaurant workers. These restaurants were concentrated in three cities: New York, San Francisco, and Los Angeles. In New York City alone, there were about 1,700 units in 1973.[1] Of this number, 250 were situated within five blocks of New York's Chinatown. Thus, the growth of New York City's restaurants reflects the developmental trend of Chinese restaurants in the United States (see Tables 17 and 18).

TABLE 17

CHINESE RESTAURANTS IN THE UNITED STATES

Year	Units
1949	4,300
1970	9,300
1972	25,000

Source: Overseas Chinese Economy Year Book (1972).

---

[1]This estimate was given to me by a spokesman for the Chinese-American Restaurant Association of Greater New York.

There are historical, economic, and gastronomic reasons for the proliferation of Chinese restaurants. Historically, Chinese restaurants had been in existence in the United States since the pioneer days, so the American public has been familiar with Chinese food. In comparison to other national cuisine, Chinese food is usually cheaper. Also, Americans are fond of Chinese food because of its tastiness and fastidious preparation. Table 18 was compiled from data obtained from the Chinese American Restaurant Association of Greater New York attempts to indicate this fast growing business.

TABLE 18

CHINESE RESTAURANTS IN NEW YORK CITY

Year	Units
1963	560
1970	1,500
1973	1,700

Source: Chinese American Restaurant Association.

The total number of Chinese in New York City who were engaged in the restaurant business in 1973 was approximately 35,000. Five thousand of them worked in restaurants in Chinatown area. Since many of the restaurant workers were new immigrants who lived in Chinatown but worked in Greater New York, they had to commute. However, special transportation arrangements were provided by the restaurant owners. Many Italian-owned limousines were chartered by the restaurant owners to transport their workers to Queens, Brooklyn and the New Jersey area. Thus, New York's

Chinatown is a manpower center for the Chinese restaurants in New York City.

Second, Chinese restaurants have been able to meet the changing demands of the American restaurant goers. Many Americans want to try Peking,Szechuan, and Hunan cuisine. Again, the relaxation of the immigration laws in 1965 made possible the entrance of many Pekinese, Shanghai-nese, Szechnuanese and Hunanese who brought with them their expertise in the restaurant field. At the moment, the Peking, Szechuan and Shanghai restaurants are prosperous. Although the present day Chinatown is dominated by the Chinese from Hong Kong and other parts of Kwangtung province, Peking, Shanghai and Szechuan restaurants have appeared in the area due to the needs of the American tourists as well as the Chinese in the area. In fact, there is such a heavy demand for chefs of Northern Chinese cuisine that many restaurant owners have to make special trips to Taiwan and Hong Kong to recruit chefs.

Third, the Chinese restaurants have met the demands of the larger society by internal renovation and re-organization. This ability to renovate fully indicates the entrepreneurial character of the Chinese restauranters. Thus, for instance, some restaurants spend more than $100,000 to redecorate, to create an oriental atmosphere with the intention of attracting more customers.

To start a modern Chinese restaurant takes a substantial amount of capital investment. That is why many newcomers pooled their resources with their friends to initiate a restaurant. Only after obtaining a handsome profit would they split to start their own businesses. However, it is said that the medium-sized restaurant with a staff of 20 is not some-

thing an ordinary family can manage. That is why most of the medium-
sized restaurants are run by groups of kinsmen or friends who are at
the same time the share holders of the restaurant. Some Chinese in
New York recently established chain restaurants such as the House of
Chan, and the Lotus restaurants. So far, however, big corporations and
chain stores have not been popular among the Chinese in New York. A
medium-sized Chinese restaurant with a staff of 20 needs at least a
capital investment of $140,000-$200,000. The net salary paid per person
ranges from $500 -$1500[1] per month, depending on qualifications and performance. At a glance, this salary seems to be high. However, since
restaurant workers have a 14 hour work day, six days a week, the salary
they receive is more than justifiable. The total investment of all the
Chinese restaurants in New York City is said to be around two hundred
and four million dollars (1973). Not only are the Chinese restaurants
a source of profit and income for a large number of restaurant owners
and restaurant workers. Chinese restaurants in New York have also had
a positive effect on the economy of the Chinese in New York. The Chinese vegetable farms in New Jersey on Long Island have been quite prosperous due to the continuous demands from the Chinese restaurants.
Trucking companies, Chinese grocery stores, construction companies, in-
terior decorators and designers have also benefitted from the Chinese
restaurant boom. However, the prosperity of the restaurant business,
as demonstrated earlier, is highly related to the larger society.

---

[1]Including tips.

The Chinese Laundry Business: In the pre-1965 era, the Chinese hand laundry was the most important Chinese business. Changes in the opportunity structure in the larger society had brought numerous changes in the Chinese Laundry business. The various machinery invented for laundry, technological developments in the textile business, ability of other economic opportunities for the second generation Chinese through Equal Opportunity Programs and Affirmative Action, all have had repercussions in the development of the Chinese hand laundry business.

First, the Chinese hand laundry business was re-organized. Traditionally, a scrub board, some soap, an iron and ironing board and a store front were all that was needed for the establishment of a Chinese hand laundry. Such laundries were usually run by one man or a family. Today, however, there is more division of labor and specialization in the laundry business. Although there are still family-owned Chinese hand laundries which perform all the services under one roof, including receiving, washing, cleaning, drying and delivering; most of the Chinese hand laundries in New York City are actually stations for collecting and distributing. Dirty laundry is collected and marked by the stores in New York City and later transported by trucks to the washer plants. After the clothes are washed by machines, they are then transferred to presser plants to be pressed by machines and finalized by hand ironing. The finished laundry is then packed by a special group of people. Finally, the laundry is returned to the stores in New York City. Thus, the use of machinery and the methods of specialization currently in the larger society were borrowed by the Chinese laundry business. Due to the invention of coin operated laundromats, some Chinese laundry firms have adopted this new mode of laundry operation. This is another example of the interrelationship between the ethnic niche and the larger society.

Second, technological improvements and policies of the larger society which affected the closing of many Chinese laundries were the invention of the wash and wear fabrics and the use of home washers and dryers. According to a spokesman for the Chinese Laundry Association of New York, there were 2,700 Chinese laundries in 1960 in New York. This number dwindled to about 1,000 in 1970. It is said that more will fold in the future. Many second generation Chinese-Americans now do not have to work in this business because it is easy for them to find jobs to their liking in fields which they were trained for. The policy of hiring minorities has forced many firms to stop their discriminatory practices. Thus, newly available economic opportunities lured the young Chinese away from the laundry business. The laundry business was and still is run mostly by the first generation Chinese who came to the United States in the era of 1870-1964. Some of them have died, some have returned to China, and many have retired. That is why people in the community call the hand laundry business "a dying business."

The Garment Business: Garment factories together with restaurants and laundries are called Wah Yan Sam Hong (in Mandarin, it is pronounced Hua Jen San Han)[1] - literally, the three trades of the Chinese,

---

[1]This is due to the large quantity of Chinese engaged in these three businesses. The corresponding Chinese characters are (華人三行).

The development of the garment factory is directly related to the immigration policy of 1965. Only after 1965, with the influx of Chinese
families to Chinatown, did women seamstresses become available. In
fact, the majority of the Chinese garment factories are run by the new
immigrants.

There were about 200 Chinese garment factories which specialize
in sportswear and skirts. These factories contract materials and
patterns from the manufacturers who are mostly Jewish Americans. The
garment factories in Chinatown are similar to the sweat shops of the
lower East Side in the early days. But then, people who worked in the
sweat shops were mainly Jewish immigrants. Today, other minority
groups have gradually taken over the business. The Italians and the
Chinese in the lower East Side have a considerable number of people
working in garment factories. Puerto Ricans and other East European
immigrants also fill up many other factories in the New York area. The
total labor pool in the Chinatown garment factories is approximately
16,000.

Almost all garment factory workers are women. Sewing is an ability
common to all Chinese women. Thus, recruiting skillful seamstresses in
the Chinatown area has not been difficult among the Chinese. Then,
there are other factors which compel the Chinese women to get employment
in Chinese factories. First, their lack of proficiency in the English
language limits their opportunities to get employment in the larger
society. Second, the garment factories are conveniently located in the
Chinatown area. Thus, mothers can take their children to the nursery,
grade schools or day care centers in the morning and have lunch with

them at noon because of the proximity between work and school.

Since the garment factories are only contracting firms, there is little control over production. They have more orders during certain months of the year and depend on the need of the larger society. In 1971-1972, quite a few garment factories closed due to lack of work. Recently, business has picked up somewhat and more people are employed as full time workers. Salaries of garment workers depend on skill since workers are paid by the piece. For some, the average weekly pay is $150, although weekly pay can go as high as $200 for some efficient workers. Since payment is by the piece, many workers put in extra hours and thus maximize their income. People who work eight hours a day, five days a week earn hardly more than $80 per week.

Two methods are used in garment production. One method is the whole garment method. Each worker does everything to finish a garment. The other method is the assembly line method which has many divisions. Each person is responsible only for a part of the garment.

Competition among the Chinese contractors is advantageous for the manufacturers. Organizing Chinese contractors has been a difficult task due to the lack of leadership and the interest of the owners. Many newly established garment factories simply do not want to have a trade association becasue they are small in size, new, and need to remain flexible. Regulatory measures imposed by a trade association are thought to be disadvantageous. However, garment workers are becoming organized and have been recruited by the Local 23-25 of the International Ladies Garment Workers Union of New York City. The collective action taken by the union members recently forced the garment contractors to give a second thought to organizing a more solid trade association or guild for themselves. The Chinese Garment Makers Association is still weak and has only a part time lawyer and a staff to take care of the affairs of the association.

So far, most of the Chinese garment factories are relatively small, few of them having more than 50 workers. Although many of these firms are registered as corporations, most of them are owned by family members or relatives. Thus, formally they give the appearance of a corporation; in practice the shares are owned by members of a family or a group of kinsmen.

Gift Shops and Grocery Stores: Aside from the three major businesses, gift shops and grocery stores are of importance to the Chinese. Like other businesses, these two are affected by the larger society. Favorable attitudes towards China crafts and gifts. There were about 30 gift shops in 1965 in Chinatown. Today, there are about 60 gift shops selling Chinese-type souvenirs, mostly imported from Hong Kong, Taiwan and China. Some of the gift items, however, are manufactured or assembled in the Chinatown area. The gift stores also supply materials for the decoration of the Chinese restaurants. In connection with the gift shops, many Chinese housewives and children are engaged in assembling jewelry and finishing gift items for the gift shops. Salaries are paid by the piece. Reward for the work is modest. For many housewives, it is considered extra income which they earn during their spare time.

Due to the increase in Chinese population after 1965 and the growing demand for Chinese restaurants, the grocery business in Chinatown has been prosperous. In 1965, there were only 50 Chinese grocery stores. Today there are about 70 Chinese grocery stores in New York Chinatown. On Saturdays and Sundays Chinese housewives come from as far away as New Jersey and Connecticut to do their grocery shopping in Chinatown.

The Chinese grocery business is a very complex business. It needs both domestic and international connections. New York's Chinatown grocery stores are related to many other grocery stores in different Chinatowns in Canada and the United States. Since the demand for Chinese groceries is relatively high in New York City, most of the imported items are shipped to New York's Chinatown. From there, grocery items are redistributed to the Chinatowns in Philadelphia, Boston, and Chicago. Furthermore, many of the ingredients necessary for Chinese cooking have to be imported from China, Taiwan, Canada, Hong Kong, Mexico and even Peru. Shops which do not have direct connections with exporting firms overseas have to get the goods from the bigger grocery stores at wholesale prices.

Other Businesses: It would be erroneous to think that every Chinese is engaged in one or another of the above businesses. All manner of conceivable goods and services which cater to the Chinese customers may be found in Chinatown. These businesses range from Chinese funeral homes to Chinese barber shops and Chinese herbal stores. Because of the existence of practically every trade in the Chinatown area, many Chinese do not have to step out of Chinatown to work or do their daily shopping According to statistics furnished by the Chinese Chamber of Commerce in New York City, a table indicating the various Chinese businesses was constructed (Table 19).

TABLE 19

CHINESE BUSINESSES OTHER THAN RESTAURANTS
LAUNDRIES, GARMENT FACTORIES, GIFT SHOPS AND GROCERY STORES (1973)

Types of Businesses	Units
Bakeries	7
Banks	1
Barber shops	13
Beauty salon	8
Chinese Book Stores	15
Candy stores	4
Carpenters, painters and plumbers	6
China and Cookery and Glassware	4
Clothing stores	5
Dentists (Chinese)	8
Drug stores	5
Employment Agencies	7
Importers and Exporters	25
Tailors	5
Fish Markets	2
Florists	6
Funeral Services	3
Furniture	4
Hardware	3
Herbalists	12
Insurance, Real Estate and Stock Brokers	30
Jewelers	5
Laundry Supply and Appliances	10
Liquor stores	4
Meat and Poultry stores	15
Mining and Manufacturing	2
Newspapers	7
Noodle Manufacturers	8
Photo Studios	5
Physicians	30
Printers	10
Radio and TV Appliances	8
Shoe stores	1
Theatres and Movie Houses	7
Chinese Closed Circuit TV Station	1
Chinese Closed Circuit Radio Station	1
Travel Agencies	7
Trucking Co. and Taxi Co.	3
Accountant Firms	10
Lawyers	25
Advertising and Art Designs	3

The fact that these various kinds of businesses exist to serve the people of Chinatown and the fact that the Chinese in the area do not have to speak English when shopping, should not be interpreted to mean that Chinatown is a self-sufficient community. It may appear self-sufficient, but its livelihood depends on the larger society. The fact that China-town has a diversity of Chinese business establishments serving the needs of the Chinese reflects the important role of the government in the Chinese migration to New York City. Because new immigrants are admitted to the United States each year, immigrants who do not speak English and are used to the traditional way of life, it is natural that many Chinese shops have been established to serve their needs.

Community Structure and Entrepreneurship

The structural changes brought about by the influx of immigrants and the changes in the attitudes and policies toward the Chinese, have had their impact on the entrepreneurial pursuit during this period. The various associations and the newly established agencies, newspapers, and labor unions have all played a role in the economic activities of the Chinese.

The Associations and Entrepreneurship: The associations which have had powerful controls on the business community still have their in-fluence. The traditional family and regional associations and the Con-solidated Chinese Benevolent Association in particular have been under attack by radical students and community workers for being too slow to adapt and meet the needs of the new immigrants. What seems to have been overlooked in their criticism is the fact that most of these associations were established in the pre-1965 era to serve the needs of the adult, male Chinese and are therefore not prepared to tackle the contemporary social problems such as housing, medicare, and youth problems. However, the traditional associations still retain their influence among the Chinese businessmen.

The Consolidated Chinese Benevolent Association remains the highest authority of the Chinese community. It arranged with the Social Security Administration to send a Chinese staff member to the association center every Sunday afternoon to help the elderly apply for social security benefits. It invited the Department of Health to send doctors twice a year to give free injections against influenza and the colds to the elderly. In 1966, the CCBA organized a successful demonstration to keep the Fifth Police Precinct in Chinatown. In the spring of 1974, the CCBA sent a petition to City Hall asking for more police protection for the deteriorating living environment in Chinatown. Recently, it cooperated with the New York Police in the arrest of those criminals who vandalized and extorted Chinese laundries and their owners. On behalf of the Chinese community the CCBA requested permission from the governor of New York State in 1973 to open their businesses on Sundays. Other matters affecting the Chinese businessmen such as traffic safety, parking, and cleanliness of streets were also brought to the attention of the proper authorities of the state or city by the Chinese Consolidated Benevolent Association.

In the area of employment, the CCBA often acts as broker. Many American firms frequently send their employment circulars to the CCBA to request assistance in their recruitment process. It cooperated with the Lower East Side City Manpower Career Development Agency to help train Chinese as key punch operators, painters, carpenters and plumbers. Thus, the CCBA still functions as a broker for the community.

The mediation service of the CCBA is frequently used by Chinese businessmen, despite the availability of legal aid agencies. Thus, for instance, wage problems of the Chinese laundrymen were brought to the CCBA for mediation.

The CCBA adopted an anti-communist stance and is a strong supporter of the Nationalist Chinese. This perhaps is due to the fact that the CCBA is controlled by the older Chinese who either suffered under communism or embraced anti-communist ideology. Historically, the CCBA assisted the Kuomingtang in their overthrow of the Manchurian government in China. There are two Kuomingtang offices located in Chinatown. Both the Chinese Consulate (from Taiwan) and the Taiwan government have intimate associations with the CCBA. When highranking government officials visit Chinatown, New York, the CCBA always has advance notice and is able to organize receptions for them on behalf of the community. The leaders of the CCBA are frequently invited to Taiwan for visits. Some were given titles and decorated by Chiang Kai Shek. The Chinese school under the control of the CCBA also receives aid from the Taiwan government. When Chinese businessmen want to import merchandise from Taiwan, they are required to produce recommendation letters from the CCBA. Thus, the CCBA is a bridge between the Chinese businessmen and the Taiwan government.

The CCBA continues to play the role of sponsor for various cultural educational and community projects. With financial support from the

Chinese-American Bank and the Chinese Chamber of Commerce, the CCBA set up a Small Business Administration training program. Because of the various community activities they perform, the Kiu Ling of the CCBA still enjoy great prestige in the community. They are the resources for the Chinese businessmen **because** these Kiu Lings are mediators and brokers, and they have good connections and valuable information.

Due to the anti-communist stance of the CCBA, it has been quite hostile to the youth groups which are sympathetic with Peking. The main reason for the CCBA's refusal to admit other associations and organizations establihsed in the recent years to its constituency is because many of these associations and groups are sympathetic toward the People's Republic of China.

Clán, Regional, and Dialect Associations: Most of these associations remain favorite places for the old immigrants and the retirees. They still render welfare and employment assistance. The bigger associations still have dormitories for the old and unemployed and give free meals to them. The traditional "credit clubs" are still organized. However, they are no longer the main source of financing. Banks and the credit unions play a more important role. With the exception of the Lee Family Association which has a credit union, other family and regional associations do nothing to assist the capital formation of the Chinese.

The important activities of these associations are the annual election of the officials and the Spring and Autumn Festivals(清明 and 重陽). The annual election in the association is attended by those who want to gain a following in the associations. In order to get elected, many donate thousands of dollars for the community activities.

The names of the donors are publicized by the local Chinese newspapers
which circulate all over the Chinese communities in the Unites States.
Thus, one can enjoy great publicity when running for office. The
elected leaders of the associations still enjoy prestige in the business
community, and such prestige can be converted for entrepreneurial pursuit. It is said that once a person is a Kiu Ling, he will be invited
to participate in partnership and other gain seeking pursuits.

During the Spring and Autumn Festivals[1] the leaders organize trips
to the cemetery where former members have been buried. After the visit
members return to the association hall for a collective ritual ceremony,
bowing in front of the portraits or the ancestral tablets of the association. A banquet is then served. Thus, group solidarity continues to
be expressed through ritual representation. Furthermore, these associations remain a center for the recreation of the old and especially for
the nostalgic Chinese who have strong emotional ties with the homeland
and with the Chinese culture. Chinese games are played, Chinese dialects are spoken; and Chinese festivals such as the Mid-Autumn Festival,
the Dragon Boat Festival, and the Chinese New Year are celebrated.

The establishment of the various social agencies has taken away
many responsibilities from the traditional family, regional and dialect
associations in the area of welfare service. Thus for instance, there
are specific social agencies such as the Golden Age Club and the Greate
Chinatown Community Association serving the senior citizens. Other
employment and social agencies, however, are far more effective in find

---

[1]The Spring Festival is also known as Ching Ming (淸明); the
Autumn Festival is sometimes called Chang Yung (重陽   ).

ing employment and obtaining health care and social security benefits.
Nevertheless, the traditional family, regional and dialect associations, as indicated earlier, remain a center of recreation for the old
and a social club for the traditional businessmen who want to establish
a following for gain pursuit activities.

The Trade Associations: These Associations are far more important
than those of previous decades. The American-Chinese Restaurant Association and the Chinese Chamber of Commerce both have increased memberships. They often negotiate with the larger society on matters concerning the Chinese Businessmen. They are information centers which channel
information and regulations on tax, sanitation, wages, and licenses.
The trade associations are also the protectors of the Chinese businessmen. For example, in 1972 the Village Voice made a derogatory remark
about Chinese restaurants, stating that most of the meats served in
Chinese restaurants was "dog meat." This remark irritated many Chinese
restauranteurs. The American-Chinese Restaurant Association immediately filed a million dollar defamation suit against the Village Voice.
Fearing disasterous consequences, the Voice apologized and asked for
forgiveness. The suit was subsequently dropped. Thus, the Restaurant
Association acts as a broker and protector for the Chinese restaurants.
Other trade associations such as the Chinese Import and Export Association have performed important services for the Chinese businessmen by
providing information, obtaining permits, and gaining favorable export
quotas from the governments concerned. Thus, the Chinese trade associations facilitated the entrepreneurial activities of the Chinese through
their brokerage activities.

Increased educational background among the Chinese businessmen is perhaps responsible for the membership increase in other businessmen's organizations such as the Chinese American Elks Club, Dragon Lodge, Lion's Club of Chinatown and the Chinese Chamber of Commerce. The most important of these is the Chinese Chamber of Commerce which recently recruited many influential Chinese businessmen. The Chinese Chamber of Commerce has acted both as patron and broker for the Chinese in recent years. Leaders of the Chamber are rich Chinese entrepreneurs who have been generous in their donations to various cultural activities in the community. These leaders are also the sponsors of many other community projects such as the construction of the twenty-nine story Confucious Plaza Cooperative, the installation of pagoda telephone booths, erection of the Chinese lantern-design street lights, and police call boxes with instructions in Chinese.

The leaders of the Chamber of Commerce are instrumental in transmitting valuable information to the community concerning economic opportunities, availability of government subsidies, and business regulations. For instance, the Chinese Chamber of Commerce recently urged the community and Chinese businessmen to take advantage of the "Mitchell-Lama Act," "The Housing Act of 1949," and the "Small Business Investment Act" to procure governmental aid to build better housing, parking facilities and to make general commercial premises improvement.[1] The community has benefitted from all this information and has used its resources under the auspices of the Chinese Chamber of Commerce.

---

[1] This information is obtained from the 60th Anniversary Journal of the Chinese Chamber of Commerce of New York, Inc., p. 85.

Thus, the leaders of the Chinese Chamber of Commerce are brokers and patrons for the community. The payoff for them is _prestige_ which can be activated for entrepreneurial pursuit. Due to their wealth, power, and possessions of valuable information, many less prosperous Chinese businessmen are envious of these leaders and try to form dyadic contracts with them.

Tongs: The Tongs still exist and some members of the Tongs are said to still be involved in many illegal activities such as gambling, prostitution, and drugs. The two powerful Tongs in today's Chinatown are the On Leong and the Hip Sing. Many times profits obtained for the illegal businesses are said to have helped quite a few Chinese entrepreneurs in the Tongs launch other legitimate enterprises. To the insiders of Chinatown, the existence of the youth gangs is correlated to the Tongs which alledgedly finances and supports them. These gangs, according to some observers are said to have economic significance for the community. These gangs are said to be "hired" by the Tongs to "police" the streets and keep the "muggers" away from Chinatown. One knowledgable informant claims that, "The youth gangs only kill each other. They have never deliberately caused any harm to the regular Chinese merchants or tourists." The youth gangs were also said to be employed to protect the gambling dens operated by members of the Tongs. These gangs are also needed to "regulate" the misbehavior of the unruly gamblers.

Not all the Chinese businesmen are members of the Tongs. Those who join the Tongs are said to be either in need of protection or are interested in engaging in clandestine profit-making activities such as drugs and gambling.

    <u>Agencies and Entrepreneurship</u>: The agencies discussed here are not social service agencies but profit making agencies such as law, acoounting, employment, travel firms, and newspapers. All of these agencies have bilingual staffs and are familiar with the larger society and the Chinese community. They have contributed to the entrepreneurial activities by rendering their services in obtaining licenses, billing, income tax reporting, sponsoring technical personnel, and translating. Since confidences are often involved in their services, most of the accountants and law firms are hired on recommendation of friends or kinsmen. Interpersonal relationships between customers and accountants or lawyers frequently lead to business partnership and other gain pursuits. It is common to find an accountant in multiple businesses. Thus, informant R has an accountant firm and a radio station. Informant A is both an accountant and a real estate salesman. The latter said that knowledge regarding his client's financial situation often helped him to sell real estate. On the other hand, the information they have on various businesses in the larger society and regulations and advantages adhered to in various policies is instrumental for the entrepreneurial pursuit of their customers. This explains why so many Chinese entrepreneurs are eager to establish dyadic contracts with people in these businesses.

    The newspapers[1] are important not only because they are the sources

---

[1]The major Chinese daily newspapers are: <u>China Times</u>, <u>China Tribune</u>, <u>Chinese Journal</u>, the <u>United Journal</u>, and the <u>China Post</u>.

of information for the Chinese entrepreneurs, they also endo.

their liking. Their endorsement in the newspapers often brings

customers. Thus, many entrepreneurs invite the Chinese press for i .g-

urations. Restauranteurs want to give them free meals. Other business-

men often create occasions to take them out to tea. Good publicity

for the entrepreneurs and their firms is thought to be essential for

their gain pursuit activities.

Labor Unions and Entrepreneurship: Labor unions in the past have had

difficulties recruiting members in the Chinese community. Since 1965,

these unions (especially the International Ladies Garment Workers

Union) have employed a Chinese-English bilingual staff, and through

their efforts many members have been recruited. The garment factory

owners attempted to discourage their employees from participating in

the unions but without much success. The unions indeed pose a threat

to the entrepreneurial activities of the Chinese businessmen. Many

entrepreneurs, instead of opposing the unions, try to establish dyadic

relationships with the union officials in order to familiarize them-

selves with the regulations and avoid unnecessary violations of contracts

as well as to discover escape routes in the filing of taxes, wages, and

social security reports.

In order to avoid confrontation between unions and employers, many

Chinese entrepreneurs also try to establish "good" relationships with

their employees by putting them in their debt in one way or another so

that they could not bring complaints to the unions.[1] Thus entrepren-

---

[1]Further discussion on this matter will be conducted in Chapter 7.

eurial activities also involve the establishment of patron-client and broker-client relationships between the employers and employees, and between employers and the union officials.

In summary, there are resources and restraints brought about by the changes in the larger society's policy toward the Chinese and by the changes in the Chinese community as well. The new resources are manpower, expertise, family firms, funds from the government, more economic opportunity. The patron-client and broker-client relationships created for entrepreneurial activities are formed and manipulated under the constraints and reinforcements of the new social economic environment.

CHAPTER 6

TRANSACTIONAL RELATIONSHIP AND THE ENTREPRENEURIAL
PURSUIT OF THE CHINESE IN A NEW ERA: 1965-1974

There is a tendency among some social scientists, especially those
who are oriented to the evolutionary approach to the study of cultures
and societies to hold the view that the traditional, broker-client and
patron-client relationships are historical vestiges, that they are replaced by party patronage in industrial societies (Wolf 1950; Silverman
1965; Weingrod 1968). Eric Wolf (1950) hypothesized that modernization
will fundamentally change the role of the patrons or the vertical com-
padre. However, studies conducted by anthropologists in different parts
of the world seem to indicate that patronage and clientage did not dis-
appear in the wake of or during modernization (Strickon 1972; Paine 1971;
Tien 1953; Coombs 1973). Patron-client relations,as shall be shown in
this chapter, continued to be formed and manipulated for various goal-
seeking activities.

What has changed in the present day Chinatown is not the fact that
the patron-client relationship does not exist, but the changed nature
of patron-client relationship and the availability of other brokerage
mechanisms such as the social agencies, brokerage firms, and kinship.
Thus, altered resources and modified community structure of New York's
Chinatown after 1965 have brought about the emergence of the non-Kiu Ling
brokers. In the pre-1965 era, the community's Kiu Ling were both patrons
and brokers. Today, there are Kiu Ling brokers and non-Kiu Ling brokers.

The purpose of the present chapter is to uncover the processes involved in the creation of patron-client and broker-client contracts and their manipulation for the establishment of firms, economic cooperation, obtainment of employment, financing, information and dispute settlement. One point has to be re-emphasized at this juncture. That is, the manipulation of interpersonal relationships such as action sets, ego centric networks or patron-client dyads for goal-seeking activities are not unique among the Chinese in New York, but common in many cultures (Barth 1966; Davenport 1960; Gould 1969; Horowitz 1967; Coombs 1973; Benedict 1968; Dirks 1972; Mayer 1966; Plotinicov 1967; Gulliver 1971; Barnes 1969; Epstein 1969; Wheeldon 1969; Kapferer 1969; Boswell 1969; and Mitchell 1969).

The present analysis focuses on the changed nature of patronage and brokerage, their formation and manipulation under the constraints and reinforcements of the new social and economic resources available to Chinese in this era. To accomplish such a purpose, the trinitarian model advocated by Strickon and Greenfield (1972) will be followed. The advantages of following the same model are: 1) it guarantees a comparative framework;[1] 2) it accentuates the transactional processes in decision-making activities; 3) it provides an opportunity to view the formation and manipulation of patronage and brokerage in a historical perspective. The last point is of importance because the various patron-client or broker-client relations existing in the present day Chinatown could have roots in the pre-1965 era. Coomb (1973: 96-112)

---

[1]This model advocated by Strickon and Greenfield (1972) was used also in Chapter 4.

suggested that the changing nature of interpersonal relationships could be viewed not only as a synchronic structure but also as an on-going process in which changes in the pattern of relationships are understandable in terms of previous patterns.

Applying the model to the analysis of patron-client and broker-client transaction means examining 1) the cultural idioms such as <u>Kam Ching</u> (trust or sentimental warmth), <u>Yee Hey</u> (trusting righteousness), and <u>face</u>, under which transactions and negitiations are conducted; 2) the system of formal positions in the traditional associations and the modern agencies; and 3) the resources available to the Chinese which include family, kinship, and friendship connections, money, manpower and expertise, and financial assistance from the larger society such as the 350 million dollars allocated to the Community Action Programs by the Economic Opportunity Act in 1963.

Our discussion begins with the manipulation of various interpersonal relationship by Chinese firms. Kinship, clanship, patron-client and broker-client relationships can be examined within the environment of the firm and/or in the firm's external relationships with the community and the larger society. At this point, it is necessary to present a discussion and analysis of various Chinese firms.

Chinese Firms: A General View

The ethnic character of the Chinese entrepreneurship is manifested both in the types of businesses they pursue and the patterns of management, transaction, and ownership. As mentioned earlier, the present day Chinese concentrate heavily in the ethnic niche encompassing laundries,

restaurants, and garment factories. In terms of management and ownership in the post-1965 era, the preferred way of organizing and establishing a firm among the Chinese was through the use of family members.
Family firms were common particularly in the Chinese garment factories,
small scale Chinese restaurants and some non-specialized Chinese hand
laundries.[1] Since the proliferation of family firms is related to the
existence of Chinese families, a brief comparison and contrast of families of these two periods follows.

    Chinese families: In the pre-1965 era, there were relatively few
families in Chinatown,[2] save those who sent for their children and wives
before the 1924 Quota Act and those who sponsored their war brides after
1945. Thus, for some time, Chinatown was labelled a Bachelor society
(Wu 1958; Heyer 1953; Schwartz 1948). Although there were some Chinese
who were married, the number of such marriages was insignificant.
Since 1965, there have been four types of Chinese families in New York's
Chinatown: 1) the old immigrant families who came before 1965; 2) the
new immigrant families who came to New York after 1965; 3) the second
generation Chinese-American families which are the result of the intermarriage between the U.S. born Chinese; and 4) the third generation Chinese families which are the result of the intermarriage between the children of the second generation Chinese-Americans. Marriage between the
Chinese and the non-Chinese exists, but it occurs more among the Chinese
students who came to this country to study in the various colleges and

---

[1]Most Chinese laundries in this era have detailed division of labo

[2]For a more complete explanation of the shortage of Chinese familie
in the pre-1965 era, see Chapters 2 and 3.

graduate schools. With the exception of the second and third generation Chinese families, the family is still a unit of production and consumption under the supervision of the family head who is usually the father or the eldest effective male. He is a decision maker. Authority is structured according to sex and birth rank.

Most of the family firms in New York are run by the new immigrant families. Second generation and third generation Chinese who are born and raised in the United States are not particularly interested in returning to Chinatown to work. Some of them went to college and were trained professionally. They prefer work with American establishments. Those second or third generation Chinese professionals who can speak the Chinese language and are familiar with the culture, often return to Chinatown to make money. It is said that Chinatown is a gold mine for bilingual, second generation Chinese lawyers and accountants. I met several Chinese lawyers who are learning the Chinese language for the sole purpose of making money from the immigrants. Family members of second and third generation Chinese are seldom involved in the business activities in Chinatown; they feel it is more rewarding (in terms of money and career promotion) and more convenient[1] to work with U.S. firms or establishment. Thus, the economy of Chinatown in the post-1965 era is controlled by the foreign born Chinese (both the old settlers and the new immigrants) and the second generation Chinese who can speak the Chi-

---

[1]Convenient in terms of language, training and even residence. Most of the second and third generation Chinese cannot speak the dialect and live outside Chinatown. They are trained professionally in fields which the larger society offers more opportunity: engineering, computer sciences, architecture, law, accounting, etc.

nese language. In a very general way, it is possible to delineate the different clusters occupied by different groups in the community (see Table 20).

Among the old settlers partnership with kinsmen and friends is still prevalent. The rich old settlers in this era tend to be partners in different businesses at the same time; thus they are multiple share holders. With the exception of traditional hand laundry stores and small scale Chop Suey Restaurants, the old settlers have very few family firms.

TABLE 20

INTERRELATIONSHIPS BETWEEN TYPES OF
CHINESE BUSINESSES AND TYPES OF CHINESE (1973)

Types of Chinese Businesses	Sub Types	Controlled by

Chinese Laundries	Washer plants
	Presser plants
	Collection and
	  delivery stores
	Complete Service
	  hand laundry
	  stores
		Old Settlers

	Laundromats	New Immigrants

Chinese Restaurants	Chop Suey Restaur-
	  ants
	Snack and Coffee
	  shops
	Cantonese Restaur-
	  ants
		Both New Immigrants
		  and Old Settlers

	Shanghai, Peking
	  Hunan, Szechuan
	  Restaurants
		New Immigrants

Garment Factories	Skirt, blouse, and sportswear	New Immigrants
Travel Agencies, Law, Accounting and Insurance Firms		Mostly Second Generation Chinese- Americans
Chinese Groceries		Both Old Settlers and New Immigrants
Chinese Gift Stores		Both Old Settlers and New Immigrants
Chinese Book Stores		Mostly New Immi- grants

However, among the new immigrants, special preference is given to the establishment of family firms. Those who cannot start their own family firm usually cooperate with other new immigrants to organize a small firm. After they have made some profit, the partners usually split. This process of fusion and fission seems to be an adaptive technique for those who do not command the necessary resources to start their own businesses. Today almost eight percent of the Chinese garment factories, ninety percent of the Chop Suey Restaurants, and ninety percent of the full-service hand laundry stores are run by family members. Of these family firms, the following major types can be found (Table 21):

TABLE 21

MAJOR TYPES OF CHINESE FAMILY FIRMS (1973)

Type 1:	Family firm	owned, managed and staffed by family members only
Type 2:	Family with hired employees	owned and managed by a core group of family members but hires employees
Type 3:	Family with a labor boss	owned and managed by a core group composed of family members but a labor boss is hired who is responsible for hiring staff

In the family firm environment, the family head is often the major decision maker. He plays the role of father, patron and friend in his relationships with his family members, employees, and labor boss. Thus, there are kinship, friendship, and patron-client relationships among the members of firms. The manipulation of these relationships for entrepreneurial pursuit is recognized by Burton Benedict (1969), Arnold Strickon

(1972), and Francis Ianni (1972) and will be discussed later in this
chapter.

In addition to family firms and partnership firms there are also
corporations formed by share holders and partners who are not related to
each other. Sometimes in the local Chinese newspapers, well known restaurants and garment factories publish notices inviting people to be
share holders. The mere fact that they do not advertise such invitations
in English newspapers indicates their preference for members of
their own ethnic group to participate. One informant confided that the
"different way of thinking, different way of organizing things, different customs, difficulty in communication, made cooperation with Sai Yan
(Westerners) difficult and a disastrous result from such cooperation
can be expected." The sharing of ideals and values and the sharing of
criteria for judgment of performance are thought by members of ethnic
groups to be the bases for business cooperation (Greely 1970; Barth
1969). Thus, non-Chinese are excluded from economic activities of the
Chinese due to strategic and practical considerations, not because of a
racist attitude. Recently, some big Chinese restaurants in New York
have tried not to offend the eager white Americans who want to be share
holders; they have made exception and accepted their investments. There
are restaurant entrepreneurs who see the advantages of having some rich
and powerful Americans who have the connections conducive for entrepreneurial activities and invite them to participate in their businesses.
However, as a rule, non-Chinese are not invited to launch economic activities with Chinese. However, this does not apply to the non-Chinatown
connected corporations such as Wang's Lab whose shares can be bought from

an OCT (Over the Counter Exchange) through any brokerage firm on Wall
Street. Since this study is concerned with the Chinese of Chinatown,
the   Chinatown-connected Chinese and their activities are beyond the
scope of the present study.

Patronage and the Operation of Chinese Firms

Economic success depends a great deal on the manipulation of human
relations. From the planning stage to the establishment and operation
of a Chinese firm, patron-client and broker-client relations are created
and manipulated. There are different types of people a Chinese businessman has to enter into dyadic contract with, types of action groups to
form, and organizations to join. Thus an individual has various sets of
networks to manipulate: personal set - linking the actor with one person;
action set - linking the actor with a group formed to pursue specific
ends; and role system set - linking the actor with an organized role
system or formal group (Wolfe 1971: 299). All these interpersonal relationships are important assets through which entrepreneurs seek to
exploit available resources and compete for customers (Barth 1962: 5-9).
The use of the family and kinship network to organize family firms will
be discussed later; what concerns us here is the general exposition of
the manipulation of action set, personal set and role system set in the
operation and the establishment of Chinese firms.

In the Chinese community of New York, there are special types of
people with whom a Chinese entrepreneur would like to have relations:
the Kiu Lings (leaders of the overseas Chinese) and the brokers. A busin
ess endorsed by the Kiu Lings is generally thought to have more prestige,

attract more cutomers, and get the approval of the community. Thus, many
newly established firms are eager to seek endoresment statements from Kiu
Lings who are friends to publish in the classified ad section of the
local Chinese newspapers. This practice is particularly common among
the Chinese physicians. One such endorsement by a Kiu Ling appeared
thus:

> Dr. Chang Ching Ming, son of
> Mr. and Mrs. Chan Ting,
> a graduate of China Medical School,
> specially recommended by the
> Chan Family Association and Kiu Lings:
> Chan Ho
> Lee Po
> Wong Ko Yan
> Eng

Thus, Dr. Chan's action set is composed mainly of Kiu Lings. In this
action set, the relationship between the actor and the others is actually
a client-patron relationship. Needless to say, the actor has to reciprocate these Kiu Lings with gifts such as money or free medical service.

During the inauguration, Kiu Lings are invited to attend the ceremony. It is said that their presence will bring special prestige to a
firm. The fact that they attend the inauguration is nurtured and publicized. It is likely that a gratitude notice will appear in the local
newspapers for several days. The public will then know the firm has
good standing and good connections.

For the purpose of pooling resources to establish a firm, action
sets are also created. For instance, some friends are solicited to form
a "hui" (credit club) with the actor to pool financial resources; some
kinsmen are asked to enter business partnership with the actor or to initiate a profit making enterprise. In general, only friends, family mem-

bers, kinsmen, and Kiu Lings are invited to form various action sets.

There are other types of people with whom the Chinese entrepreneurs are eager to enter dyadic contracts. These are the bilingual Chinese lawyers, accountants, union officials and even the brokers of the employment firms. The advantages of having such networks are obvious. It is an asset for a Chinese entrepreneur to have a friend who is a lawyer to straighten out business problems in the firm or the immigration problems of some of his employees. An accountant friend is expected to keep the secrets of the financial situation of the firm and to direct bookkeeping as well as give information of tax loopholes. It is advantageous to have a friend who is an employment broker who can be relied upon to find employees to fill in vacancies during crises situations such as employee walkouts or sickness. Union officials are useful in that they can help entrepreneurs alleviate many labor problems. Chinese lawyers, accountants, union officials and employment brokers can be considered as belonging to one type: brokers. They act as mediators between the entrepreneurs and the community, and between the entrepreneurs and the community, and between the entrepreneurs and the larger society.

Traditionally, business transactions, such as the closing of opening of stores, has to be performed in front of the Chinese officials of the Consolidated Chinese Benevolent Association (Cf. Chapter 3). Today, such transactions are performed mainly in the Chinese lawyer's office. However, to validate such a transaction, they must publicize it in the local Chinese newspapers.

Except for the garment factories and the Chinese laundries (both
of which have unions) it is customary for the Chinese businessmen to
file income tax reports for employees to such an extent that they do not
represent the salary received by the employees. An employer is required
by law to have funds put aside for the payment of income tax and social
security. This amount is in proportion to the salaries paid. Thus, if
an employee receives a large salary, then the employer has to withhold
more for various taxes and social security, and vice versa. In order
to maximize gain for the employer, it is customary for an employer to
report a fraction of the income he pays to his employees and thus withhold less and pay less to the government. Through this practice, the
employee has to pay less than his legal share of social security, tax,
but from retirement the employee receives less from the government than
he ought to get. The advantage here is that the employer, instead of
paying, say $1,000 tax and social security to the government, pays $500
since he reported only a fraction of the income tax of his employees.
In the long run, the employees are the ones who suffer because they will
receive smaller security benefits. The employer profits from the system
by "pocketing" a portion of the money which technically belongs to the
government and the social security bureau and the employee. To avoid
detection and prosecution, employers rely on friends who are smart
lawyers and accountants to help perpetrate the frauds.

The common methods resorted to for the maintenance of the broker-
client relationships are mutual gift giving, mutual help, and occasional
mutual invitations to tea or lunch. In order to make the other parties
indebted and therefore insure future interaction or reciprocation from

the other party, it is frequently thought necessary to take the first move of making prestation. Further, the initiation of prestation (such as paying the bill for dinners) is interpreted as an act of friendship, generosity, and even righteousness. Persons with these qualities are thought to be worthy of further business interactions.

In restaurants, friendly competition is often seen as Chinese fight to pay the bill. The scene is difficult for outsiders to comprehend. I have accompanied several businessmen to dinner on different occasions and noticed that if some of the diners are important friends who are lawyers, bank officials, or Kiu Lings, the person making the prestation will immediately rush to pay the cashier and ask him or her to inform these friends that their bill has been taken care of. During my fieldwork in New York, I also encountered situations where my bill was paid by my partner's friend before I realized it. My bill was also paid, not because I am an anthropologist, but because my dinner partner was in the action set of the person who paid the bill. My friend does the same for other friends occasionally too; for otherwise it would be said that he lacked Yee Hey (trusting righteousness), Kam Ching (friendship or trust) which are important in social interactions in Chinatown.

Thus, prestation and counter prestations are made to reinforce and maintain friendship and patron-client dyads in the action set and other social networks. The actual manipulation of these patron-client dyads, broker-client dyads, and action sets for the establishment and maintenance of family firms, financing, employment and mediation settlements in this era will be discussed in the following sections.

The social occasions for the contraction of patron-client dyads

and broker-client dyads in today's Chinatown are: 1) the celebration
of a one month old grandchild; 2) the engagement ceremony of a son or
daughter; 3) a marriage ceremony; 4) the inauguration of a new firm, and
4) the Chinese New Year's celebration in the associations. There are
rules governing the interactions. Tokens of gratitude have to be shown.

On the occasion of the celebration of the one month old grandchild,
it is common for the rich grandfather to invite his colleagues, friends,
Kiu Lings, other kinsmen and prospective candidates for dyadic contracts
to participate in the celebration. The affair is usually held at a
Chinese restaurant with Chinese decor and arranged with proper symbols
on the walls. The invitations are printed in gold characters on red
cards. People who attend to the banquet are expected to bring presents,
usually in the form of money wrapped in red paper or gift certificates
in envelopes. The banquet begins with a kinsman or friend who acts as
M.C., introduces the guests to each other. Toward the end of the banquet, the host is expected to show his gratitude for giving him face by
announcing that he is giving a donation to his family association or to
the Chinese school. Usually the leaders of the CCBA and the president
of the respective family association are expected to receive the donation.
In addition to this, the host is expected to publish a "thank you" note
in the local Chinese newspaper. During the banquet, the prospective
candidates for dyadic contract are given special attention. Toasts will
be offered to them. More conversation is exchanged. Family members are
instructed to be more respectful to these future friends.

On the occasion of the engagement or marriage ceremony of one's son
or daughter, the procedures for inviting guests are similar to those

mentioned in the celebration of the one month old grandchild. Friends,
kinsmen, and prospective candidates for the formation of patron-client
dyads are invited to both the ceremony and the banquet that follows.
Even if one cannot attend the ceremony, one must go to the banquet. Not
attending without a good excuse is considered rude and not giving face;
future interaction could be jeopardized. The invited guests are supposed
to bring gifts, this time, not for the host families but for the married
or engaged couple. However, their families are responsible for the an-
nouncement of the news, payment for the banquet, and a donation to the
community and family association as a token of gratitude and as a symbol
of concern for kinsmen and members in the community. That is why the
donation is often given to the family association and the Chinese Consolidated Benevolent Association. A note of appreciation is also published
in the local Chinese newspapers. Not all the people present are concerned
with creating dyadic contracts. Some are there for the good food. Some
have to be there because they have to give face to their host who could
be their employer, their kinsmen or their friend. At any rate, the
guests are aware that they can make more friends which is useful in their
goal-seeking activities.

The various celebrations held by the associations on the occasion of
Chinese New Year, Spring Banquet, Celebration of Founder's Day, etc.,
are important for the members of the association to renew their friendships. The more prosperous clansmen or members can make use of the situation to recruit a larger following. The leaders or Kiu Lings have a
chance to exchange business and political information. The less prosperous clansmen can meet "rich" clansmen. Dyadic contracts are created in

these situations. While it is true that many of the new immigrants
are not particularly interested in joining the associations at first,
after staying in Chinatown for a while, many change their minds and
join some of these associations. In the past, only the old Chinese
joined them. Recently, I have seen members bring their children and
family to some associations. The Lung Kon Association (Four Brothers
Association) has a youth committee. The Haka Association has children and women participating in the events of the association. Thus,
the celebrations held by the various associations are social occasions
for members and their families. Old friendships are renewed; new
friendships are made. Etiquette also requires the publication of a
notice thanking the Kiu Lings of the community and the leaders or "big
shots" for attending the events.

Inauguration of a new firm is also an occasion to invite the Kiu
Lings, friends, kinsmen, and newspaper reporters. Kiu Lings or friends
are expected to send some tokens of friendship and good will. Bouquets
of flowers or pots of flowers carrying ribbons with congratulatory
words are the appropriate gifts to wish the newly established firms
well. The owner will usually give a cocktail party or dinner party
for those who attend. To reciprocate the kindness of the Kiu Lings or
friends who attended, a note of thanks is published by the owner in the
local Chinese newspapers. This notice is more than just a "thank you
note," it has the effect of an advertisement. The occasion of inauguration is a time to express mutual appreciation and recruit candidates
(patrons and brokers) for dyadic contracts.

The formation and manipulation of various patron-client relations
does not stop at the inauguration ceremony, nor is it limited to the
celebrations of birthdays and marriages and engagements. On the contrary, the dyadic contracts created at these occasions are instrumental to the entrepreneurial pursuit: financing, employment, obtainment of information, and settlement of disputes.

Family Firm

Following the suggestion of Benedict (1968), Strickon (1971; 1973)
and Belshaw (1967), family is not to be viewed here as an institution
abstracted from the behavior of the individuals that constitute it, but
as a network of interpersonal relations. Like other social networks,
there are constraints in the familial network: rules, expectations and
values (Benedict 1968). Because of the familial obligations and constraints, many social scientists are led to hypothesize that family and
kinship ties are incompatible with economic development. Ethnographic
evidence obtained from their studies of family firms in different parts
of the world (Benedict 1968; Khuri 1965; Desai 1965) certainly
have indicated that such a view is untenable. Benedict (1968) even
went so far as to use the transactional analysis of Fredrik Barth (1966)
to demonstrate why the family firm is a vehicle for the maximization
of gain.

Instead of viewing the family as an institution which "uses people"
(Coomb 1973: 110), it shall be demonstrated that the family as a network of interpersonal relations can be used for decision making activities. More and more anthropologists have come to the realization that
decision making activities use social relationships but at the same

time are constrained by the rules, expectation and values adhered to in these social relations (Barth. 1963; Benedict 1968; Strickon 1971, 1973; Coomb **1973).** Benedict (1968) showed the familiar ties of trust and obligation by illustrating the "transactional" behavior process between the family members. Thus, the reciprocal behavior between the father and son is seen as a process of mutual <u>prestations</u>. It is through the process of prestation and counter prestation of trust and responsibility in the family firm environment that maintains operation of the family firm. This by no means suggests that every act of prestation has to be performed on a conscious level. Some are; some are not. Coomb (1973) suggested that manipulation of rules and social relationships may proceed on a relatively un conscious level. Actors may make their decisions without being consciously aware that they are influenced by ties of trust and obligation. Nevertheless, these constraints and reinforcements are present unconsciously and are recognized when they are pointed out to the actors (Coomb 1973: 96-112).

The use of family ties in the family firm environment brings numerous advantages: 1) training of family members in business operations; 2) control of information; 3) family members can put in more hours; 4) families are an important source of financing; 5) and kinsmen of the family also constitute an **important labor pool** (Benedict 1968). In addition to these advantages enumerated by Benedict, the Chinese family firm offers the greatest flexibility needed for survival. This is particularly important in an urban situation with keen competiton and with fluctuating demands of goods and services. The seasonal nature of the garment industries in New York City has caused many Chinese garment factories to go bankrupt. However, those Chinese garment factories which are run by the family have greater endurance and flexibility. When business is slow, family members do everything themselves and thus cut down on outside help. In adverse situations family members can simply stop their salaries from the factory or reduce the profit for every garment. Low profit margin and reduced production costs in the family firm environment have enabled the survival of many Chinese garment factories during the slow seasons. Sixty percent of the businesses which failed, according to my informants, are usually those run by partners. The family firm is therefore an adaptive technique for many Chinese businessmen. The consideration of financial gain, flexibility and other advantages mentioned earlier have made Chinese businessmen give priority to the establishment of family firms.

Processes involved in the Establishment of the Family Firm: The different family firms owe their existence to the efforts of their founders who are usually the heads of the families. In the post-1965 era there are several ways to start a family firm. One is by pooling the resources of the family members who can help to work in the family firm environment. Captial, equipment, and personnel are all supplied by family members. The second way of starting a firm involves several years of hard work on the part of the family head. After he accumulated enough savings and with funds borrowed from his friends, he then sponsors his family to come to New York. All the family members live under one roof, if possible. Otherwise, the family members will try to live in the same neighborhood and come eat at the parents' house during the day.

The third way of starting a firm is via a process of fusion and fission. A person will cooperate with friends or kinsmen to start a firm. After making some profits, one of them will buy the whole firm and the rest of the partners will get their own share of profits and leave. The process of fission is not always smooth. If the partners consent to the dissolvement of partnership, one of the partners can just buy up the firm. If there is no consent, there will be bad feelings and the split will not take place for a while. Lack of cooperation will result and the business will suffer. It is said that partnerships sooner or later dissolve if the partners are not happy with the business. Allegations of all kinds can always be found before fission. Dissatisfaction with each other's performance is experssed publicly or privately. The business will drag on for a period of time, but finally the partners will either ask mediation from friends or relatives or simply agree to split. The one who has the resources can then offer to buy the firm. After buying the firm, he will have three alternatives for re-organizing the firm: 1) have it run by family members under supervision; 2) have it run by core groups of family members with employees; or 3) have it supervised by the family head and his immediate family and a staff of personnel under the control of a labor boss.

Type 1 is that run by the family members under the supervision of the family head who is usually the father or the oldest effective male. The family is an economic unit both in production and consumption. Every family member who can help, works in the firm and contributes to the common resources. Wives and children usually get only what is needed for their daily necessities. Those who work in the firm take their

meals together; food is provided from the common kitchen. Taking meals
together has several advantages. First, it saves manpower. It engages
only one person for cooking and shopping. Second, it saves money in
the purchasing of costly equipment and food can be bought in bulk. Although family members can bring expenditures up for discussion, the
decision is generally made by the family head. Thus, for example, buying a family car results in a general consultation on the proper size,
model, brand and cost. It is the family head who finally makes the
decision and makes the payments. Day to day, routine business operations are delegated to family members. Trust between family members
provides security and support for the possible consequences of such
decisions (Benedict 1968). A mistake by a son is tolerated, and he will
be given another chance since he learns from mistakes. Thus, this kind
of family firm becomes a business training center for the family members.

Family firms are thought by the Chinese to be the most durable
type of business. As mentioned earlier, the family firm can endure
during sagging economic conditions and slow business seasons. The
family firm is also a device for the generation of family wealth, since
everyone contributes to the family resources by savings, supplying
free labor, and common expenditures. The wealth accumulated by the
family firm is generally spent for purchasing family necessities such
as houses, cars, or electrical appliances.

The transactional behavior between father and children or family
head and family members in the Chinese family firm is similar to that
which Benedict (1968) described. The father of the family firm is more
than a father; he is a manager, a patron. To illustrate the process

and operation of this kind of family firm, the Chan family and their
family firm, Oriental Star, shall be used as an **example.**

The family head who founded the firm in 1968 was Mr. Chan Sr. Like
many other new immigrants, Mr. Chan Sr. had to work as an employee for
four years, he observed and learned the operation of a restaurant. In
order to avoid any misunderstanding, and the breach of Yee Hey, he told
his kinsmen shortly after his arrival in New York that he intended to
work only for a couple of years. After he had settled down and accumulated enough money, he wanted to sponsor his wife and six children to
come to the United States. It is said that these Tung Hung Hing Dai
(cousins from the same village) who owned the restaurant in which Mr.
Chan Sr. worked were grateful to Mr. Chan for past favors done for them
in mainland China, and wanted to reciprocate. After four years of work
in the restaurant, he sponsored all his family to come to the United
States. In 1968 he established a take-out-order Chinese restaurant
with the help of all the family members. The father himself now acts
as the over-all supervisor and treasurer. He decides what course is to
be taken at the beginning because he is the only expert in the restaurant business. The wife acts as chief cook and has three sons assisting
her in the kitchen. One of the sons is a delivery boy. Another son
does all the ordering and purchasing. The third son assists the father
at the store front. In order to give all children an equal opportunity
to learn, duties are rotated. All six children attended Chinese high
schools in Hong Kong but are not interested in pursuing further studies
in the United States. Their ambitions mirror their father's, to make
money in the restaurant business. For them the only opportunity open is

the establishment of Chinese restaurants in the United States. After
three years of hard work, one of the sons told me that the family firm is
planning to open another restaurant and is in the process of selecting
a location, preferably not in New York State, which already has too many
Chinese restaurants. Each of the sons dreams of having one restaurant
for himself. In fact, this is one of the motivations which induces them
to pay attention to every detail of restaurant operation.

Recently, the restaurant has been redecorated and some space has
been made available for customers to take their meals there. The father
is still the expert. He cooks; he knows how to greet the customers and
how to establish rapport with them. He also directs the kitchen staff.
Thus, the father is a teacher from whom the children learn serving, bookkeeping, and cooking. Since there is no clear division of labor, each
of the sons is expected to learn every aspect of the restuarant trade
through work in the family firm environment. The mother, however, is
the permanent chef for the restaurant since she speaks little English
but cooks well. All those who do not receive salaries but draw what
they need for entertainment, education, and other necessities. The
father reciprocates by passing on his knowledge to the children, by
training them to be successful restaurant owners, by encouraging them
to start their own restaurants as soon as they can handle them, and by
promising all the financial support for such ventures. It is said that
the father is now sponsoring more relatives from Hong Kong to assist
future expansion. The eldest son is expected to head the new restaurant
When asked his feelings on being unsalaried, one son said, "We are all
of the same family. The money of the family is ours. Why should we

divide all the family wealth at the moment we need it to expand our business? We need the cooperation of all the family members to build our future in this foreign land. Otherwise, we will be like those dogs who scavenge their own kinds." Thus, family solidarity and the necessity of common fate for all members permeates the family firm environment.

Another factor which induces all the children to stay in the restaurant trade is the realization that the Chinese restaurant is the ethnic niche for the Chinese. As one of the sons said, "Where else can we excel? We have no high education. We have no training in other professions, and we are too old to go to college; and as I see it, our future is in the restaurant trade. People can do well in different professions and trades, I believe that Chinese restaurants really have future for us."

Thus, the founder of the family manipulates several network relations for his economic activities. He manipulates the traditional clanship to migrate to the United States and employs them. After he had acquired sufficient capital and knowledge, he uses the family members to establish a family firm which is an adaptive device for competition, for giving complete business training to his children to insure their future careers, for preparing the family members for future business exploitation of the ethnic niche of the Chinese. For future expansion, he is recruiting some trustworthy relatives from Hong Kong. Hence, the patterns of recruiting kinsmen and the patterns of family firms are the consequence of economic decision making activities. In other words the behavioral regularities or "social forms" are the result of strategic and adaptive activities of the actors (Barth 1963; 1966; Bennett 1969).

In the case of the Oriental Star, the children were all teenagers or above twenty. In the following case, the children are younger, yet they help around the restaurant and learn about the business by doing it. This is a case reported by Carol Sperber of New York Times (April 26, 1973, p. 50). According to her report, there is a restaurant owner by the name of Kow Cheng Lee who has a family of eight: six children and a wife. The two oldest children live in Hong Kong with their grandparents but are expected to come to the United States shortly. The other children are Mei Ling, 10; Mei Lee, 7; Chung Ming, 9; and Mei Yee, six months old. With the exception of the youngest whose swinging crib is in the kitchen, the rest of the children all assist in the family restaurant. The father came to the U.S. in 1969 and lived in Chinatown beofre moving to Plainfield, New Jersey. After his arrival, he worked as a cook in a Chinese restaurant in Chinatown. The Lees purchased the restaurant in November, 1971. After renovating this former pizza parlor, Mr. Lee opened for business in 1972. The Lees live in an apartment above the premises and every one who can help work in the restaurant does. Ten year old Mei Ling has already become one of the most resourceful workers in the family's restaurant:

Mei Ling Lee is the hostess at the Shanghai Restaurant here. With a smile, she shows customers to their tables and asks who recommende the patrons to this fairly new establishment, and then passes throug a mental inventory of guests, trying to remember her customers.
She also acts as cashier, explains to customers the ingredients of various dishes, handles phone orders, writes out checks for her father to sign and, with her brother and sister, occasionally plays jacks with customers waiting for takeout orders. Mei Ling is all of 10 years old. The fifth grader at St. Mary's Roman Catholic School has to take care of the customers because she is the oldest member of the family who speaks English (New York Times, p. 50, April 26, 1973).

Other children also help; nine year old Chung Ming helps with the take out orders; seven year old Mei Lee helps wash dishes. Both the father, Kow Cheng Lee, and the mother, Tai Kui Lee, do all the cooking but speak practically no English. Everyday after school, Mei Ling is in the restaurant to act as liaison. When she has some free time, she sits at one of the tables and concentrates on her homework. The point here is that many family businesses could not be operated without the help of family members. There is too much stress on the businesses, especially at the beginning when customers are few and much money has been spent in the renovation of the restaurant. In the case of the Lees, the ten year old daughter contributes to the family firm both with her charm and her expertise in speaking English.

What has not been analyzed is the mechanism involved in the pattern of transaction in the family firm environment. The maintenance of the family firm depends on the relations between the actors. Like the Chan family firm and other Chinese family firms, it is through the transactional _prestation_ that the Lee family firm is maintained and perpetuated. Further, a break from the business is not just a break from ordinary business associates; it involves family members. Business ties are bound to many other ties: blood ties, manager-trainee ties and even patron-client ties.[1]

Type 2: This second type of family firm includes a core group composed of family members and employees who are **nonmembers** of the family. This kind of set up is similar to the Nakama system in the Japanese

[1]This is particularly clear in the case where the parents give full financial support for future economic activities such as opening a new business.

forestry industry (Bennett and Ishino 1963). In the Nakama system,
there is an employer-patron, a core group of professionals who are related by filial or blood ties, and a peripheral and mobile group
(Bennett and Ishino 1963: 176-200). The authors found extensive patron-
client relationships both in the formation of the Nakama and the interaction pattern within it. The difference between Type 1 family firm and
Type 2 family firm is that the former consists entirely of family members
while the latter is built upon a core of kinsmen. The employer or boss
of both types of family firms is always the head of the family. Outside
employees are hired because of the lack of manpower within the family.

The core group in the Chinese Type 2 family firm is under the supervision of the family head. Members of the core group are insiders
and are familiar with the business routines and have the delegated
power to make the day-to-day routine decisions. The family members
usually contribute both capital and expertise to the firm. Thus, they
are both share holders and workers.

Processes involved in the establishment of this type of firm are:
1) pooling of resources with the adult family members; 2) organization
and recruitment of employees under the family head's efforts and plans'
3) mobilization of a publicity campaign again under the family head; and
4) development of business connections. The connections ought to include
the formation of dyadic contracts between the firm and its customers,
the head of the firm and its workers, the head of the firm and its whole-
salers or manufacturers, and the head of the firm and its unions and
transportation companies. A family will not plunge blindly into a business of which it has no knowledge. Economic alternatives are first

investigated and weighed. The amount of capital needed and the kinds of
skill required are assessed. Since most of the new immigrants have to
spend several years working before they can have their own firms, many
use these years to save money and learn all the practical skills and
knowledge related to their future enterprises. Thus, a person who has
the ambition to start a restaurant of his own will seek work in a restaurant. He will observe every detail and learn as much as possible from the
work. A person who wants to start a garment factory will work in a garment factory for some time or establish dyadic relations with people who
are in the business so he can learn from them about the business operation.

An example of this type of family firm is the Eastern Continent[1]
which is a garment factory. The firm was incorporated in 1968. The
family head and founder of the firm is the oldest brother who was
sponsored by his older sister who worked at one of the universities in
the United States in 1965. He wanted to go into business but lacked the
necessary capital and skills. After his arrival here he discussed his
plans with friends. Observing the general economic situation, he felt
that his future lay somewhere in the restaurant or garment business.
He went to Chinatown and got a job working in a Chinese restaurant
through the help of his former classmates. He moved up the ladder
quite rapidly in the restaurant from washing dishes to bus boy, to
waiter, to chief waiter. While he was working he closely studied the
restaurant and garment trades.

---

[1]The firm's name has been changed to preserve anonymity.

Having decided that he would go to the garment business, he sent word to his three younger sisters and his fiancee in Hong Kong to learn sewing. He even subsidized them in sewing school. In 1967 he changed his job and took up employment in a garment factory as a garment presser with the intention of observing the general operation of the business. Meanwhile, he sponsored his fiancee and his sisters to the United States and was able to persuade them to seek employment in garment factories. After one year of working in the garment factory, he pooled all his available resources and bought a garment factory which had gone out of business due to mismanagement. It is said that the brother and his wife owned sixty percent and the other three sisters owned forty percent of the shares of the firm. Legally, Eastern Continent incorporated, although it was run as a family firm. The past four years have brought success through sound management and hard work. The brother's wife now runs a boutique. The brother has also incorporated a real estate firm. Since expansion required more manpower, more relatives were sponsored to the United States. Since all the relatives on his side of the family have come to the United States, he then sponsored the relatives on his wife's side. Thus, patrilineal relatives are given priority before matrilineal relatives in employment and sponsorship of immigration. This pattern is similar to that of the pre-1965 era of Chinatown.

In Eastern Continent, there are two groups of people. One is the core group composed of three sisters; the peripheral group consists of the non-family members. The brother is the major decision maker.

Minor business decisions are delegated to the sisters who are also the principal technical personnel of the firm. In this internal relationships within the firm, the brother is the owner, boss, employer, and patron. He feels that he is the protector for the family business. If he fails, the family firm fails and the family fails. He is the overall supervisor of production. His sisters are assistant supervisors who take care of several sections (See Diagram 2). While he is around the factory, he takes care of the final products, including pressing and inspection to make sure that defects have either been removed or corrected. Constant favors and reciprocal benefits pass between the boss-patron and the members of the firm. The brother takes all family members out every Sunday to a Chinese restaurant and then drives them around sight seeing. However, when the firm is very busy, the family members are expected to forgo all these Sunday entertainments and work. Non-family employees are not expected to work on holidays because it would constitute a violation of work contracts and the union would object. The owner is a patron of his non-family member employees in many ways. He is a counselor on matters like schooling for children and getting driver's licenses. He often gets information for his employees on the latest immigration rulings, investments, and housing. He recommends lawyers, investment brokers, and tutors to teach English. His employees reciprocate by working harder by staying with the firm even during the slow seasons. They also send some gifts during the Chinese festivals. Thus, Kam Ching develops in the interaction between boss and employee. "All the problems in the firm will be solved if there is Kam Ching between the employer and employee." He is aware that he is more than an employer to them and that he is consciously cultivating Kam

Ching with the workers:

> When I select certain people to work I know they are useful and
> good to the firm. I don't want to lose them. If they are used
> to the machine, the people in the firm, they would have more
> efficiency. That is why I prefer to keep all the employees. As
> you know, the garment industry is constantly undermanned. Every
> employer is devising gimmicks to attract workers. I feel that I
> have to do some things for them too. Personally, I feel that if
> you treat the workers well, then you can win their loyalty. My
> workers seldom leave the firm because I take care of them. I
> keep them at work, and I see that their family problems such as
> schooling of their children and housing are solved. I taught
> them driving cars. I give them a bonus if a job has been profit-
> able.

Out of necessity the specific patron-client relationship is nurtured

and cultivated. Thus, maximization activities require a specific struc-

turing of social relationships (Barth 1963, 1966; Bennett 1969;

Strickon 1972). Eastern Continent's management and production

methods have been selected to fully demonstrate the internal relation-

ships within the firm. There are two production methods in the Chi-

nese garment factories. One is the whole garment method or complete

garment method. The management only has to bunch the parts together

and give them to the workers to assemble into finished garments. The

second method is called section work or assembly line method. Each

worker is responsible for and specializes in sewing parts of the gar-

ment. Different managements have different preferences.

The Eastern Continent selected the second method for a variety

of reasons. The whole garment method is easy for the management but

quality control is difficult, since it depends on the skill of each

worker. The owner manager told me that the assembly line method can

help control the over-all quality. More uniform quality can be expected. Difficulties in the assembly line method lie in the mangerial skills, discipline among workers, and commitment to the firm. If two workers who specialize in parts of the garment resign, the whole production process could be paralyzed. It is for this reason that informant X has used all possible methods to instill loyalty among his workers. He has had them since 1969. Kinship terminology such as <u>Che</u>, <u>Muy</u>, <u>Ko</u>, <u>Dai</u>, <u>So</u>, <u>Suk</u>, <u>Sum</u> and <u>Po</u> are deliberately used.[1] He often tells them that, "we are of one family. You can depend on me for everything!" The factory has also a Mahjong table which the workers can use during their free time. Some workers are invited with the family to participate in family activities such as marriage celebrations, birthday celebrations, etc. However, in the family firm, the important positions are occupied by the family members, in the case of the Eastern Continental, by the three sisters (See Diagram 2). In Diagram 2, steps 1, 2, 3, and 8 are supervised by family members. The owner-manager is in charge of inspection and general factory operation.

---

[1]The corresponding characters for Che, Muy, Ko, Dai, So, Suk, Sum and Po are 姊 (older sister), 妹 (younger sister), 哥 (older brother), 弟 (younger brother), 嫂 (wife of older brother), 叔 (father's younger brother), 嬸 (father's younger brother's wife), and 婆 (grand-mother).

Diagram 2

Production Line in a Garment Factory

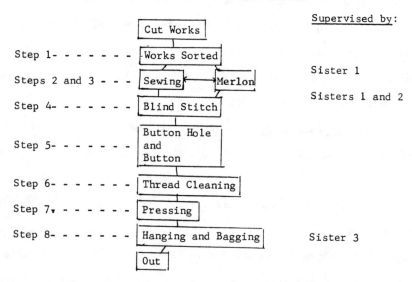

Supervised by:

Step 1 - - - - - - -

Steps 2 and 3 - - -   Sister 1

Step 4 - - - - - -   Sisters 1 and 2

Step 5 - - - - - -

Step 6 - - - - - -

Step 7 - - - - - -

Step 8 - - - - - -   Sister 3

Since informant X can speak English and wants to maximize his profits by using few or no middlemen to get the bundles (orders), he himself often deals with the manufacturers directly. Competition among the Chinese garment factories is keen, and many of them have to lower their prices in order to get the bundles from the manufacturers. To insure the normal flow of materials, the owner of Eastern Continent makes a series of prestations to maintain his dydadic contracts with manufacturers.[1] Prestations are made in the form of gift giving during the Christmas season. On the average, he spends $100 to buy expensive Chinaware and liquor to give to each manufacturer with whom he has contracts. In return, these manufacturers give him the bundles and recom-

---

[1] Almost all the garment manufacturers whom the Chinese contractors deal with are Jewish-Americans.

mend patterns which can be sewed easily and thus generate more profit.

In addition to the patron-client relationship between the owner and the manufacturers, the owner has to foster "working" relationships with the truckers. It is said that sometimes garments can be stolen or lost on the way to the manufacturers. No one can be sure what has happened to these garments. Thus, informant X spends time with the truckers, talks with them, cracks jokes and occasionally gives them one or two dresses for their wives; thus he binds the truckers to be more "careful" with his shipments. The proper functioning and the smooth operation of his garment business requires the formation and manipulation of various interpersonal relationships: kinship and patron-client relationships.

Idioms and Ritual. To tie some individuals to a more permanent bond, ritual brotherhood or sisterhood is used. The kinds of ceremonies for ritual brotherhood or sisterhood vary. For some, the ceremony is conducted in the family home in front of the members of both families. A handshake between the candidates and a bow to the portrait of the God of Justice, Kwang Kung are the common elements of the ritual. For others, it is just a dinner to which friends and relatives are invited. Shortly before the dinner, the M.C. announces the intent of the occasion; then people celebrate informally. In Eastern Continent, an employee enters ritual sisterhood with one of the assistant supervisors who is a member of the core group in the family firm. It is uncommon for Chinese to use Catholic baptism for the godfather/son relationship since it is a goal-seeking activity rather than a religious activity. However, making vows together in front of the portrait of Kwang Kung, God of Justice, Hero of Yee Hey, is common among members of the same association when entering

the alliance of brotherhood. From then on , individuals are expected
to consider, "each other's life as my life," and are obligated to assist
each other when called for.

The idioms for the operation of the patron-client relationship, kinship and ritual relationships are: <u>Yee Hey</u> (trusting righteousness), <u>Yam
Ching Mei</u> (human sentiment), <u>Kam Ching</u> (friendship), and <u>Chan Ching</u>
(warmth of kinship). These are the idioms which enable the smooth interaction between patron-client and kinsmen and friends. The importance
of these cultural values can be seen in the following statement made by
one informant:

> If there is enough <u>Yee Hey</u> and <u>Kam Ching</u> between the employer and
> employees, there will not be unsolvable labor problems. If there
> are <u>Chan Ching</u> and <u>Kam Ching</u> among the family members, no serious
> lack of cooperation will occur. <u>Yee Hey</u> and <u>Kam Ching</u> existing
> between friends is even more valuable than kinship. You can al-
> ways depend on a friend with <u>Kam Ching</u> and <u>Yee Hey</u>.

The same informant also lamented that these values are vanishing in
Chinatown. However, upon closer investigation, it was found that these
values are still held by many Chinese. In fact the manipulation of these
values is particularly obvious in the Chinese family firm environment.

It is the successful manipulation of kinship and patron-client relationships which enables the continual success of Eastern Continent. During the past five years many Chinese garment factories changed hands or
went bankrupt due to their inability to survive during the slow seasons.
Those firms which are best suited for survival during the slow seasons
are firms like Eastern Continent which are family run or have substantial
numbers of family members or kinsmen to man the production staff.

The competitive nature of the Chinese garment industry should be viewed in relation to the opportunity structure. First, the demand of the larger society for clothing depends on the general economy and consumption patterns. Americans are not bound as much by fashions as in the old days. Inflation has been rather rapid in the past several years. The clothing business has been slow. Second, the rapid increase of Chinese garment factories in Chinatown is responsible for the spirit of competition. In 1965, there were about 20 Chinese garment factories in Chinatown. Since garment factories do make profits and require relatively small capital investment, many Chinese laundry owners have switched to this new trade. The industry multiplied ten times in less than ten years. Workers' salaries are paid by the piece. To ensure a continuous flow of work in the garment factory, it is necessary to have continuous supplies and orders from the manufacturers. Many garment factory owners have to compete with each other to ensure the supplies of orders from their manufacturers. In addition to cutting down the price, they have to build interpersonal relationships such as patron-client relationships or friendships with the manufacturers and patron-client relationships with the workers. All this consumes time and money. However, these relationships have to be manipulated for the economic activities of the Chinese. Strategic manipulation of these relationships is the key to success. The Eastern Continent is a living example of such a strategic adaptation.

Type 3: Family members with a labor boss and his staff. This kind of family firm differs from type 2 in that the former has a core group of kinsmen with an organized peripheral group of outsiders, while type 3

has two important groups of personnel in the firm. One of the groups is
headed by a labor boss in charge of his hired employees. The other is
a group headed by the family head who is the super-boss responsible for
the management and operation of the whole firm. This type of arrangement is common in the medium sized Chinese restaurants such as the Mandarin Restaurant and the King Wah restaurant. In terms of authority
structure, the family head is the supreme authority in this type of
family firm (see Diagram 3).

Diagram 3

Authority Structure of a Family Firm (Type 2)

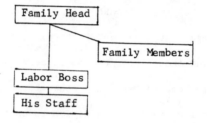

A system of patronage developed in this kind of family firm. The family
head is the super-patron for everyone in the firm. The labor boss is a
patron for his staff. The development of patronage within the labor bos
system was observed by Bennett and Ishino in their study of the Japanese
forestry industry (Bennett and Ishino 1963). Relevant to the present
discussion is the fact that the labor boss may work along side his sub-
ordinates and develop a very close _esprit de corps_. He trains his
employees. At times, he even assumes the position of foster-father-cum-
teacher of his younger staff members. To demonstrate the operation of
the patron-client relationship in this kind of family firm, the Mandari

Restaurant[1] will serve as an example.

Due to lack of technical personnel and expertise, the family members can take care of the dining area and the cash register only. The kitchen is commanded by a chef and his own staff. The chef is responsible for setting up his staff, screening and hiring the help. He oversees the operation in the kitchen, estimates,the amount of food served, directs the preparation of various courses, keeps the kitchen clean and in good order. He is responsible for the staff. He can relocate or fire them. In this kind of family firm it is said that the chef often forms his staff by recruiting his own relatives, friends and people with whom he has some ties based on locality of origin or dialect. In a word, he has to coordinate a network of interpersonal relationships within the firm.

The family head is responsible for supervising the "front" of the restaurant, its atmosphere and decoration, and publicity. He has to coordinate his group, the family members, in ushering, serving, and collecting. The interrelationship between the father and the family members is similar to that mentioned in Type 1. All the family members who can, help in the family firm. In the Mandarin Restaurant, the wife works as cashier, one of the sons works part time in the evenings as a waiter since he has to attend school during the day. The family head also makes it a point to know restaurant management, and he wants his children to learn management techniques from him. These techniques include personnel management, advertising techniques, treatment of customers,

---

[1]This is a ficticious name.

and "diplomacy" in dealing with outsiders, systems of bookkeeping, and taxes. Responsibility and trust, shown on the part of the family head, will be seen as prestations by sons who will reciprocate by doing their jobs well and making a commitment to the firm.

All the people who work in the firm take their meals together. Breakfast is at 11 a.m., lunch at 4 p.m., and dinner at midnight. Taking meals together can maximize savings and time. From the employee's point of view, it is a device which saves labor resources and wins staff loyalty. Taking meals together also prevents people from returning to work late. The owner of Mandarin Restaurant said that he made a deliberate effort to keep his staff by providing good benefits. He instructs the labor boss (chef) to prepare extra dishes on the first and fifteenth days of the month for the common meals. He also has a dormitory for unmarried employees. However, normally, he does not "boss" the employees around, for it will create friction with the labor boss.

The labor boss does a great deal to promote both efficiency and solidarity or esprit de corps within his staff. He takes care of their welfare and personal problems, as well as supervises their work. In the case of the Mandarin Restaurant, the labor boss is given a share of stock in the firm. As a chef, he has three assistant chefs, three bus boys, and one receiver/cleaner. His relationship with the staff members is teacher, leader, patron, friend, and brother. Since he is made part share holder, he is also concerned with the profit of the firm. He takes special precautions not to waste materials in the kitchen and not to

overwork the staff.[1] If he notices someone with a morale problem, he
asks him to take a break or a trip. The spirit of brotherhood is deliberately cultivated. Everyone is expected to be fair with one another.
The Yee Hey (trusting righteousness) is welcomed. In the kitchens of
many restaurants, the portrait of the God of Justice, Kwang Kung, is
hung in a visible place. Some restaurants even have an alter of Kwang
Kung which serves as a reminder that everyone should be just to each
other so that the deity will not be offended.

Idioms: The idioms used among the family members in the firm are
similar to those mentioned earlier in this chapter: Kam Ching (trusting
friendship), Chan Ching (warmth of kinship). The idioms used in the
maintenance of the patron-client relationships between the labor boss and
his staff, between the owner and the staff, between the owner and the
labor boss are Kam Ching (trusting friendship, Yee Hey (trusting righteousness), and Yam Ching Mei (Human sentiment).

To sum up then, kinship and patron-client relationships are used in
all three types of family firms. Because of the continued use of the
traditional idioms in the manipulation of kinship and patronage, these
values are preserved in the Chinese community of New York. Thus, both
the instrumental goals (the production and sale of goods and services)
and the expressive goals (the promotion of solidarity and common orien-
tations) are achieved by the manipulation of kinship and patronage in
the family firm environment.

---

[1]The normal work day in a Chinese restaurant is 12 hours. Overwork
means more than 12 hours per day.

Kinship, Patronage and Brokerage in Employment

There are no official statistical data on the unemployment situation
in Chinatown. From interviews with employment and social agencies, it
seems that unemployment is relatively low. However, there is a great
deal of under-employment; that is, many are not working according to their
capacity, potential, education or training. Former Chinese classics pro-
fessors may work in grocery stores because they cannot speak a word of
English. Obtaining employment in Chinatown is not difficult. The methods
of employment are mainly through the following: alumni associations,
the Consolidated Chinese Benevolent Association, various alumni associations, and employment agencies.

Jobs in Chinatown are obtained mainly through kinship and friendship networks. Jobs outside of Chinatown and in the larger society are
obtained mainly through social agencies, the Consolidated Chinese Benevolent Association, various alumni associations and employment agencies.
The Chinatown Study Group (1969) found that the major reasons for the
Chinese migration to Chinatown are friends and relatives in Chinatown,
common and familiar culture, and job opportunities in the area (Table
22).

Family members, kinsmen, and friends in the Chinese community of
New York, as in other overseas Chinese communities elsewhere (Tien 1956;
Amyot 1960 Ng 1958; Huck 1968), are given priority in employment. The
unique aspect of employment in the Chinese community of New York today
is the special preference given family members and relatives who may
or may not be in the United States. That is, the cohesiveness of the
kinship network is not necessarily diminished by geographical distance.

TABLE 22

REASONS FOR COMING TO LIVE IN CHINATOWN

Question: What is the most important single reason that you
and your family came to Chinatown to live?

Answers:	Friends and/or relatives in Chinatown	182	32.2%
	Common and familiar culture	164	29.0
	Job Opportunities in the area	126	22.3
	Easy to find place to live	15	2.7
	Other	25	4.5
	No response	25	4.5
	Total sample	565	100%

Source: Chinatown Study Group Report (1969: 15).

The Chinese businessmen, especially after they have firms of their
own, want to sponsor some relatives from Hong Kong or Taiwan. The major
reasons for such preferences are: 1) family members and kinsmen are
more trustworthy than outsiders; 2) kinsmen are expected to work harder;
3) there is the expectation that a successful Chinese would sponsor his
close relatives to migrate to the United States, and 4) it is cheaper
for a businessman to sponsor kinsmen employees from Hong Kong or Taiwan
than to hire a Chinese or an American from this country. However, in
order to activate this kind of employment, one of the parties has to
activate the kinship relation by means of correspondence. The unstable
political situation in Hong Kong (the threat that British control will

be taken over by Communist China) induces many refugees to look for opportunities to migrate overseas. The United States immigration policy
since 1965 favors the migration of immediate relatives of many Chinese
who want to migrate to the United States.

Thus, both the kinship obligation and consideration of gain motivate
sponsorship by businessmen-kinsmen. Through the act of sponsorship, relationships between kinsmen have become more than kinship; there are also
sponsor-sponsored employer-employee and patron-client relationships.
The newly arrivec kinsmen are thus tied to the employers and are expected
to work hard and get little pay in order to reciprocate the kindness of
the sponsor. A Kinsmen sometimes can remain in such a client-employee
status for many years to be "milked" by the employer-patron. In order
to maintain a harmonious relationship, further prestation on the part
of the employer is expected. If new prestation is not extended, the
employee-kinsman will leave the firm and attempt to find employment esle-
where.

Another way of securing employment is through the social networks
within the defined associational structure (Little 1957; Banton 1957;
P. Mayer 1961; Fraenkel 1964; Gugler 1965). The temporarily unemployed can still get lodging in the big family associations in New York's
Chinatown where free meals are provided. The job hunter can go to the
association and leave word for individuals in his social network. It is
frequently found that members in the social network employ the jobless
or transmit job information to the job hunter. Sometimes, some "generous" and "righteous" Kiu Ling will come forward to take someone into his
firm. In doing so, the Kiu Ling is recruiting at once an employee, a

follower, and a <u>client</u> which is useful for various goal-seeking activities.

The third way of obtaining employment is through the manipulation of friendship networks. Friends who were former region-mates, classmates, office mates, or business partners are given special consideration. This preference in giving employment or in assisting in the obtainment of employment for old friends is a characteristic of Chinese friendship. Francis Hsu (1971) noted the permanence of Chinese friendship, the tendency to bring friends into one's primary network, and the impulse to expand one's kinship-like relations with friends through the Chinese institution of ritual-parenthood or dry parenthood[1] (Hsu 1971: 71-72). The practice of ritual brotherhood and sisterhood was discussed previously, and the procedure in contracting dry parenthood is basically the same. In the case of dry parenthood, however, the relationships contracted and implied are not only between the two pair of parents but between their children as well. In New York's Chinatown, one does not rush into dry parenthood. More <u>Kam Ching</u> (trusting friendship) and more <u>common interests</u> should first exist.

Two points have to be reemphasized. Friendship among the overseas Chinese does not dilute and replace kinship ties; it merely extends these ties. Friendship networks do not necessarily imply the similarity of social status. Although a frienship network could be an effective network providing more connectedness and cohesiveness (Epstein 1961; Boswell 1969), in the case of the Chinese in New York, this does not

---

[1]The Chinese term is <u>Kan</u> <u>De</u> <u>Neng</u> in Mandarin (乾爹娘) and <u>Kai</u> <u>Ka</u> in Cantonese (契家).

necessarily imply the elimination of status differentiation. That is to say, in effective friendship networks, contrary to Epstein's (1961) and Boswell's (1969) expectations, there may be **asymmetry in social** status and patron-client relationships although couched in the idiom of friendship. All things being equal, employment preferences are given in the following ranked order:

1. members of the immediate family
2. patrilineal kinsmen
3. matrilineal kinsmen
4. old friends
5. new friends
6. friend's friend
7. Chinese who migrated from the same region
8. Chinese who speak the same dialect
9. other Chinese
10. non-Chinese

There is no high degree of specialization of occupation along clanship lines in today's Chinatown. For instance, one cannot assume that the Chan clan dominates the garment factories or that the Lee clan controls the restaurant business. Specialization along regional and linguistic lines does exist. All Cantonese hand laundries are run by people from Kwangtung Province. Most Chinese hand laundries are run by Toysanese speaking Chinese. Shanghainese, Szechuan and Peking restaurants are run by Mandarin speaking people. Thus, cooperation along regional and dialect lines among the Chinese in New York does exist.

Idioms: Finding jobs for one's family members, kinsmen and friends is expected. Further, an employer in the position to hire but choosing not to is criticized for lacking Chan Ching (familier warmth), and Kam Ching (trusting friendship), Yee Hey (trusting righteousness), and Yan Ching (human feelings). Sometimes, a go-between (mutual kinsman or friend to both the prospective employer and employee) will interview and

persuade the employer to hire and the employee to accept the offer. If
the intervention is successful, the two parties are expected to reciprocate the efforts of the go-between by taking him for tea or to dinner
separately. Such a gesture is interpreted as a token of appreciation
and a symbol of Yee Hey. Employers are also expected to give the employees who are kinsmen, friends and family members more trust and responsibility. Employees are expected to work harder and complain less.
During the major Chinese festivals such as the Moon Cake Festival, the
Dragon Boat Festival and the celebration of New Year , the employer is
expected to let his employees leave work earlier so that they can join
their families for these festive celebrations. Sometimes, all the kinsmen and friends working in the firm are invited over to the employer's
house to play Mahjong and have dinner. At least, the employer is expected to show token concern and appreciation for his employees' happiness
during these important Chinese festivals by **giving** bonuses or seasonable
presents like moon cakes or just by giving half a day holiday.[1] Among
the kinsmen and friends in the firm, exchange of invitation to meals or
tea is common. During the major Chinese holidays, mutual visits are
also practiced among the kinsmen and friends in the firm. The employees and their families are expected to extend their "greetings" and
to visit the employer-kinsman on or during the Chinese New Year.

   In addition to the traditional ways of obtaining employment through
familial, kinship and friendship networks, there are other avenues which
are available to the present day Chinese: 1) Chinese employment agencies;

---

[1]If this cannot be done, a make-up holiday will be given some time
during the year.

2) social agencies in Chinatown; 3) newly established cultural or student associations; and 4) traditional associations such as the Consolidated Chinese Benevolent Association. These agencies and associations are particularly instrumental in obtaining jobs from the larger society for the Chinese. Both the local Chinese newspapers and the New York Times classified ads are important sources of information for employment as well.

Employment Agencies: the important employment agencies in the Chinatown area are Claremont Majestic, China Employment Agency, and Chinese Central Employment Service. The employment brokers are bilingual Chinese who are familiar with the employment situation in both Chinatown and the larger society. These bilingual brokers are able to negotiate with larger American brokers in mid-Manhatten area which provides job information to the former. When suitable Chinese applicants come along, they will be referred to the mid-Manhattan American brokers. A commission fee is arranged and given to the Chinese brokers for referral to the American brokers. Thus, there is a broker-network among the employment brokers. The Chinese employment brokers also have connections with the employers in Chinatown, especially with the restaurant and garment factory owners. Any Chinese who wants to get a job through these Chinese employment brokers must pay a fee. The relationship between the job applicants and the brokers is stricly a cash or business relationship. Some informants prefer this form of obtaining employment. The advantages can be seen in the following statement made by one informant:

> I prefer to go to the employment broker for jobs in the restaurants. I just pay him some money and don't owe anybody anything. If I am not satisfied with my job, I can just quit my job and get another

one through another employment broker. In case I quit, I will not
have to embarrass my friends or kinsmen who got me the job.

Thus, one is not "tied" to any relationship and will not cause loss of
face to one's friends or relatives. This non-concerned attitude of some
employees has been noted by employers in Chinatown. That is why they
still prefer kinsmen and friends for employment for they are more responsible and more loyal. Some employers complain that there is such an
erosion of Yee Hey (trusting righteousness) and Kam Ching (trusting friendship) in present day Chinatown that they find it difficult to trust
people they don't know. One of the local Chinese newspapers, the China
Times, noticing the erosion of the traditional closed knit patron-client
bond had this editorial comment on May 17, 1973:

> There are two major problems in present day Chinatown. First is
> the parking problem. . . Second is the necessity of establishing
> good relationship between employer and employees. Twenty years
> ago, most of the employees in Chinatown's establishments were kins-
> men or village-mates and Chan Ching (warmth of kinship), Heung Ching
> (locality ties) were the pivoting points of patron-client relations.
> Due to the rapid increase of population and the hastened economic
> development in recent years, the circle of employment has trans-
> scended the traditional circle of kinsmen and village-mates. Hence
> patron-client relations are diminished. The traditional patron-
> client and host-guest relations are transformed into the common
> boss-labor relations. . . . This rapid change of human relation-
> ships could bring disastrous effects to the commercial activities
> of the Chinese which depends on the bond of Kam Ching (trusting
> friendship) and Chan Ching (warmth of kinship). Therefore, we
> caution all the employers to initiate realistic plans to face the
> eroding patron-client[1] relations (China Times, May 17, 1973).

Social Agencies as Employment Brokers: Social workers in Chinatown social agencies such as the Chinese Development Council and Chinatown Planning Council are instrumental in assisting Chinese to obtain

---

[1]The exact erm used by the China Times in this editorial is Bung Chu
Kwang Hei (賓主関係 - literally, guest-host relation). The closest
equivalent of this term in the phraseology of social science is, in my
opinion, patron-client relation.

jobs from the larger society. Thus, these social workers are not just employment brokers but culture brokers, bridging the Chinese community to the outside world. Traditionally this function was performed mainly by the Consolidated Chinese Benevolent Association. Today, due to the funding available from the federal and state agencies, many bilingual social workers are able to establish these social agencies to serve the Chinese community. Thus, for instance, the Chinatown Planning Council is able to find jobs for thirty to forty Chinese per month. The Chinese Development Council has been soliciting jobs from big American firms and government offices for the Chinese. These social agencies are generally quite alert to employment opportunities in government and commercial establishments for minority groups. The Chinatown Man Power Project has organized training programs for different American establishments such as banks and telephone and electric companies. Due to the brokerage activities of these social workers, there are more Chinese participating in the economic activities of the larger society. Thus present day Chinatown has become more outwardly oriented.

The Newly Established Associations as Employment Brokers: One of the more active agencies which assists employment and disseminates information to Chinese about job opportunities in the larger society is the Hong Kong Student Association. It organizes seminars on "employment opportunity" and publishes information on available economic opportunities for the Chinese in New York. Association of this kind are interested in building up "ethnic power" (Chinese power) by having more Chinese participate in the political and economic life of America. These associations are, by and large, not radical organizations. They are

interested in fighting for more economic opportunity for the Chinese.
The leaders or officials of these associations are usually bilingual,
college educated Chinese, inspired by the Black and Puerto Rican movements, to return to Chinatown to serve the less privileged Chinese.
Many of these associations have monthly journals which carry employment information. The leaders of these associations are active in
soliciting jobs from big American firms. There is no service charge
for this brokerage function. However, it is customary for the employee-
to-be to take these "devoted leaders" out for a meal, as a gesture of
appreciation. The idioms of Yee Hey and Yau Sum (devotion) are used to
praise these leaders by the favor receivers.

Consolidated Chinese Benevolent Association as Employment Broker:
Since this association is known to the American public as the informal
government and highest authority of Chinatown, many American business
establishments in New York send their requests to the CCBA when they are
interested in employing Chinese from Chinatown. However, the CCBA is
not known to be active in soliciting jobs from the larger society for
the Chinese. This is said to be due to lack of manpower and financial
resources. When employment notices and requests are sent to the CCBA,
they are generally published in the local Chinese newspapers, which advise the Chinese to send their applications. The CCBA is not only asked
to disseminate employment information by the larger society but also to
conduct employment training programs, English classes for Chinese, and
job interviews. Thus, the CCBA is a bridge for the Chinese to obtain
employment from the larger society. It is said that the CCBA could play
a larger and more active role in soliciting job opportunities for the

Chinese and in soliciting funds to establish employment training.
Limited staff resources and the general fear of losing its autonomy had
kept the CCBA cautious in accepting funds from the government. This
fear of losing its control over its affairs is expressed by one of the
high ranking officials of the CCBA thus:

> I know there is possibility in getting fundings from the government
> for different programs of CCBA. The board members and I decided not
> to accept any grants unles there are no "strings attached" to the
> grants. We want to have a say on whatever programs we are under-
> taking and sponsoring. If outsiders are running our affairs,
> there will not be any Consolidated Chinese Benevolent Association.

Thus, some economic opportunities are sacrificed for the preservation of
autonomy of the CCBA, the supreme organization of the ethnic Chinese in
New York.

Newspapers and Employment: More employers use the classified ads to
announce vacancies than people using "position wanted" ads. This is perhaps due partly to the availability of positions and partly due to sus-
picions on the part of Chinese job hunters who are afraid of being taken
advantage of in so doing. This feeling is expressed by one of my informants Job Hunter: "We have to do our duties and watch ourselves more, so
we don't want to get into any trouble. If we advertise ourselves, we
may fall into a trap set up by some bad people." However, the job
hunters do look up the Chinese newspapers' "positions available" ads,
and some of them obtain employment through these advertisements. Inter-
estingly enough, more Chinese trust the New York Times than any local
Chinese newspaper on employment ads. However, only the bilingual Chines
can read the New York Times, and only they are qualified for those jobs
advertised in the New York Times.

Summary: The **Chinese** in this era have avenues for employment which they did not have in the 1870-1964 era. In the past, kinship, friendship, and patron-client networks were the main sources for employment. In the present day Chinese community, in addition to the family, kinship, friendship and patron-client networks, Chinese can work through other formal corporate structures such as social agencies, associations and commercial employment organizations. Employment patterns are also related to the different resources or opportunity structures. In the pre-1965 era most of the Chinese worked within the community. In the post-1965 era more jobs are available in the Chinatown area as well as in the larger society. Brokerage institutions such as employment agencies, social agencies, associations, and newspapers have played instrumental roles in obtaining jobs in the larger society. Thus, it seems that while kinship, friendship, and patron-client networks are best suited for employment in the Chinese **firms,** formal groups such as social agencies and associations are useful in assisting the Chinese in employment in the larger society. The implication of this is that personal networks and formal groups have different adaptive advantages (Dirks 1972: 565-585). Their contributions to the various decision making networks vary depending on the resource structures.

Informal Realtionships and Financing

Sources of financing for the Chinese in this period are personal savings, family members, kinsmen, friends, informal credit clubs (hui), credit unions in the family associations and labor unions, loan sharks and banks.

Borrowing money from the banks always requires permanent residency, citizenship, collateral, co-signers. Another important element in financing through a bank is interpersonal relationships. Both high ranking banking officials and borrowers say that some knowledge about both parties, some relationship between the two is instrumental in the formation of broker-client relation. A branch manager[1] of an American bank in the area admitted that he has to have a fair knowledge about the borrower, his collateral, means of livelihood, character and connections as well. "If they do not have collateral, but I know the person and am sure that he will return the debt, I will recommend and approve the loan." Another bank official[2] also said that, "If I know the person to be reliable, I will even pay his bounced check with money from the bank or from my pocket." The idiom used in the operation and maintenance of this kind of broker-client relationship is <u>Shung Yung</u> (**reliability and trust**). Not all bank officials will risk as much for their clients as those quoted above. A closer relationship between the businessman-customers and the bank officials is necessary. Bank officials are eager to meet important businessmen in the community or potential entrepreneurs, for the friendship created can bring more profit to the bank and reward to themselves. Entrepreneurs are interested in knowing the bankers for possible favorable treatment by the banks. To contract such a relationship, one needs a go-between such as a friend who is a mutual friend of both parties. For some, it is a mutual friend of both parties. For some, it is a renewal of an old friendship in China.

---

[1] He is a foreign born Chinese.

[2] He is a second generation Chinese-American.

The mechanisms involved in the functioning of the broker-client
relationship between a customer and a bank can be illustrated with the
following case. $\underline{A}$ is a customer who is owner of a garment factory. His
difficulty is that he cannot collect his payment until he has delivered
the finished products. Sometimes, knowing that he may not have enough
funds in the bank, he still has to continue distributing the salary checks
to the employees. His friend in the bank realizes the difficulties and
made arrangements to advance the payment for these payroll checks. However, $\underline{A}$ is expected to deposit the necessary funds as soon as he has
made the collection from the manufacturers. Informant $\underline{A}$ has told me
that the arrangement so far has worked out perfectly, and he has not be-
trayed his friend's Shung Yung even once. He attributes this trust to
old friendship. The bank official and Informant A were former office
mates in a firm in Hong Kong. Even while they were in Hong Kong, they
solidified the friendship and addressed each other as "brothers-sharing-
the-same-master" (Shi Heng Dai).

The idioms used in the interaction between the broker-clients are
Shung Yung (reliability) and Yee Hey (trusting righteousness). In the
case related, Informant A's relationship with the banking official was
more than just a broker-client relationship but friendship as well.
When friendship is absent in the broker-client relationship, the loan can
still be secured provided that all the requirements are met. From interviews with the banking officials in the different banks in Chinatown, it
appears that there have been practically no cases of non-payment of loans
so far. The banks attribute this success to the traditional values of
Sung Yung (reliability) and face. Nobody wants to lose face in the

community. The banking business has been in the upswing in Chinatown, and more banks want to have their branches established there.

A major reason for the extensive use of the banks recently is the generally high educational standards of new immigrants who are familiar with banking procedures and can speak both Chinese and English. Interest rates are standardized, so one does not have to worry about being cheated. Whereas in the case of the informal credit club (hui), sometimes because of the competition in bidding, the interest rates could be much higher than in the bank. Although credit unions are another alternative for obtaining financing, not all the people have access to credit unions. So far, only the Lee Association and the Chinese Laundry Association have credit unions. People who are not members of the associations are not qualified to participate in the credit unions.

In order to get a loan from the Lee credit union, one first must be a Lee, pay membership dues, and have a share in the credit union. The borrower should have some Kiu Lings or two Chinese shop owners as guarantors. Thus, they way to secure references is similar to the tradition al financial institution. Persons unknown to the officials of the famil associations are not accepted as references. Foreigners are also excluded as references. It is said that in the Lee Family Association, th credit union has been functioning well because there are many Lees who are accountants and lawyers and are familiar with every aspect of financing.

The credit unions and the banks do not replace the traditional loar habits of the Chinese in the present day Chinatown. Family, kinship, a friendship networks are still used for financing. For some Chinese suc

as illegal immigrants and jumped-ship **sailors,** kinship and friendship
networks are used exclusively for financing. Some older Chinese immigrants who entered the country illegally many years ago (though they have
been pardoned by the Kennedy Administration) and less educated Chinese
feel safer borrowing money from kinsmen or friends. The hui is used
today mainly as a savings society, not as an important source for financing. Again, the hui is popular among the older immigrants who had participated in their respective family associations or in the home villages
in traditional China.

In view of the fact that only the Lees and the Chinese laundrymen
can benfit from their associations' credit unions, some major social
agencies in Chinatown are contemplating organization of credit unions
for the Chinese. It is said that the Chinese Development Council has
obtained all the technical advice and assistance from the larger society
and is about to put into operation a credit union for all Chinese.

Thus, banks, credit unions and social agencies are assisting the
Chinese to obtain financing from the larger society and members of the
community as well. In this respect, the United States banks and the
social agencies are integrating the Chinese with the larger society. More
participation in these financial facilities is expected in the near
future.

Dispute Settlement

There are more avenues open to the Chinese in the settlement of
disputes during this period. In addition to the use of go-betweens who
are friends or kinsmen, the network within the various associations and

the Kiu Ling patrons of the Consolidated Chinese Benevolent Association
and the family associations, there are more and more Chinese using the
United States courts, lawyers, social agencies, and the Legal Aid Society
in Chinatown to solve their disputes.

In most cases, a Chinese will prefer to solve his problmes with
another Chinese through the use of the friendship and kinship networks.
Kinsmen and mutual friends, when asked to mediate disputes, are expected
to come forward to hear the differences and to achieve a compromise between the disputing parties. The traditional pattern of solving disputes is still followed.

Family associations and the Chinese Consolidated Benevolent Associations continue to perform their mediating functions for the Chinese in
this era. However, the younger Chinese and the new immigrants are not
interested in joining these associations. The second and third generations Chinese-Americans simply do not speak the dialects used for mediation by these associations. As for the new immigrants, they are not
used to these village-like associations such as family (or clan) or the
CCBA, since they migrated mainly from the larger cities such as Hong
Kong or Taipei. In the past several years, these associations solved
less than a dozen cases per year. People who used the mediation services are the old settlers. In the pre-1975 era, cases like labor disputes, unpaid debts, share of business and even family quarrels were
brought to the family associations first. If unsettled, the cases will
then go to the final dispute settlement organization, the CCBA. As
mentioned earlier, in the 1870-1964 era, business transactions such as
the sale of a store had to be performed in the CCBA. A new Chinese stor

owner had to register with the CCBA and pay a fee every year. Such a

practice is **ignored** by the new immigrants. Business transactions are

often conducted in law offices. In order to avoid a misunderstanding,

it is customary for a Chinese who sells his property or store to run

a notice in a local Chinese newspaper. The publication of such a

notice is **regarded** by the Chinese as "legal" proof.

> To whom it may concern: I prepare to buy the undersigned Chinese
> restaurant including its site, property and its profit-making
> equipment . All transactions will be conducted with the former
> owner, Mr. Lee Hoi Shui, at 10 a.m. on March 31, 1971, in the
> attorney's office of Norman Lau Kee. Unpaid debts and other un-
> resolved matters relating to the former owner should be brought
> forward and cleared with the former owner. After the said trans-
> action, I shall not be responsible for business matters related to
> the former owner.
> Former onwer: Lee Hoi Shui
>   Purchaser: Sum Siu Lung
> Address of
> Restaurant: Long River Kitchen, New York
> Lawyer's address: Norman Lau Kee, 11 Mott St., N.Y.C.[1]

Similar notices on transactions were found daily in other local Chinese

newspapers. This indicates that the Chinese prefer to use the lawyer's

office to conduct their transactions and to clear up possibly business

disputes. One advantage in using the lawyers in Chinatown is that one

is not obligated to the Kiu Ling in the CCBA. One informant told me

that he does not have to worry about grievances and unfair settlement

by the Kiu Lings any more, because there are laws and lawyers who know

how to take care of business disputes more equitably. Due to the demand

for bilingual lawyers, many American-Chinese have returned to Chinatown

---

[1]This is not a literal translation, although efforts were made to
approximate the exact wordings in the original text in United Journal,
(March 3, 1971).

to open offices in recent years. Those Chinese-American who are not
familiar with the Chinese language are taking Chinese classes to learn
or to polish their rusty Chinese.

The United States courts are also used by the Chinese in the community today. Family courts, small claims courts, and municipal courts are
used to solve family problems, business problems, and other disputes.
In the pre-1965 era, there were virtually no Chinese civil cases going to
the United States courts. The main reasons for not using the court facil
ities were that very few Chinese could speak English well, and it was
difficult for the American judges to understand Chinese customs. Then,
the CCBA often was asked to provide translators and background information concerning the disputants. Thus, many Chinese disputants felt that
there was no difference between using the U.S. courts or the CCBA. Moreover, there was an enormous amount of social pressure on the disputants
to solve their disputes within the community. One had to bring the case
to the family association or the CCBA. Today, many new immigrants can
speak English. The legal aid agencies and the various social agencies
also assist in the settlement of the disputes of the Chinese. If the
disputes have to be solved in courts, translators can be provided and
free advice given by these social agencies.

In the cases where the rights of the Chinese are violated in the
area of housing and employment, the various social agencies are far more
effective than the traditional associations and their Kiu Ling patrons.
The agencies are more well versed with the anti-discrimination laws and
have the connections with the New York Commission on Human Rights.

The social agencies, legal aid societies and law offices have not
replaced the family association and the CCBA entirely. There still are
individuals who want to settle their disputes within the community.
These individuals are usually the old immigrants who prefer to use the
Kiu Lings of the community.

Summary

To summarize, then interpersonal relationships have an important role
to play in the economic activities of the Chinese. Family, kinship,
friendship, patron-client relationship, and broker-client relationship
are all used for the establishment of firms, for financing, for securing
employment, for obtaining dispute settlement. One of the major differences between the pre and post 1965's is the gradual replacement of the
patron-client relationship by the broker-client relationship. Members
of the community do not have to depend solely on the Kiu Lings. The
officials of the social agencies, banks, and brokerage firms such as
accounting, law, and employment offices are far more effective in affecting assistance in many of the goal-seeking activities of the Chinese.

The interpersonal relationship between the officials or directors
of social agencies, law and accounting offices and the Chinese can best
be characterized as a broker-client relationship due to the fact that
these social workers and officials of agencies do not have the wealth
and direct access to the resources necessary for the obtainment of
goals sought by their clients. However, they have the ability to assist
the Chinese to reach those who have the resources. Thus, social workers
and officials of these agencies can be called "brokers" in both the

cultural and economic sense (Wolfe 1956, 1966; Mayer 1966; Silverman 1965; Paine 1971; Barth 1963). Culturally, they are mediators between the two cultures. They are the bridges between the Chinese and the larger society. Economically, the assist members of the Chinese community to obtain employment, financing, and dispute settlements from the larger society and thus enable the **participation** of the Chinese in American society, its resources and its way of living. Hence, these brokers are agents of cultural change.

CHAPTER 7

PATRONAGE, BROKERAGE AND ETHNIC BOUNDARY

This chapter will concentrate on the role of patrons and
brokers in the maintenance of the Chinese ethnic boundary in
New York City. Needless to say, the ethnic boundary referred
to here is not a geographical boundary but a social boundary
that defines the Chinese ethnic group (Barth 1965: 15). As
mentioned earlier, the patrons of the Chinese community are
called Kiu Ling which literally means "the leaders of the
overseas Chinese." Brokers, as used in this paper, are
middle-men who attract followers through their ability to
influence persons in control (Mayer 1967: 198). In the
community, brokers are social workers and volunteers who
affiliate themselves with social agencies and other brokerage
institutions. The Kiu Ling are affiliated mainly with the
traditional associations. These Kiu Ling-Patrons and the
agency-brokers differ not only in social, economic, and
educational backgrounds but also in their conceptions of the
Chinese ethnic boundary; the differential use of ethnic
symbols and ethnic identity; their views of internal social
order; and in the adoption of different strategies for
dealing with outsiders.

I. Kiu Ling - Patrons, Traditional Associations and Ethnic
Boundary

Kiu Lings are first generation chinese who are generally
well established economically and are concerned with gaining
a name for themselves through activities in the family,
dialect, and regional associations and the Consolidated
Chinese Benevolent Associations. A survey of sixty patron-
Kiu Ling from these traditional associations revealed that
the majority possess similar social, economic, and
demographic characteristics: 1) the majority are between 50-
70 years old; 2) all were born in China; 3) the majority have
little formal education; 4) more than two thirds have spent
more than 20 years in the United States; and 5) the majority
are entrepreneurs in Chinese restaurants, laundries, garment
factories, groceries, and gift stores. Out of these sixty
recognized Kiu Ling patrons, only four have college
educations (two were educated in China, the other two were
educated partially in the U.S.). Thus, these patrons are
familiar with two cultural systems: Chinese and the United
States, and are entrepreneurs engaged economically in ethnic
enterprises. These social, economic and demographic
characteristics, as will be shown, are related to the kinds of
impressions management these people have undertaken, symbols

and validations resorted to for the preservation of Chinese
culture, and strategies adapted in dealing with the members
of the community and with the larger society.

Mangement of Ethnic Identity and the Goal-Seeking Activities
of the Kiu Ling

Jean Briggs (1971: 55-73) has shown with ethnograph
data from the East Arctic that a patron's goals, the
strategies available to him, and the likelihood of his
achieving his goals are influenced by the identity or
identities he has chosen and that others have attributed to
him. The identities selected by the Kiu Ling are many-fold.
When they make transactions with the Taiwan government, they
assume the identity of overseas Chinese because they are
given special preference by the Taiwan government in all
official interactions; in dealing with the members of the
community, they consider themselves as the "real Chinese;" in
dealing with the United States government, the Kiu Ling
simply consider themselves as Chinese-Americans speaking for
the community. Historically, the word Kiu Ling was used by
the Nationalist Government to refer to the exemplary overseas
Chinese who were leaders of the overseas Chinese and were
active in championing the causes of the Kuomintang such as
the anti-Manchurian, anti-communist movements. The mother

country expects the Kiu Ling to play the bridging role
between the community and the Nationalist Government and its
representatives. This explains why the Kiu Ling in New York
are so respectful to all high ranking officials from the
Taiwan government who visit Chinatown. Because of this
expectation, the Kiu Ling all take up the anti-communist
ideology and are hostile to groups which are sympathetic to
the People's Republic of China. They have made sure that the
newly established organizations in Chinatown are not admitted
to the Chinese Consolidated Benevolent Association. As
leaders of the overseas Chinese, Kiu Ling can obtain visas,
export permits, and favorable export quotas for certain
merchandise such as mushrooms from Taiwan.

Taking up the identity of a Chinese-American is a
necessity in dealing with the United States Government. Only
a citizen can benefit from the privileges and rights extended
to Americans. When the Kiu Ling works with the United States
government on behalf of the Chinese to protect their economic
or political interests or their well-being, they have to
assume their Chinese-American identity. Thus, for obtaining
such goals as power, privilege, and prestige, the Kiu Ling
have to assume three identities: overseas Chinese, real
Chinese, and Chinese-American.

Values and Symbols Circulated and Resorted to by the Kiu

Lings for the Preservation of Chinese Culture

The Kiu Ling are particularly concerned about their role
as preservers of Chinese culture. They envision themselves
as the real Chinese and are "models to copy" by members of
the community. To show their "Chineseness," they are eager
to: 1) participate in the twice-a-year ancestor worship and
to direct the celebration of the traditional Chinese
festivals; 2) to secure membership in many traditional
associations; and 3) to involve themselves in the affairs of
these associations. It is not uncommon to find a Kiu Ling
simultaneously holding membership and offices in four or
five associations. Membership and offical titles in many
associations are not only signs of popularity, but also
symbols of wealth, power, and "Chineseness."

Participation in associations and organizing the Spring
and Autumn Festivals and other ancestor worship rituals are
activities that Kiu Ling use to validate their roles as
culture preservers and to express their devotion to the
traditional customs of China. Usually a Sunday during spring
and a Sunday during autumn are selected by Kiu Ling to bring
members of the associations in chartered buses to visit the
graves of former members in Brooklyn's Evergreen Cemetery.
Every family association also has an elaborately decorated
altar constructed to conduct the ancestor worship rituals.

The Kiu Ling usually makes generous contributions to the spring and autumn "sweeping the graves" activities and related ancestor worship activities. The Kiu Ling are also patrons for many other traditional celebrations such as the Chinese New Year. The colorful banners, the Lion Dance Troupe and the Chinese fire crackers used for the Chinese New year are chiefly financed by the voluntary contributions of the Kiu Lings.

The Kiu Lings are the patrons of many community projects, including construction, maintenance, and furnishing the associations' buildings. Thus, the Kiu Ling of the Eng have financed the oriental architectural addition to the association's building, the rich Kiu Ling of the On Leong Association were instrumental in the construction of the Chinese looking building at Mott and Canal Streets and the leaders of the Lun Kong Associations were the donors of the expensive Chinese furniture (made of mahogany and marble) in their Association.

As mentioned earlier, the Kiu Ling are usually older Chinese who are pro-Nationalist China (Taiwan). They are not hesitant in using symbols to demonstrate their pro-Kuomintang ideology. Pictures of Chang Kai Shek and Sun Yat Sen are displayed in the offices of the various family, regional, and dialect associations and the Chinese Consolidated Benevolent Association. Both the Chinese (Kuomintang) and Amercan Flags are prominently displayed in the various parades that the Kiu

Ling sponsor.

Not only do the Kiu Ling validate their "Chineseness"

and their "prestige" through their active participation in

Chinese festivals and their extravagant donations to

cultural activities, they also promote tradtional Chinese

values. Robert Paine (1971: 17-19) and Jean Briggs (1971:

55-73) both contend that the word "patron," by definition, is

a person who chooses the values, or prestations and puts them

into circulation:

> The patron chooses for the client those values in
> relation to which, the patron protects the client;
> moreover, the patron expects the client himself to
> embrace these values (Robert Paine 1971: 19).

The values selected by the Kiu Ling are traditional

values: Lai (or Li in Mandarin), politeness and propriety;

Yee Hey, trusting righteousness; Kam Ching, sentimental

friendship; Yan Ching, human feelings; face, and Chan Ching,

warmth of kinship. These values are the basis for patron-

client transactions in the community. Thus, in the

manipulation of patronage for gain seeking activities, many

traditional Chinese values are used and maintained. The Kiu

Ling or patrons of the community are the stabilizers of the

traditional Chinese values. Although Strickon and Greenfield

(1973) did not deal with the maintenance of the ethnic values

or idioms as bases for patron-clients, they state, however,

the existence of certain values or idioms as bases for
patron-client transactions (Strickon and Greenfield 1973:
15). In the case of the Chinese, the continual patron-client
transactions require these values as prerequisites. In fact,
many of the Kiu Ling interviewed lamented that all these
basic values have become alien to many second and third
generation Chinese and that they do not feel confident in
conducting transactions and negotiations with them. Hence,
the manipulation of patronage for goal seeking pursuits, in
turn stabilizes these traditional Chinese values.

The Concept of the Chinese Community and Rules Governing the Contact of the Members of the Community

The Kiu Ling's concepts of the Chinese ethnic group
differ from that of the brokers. To the Kiu Ling, the
Chinese community is for the real Chinese. Second and third
generation Chinese are "Americanized Chinese" and are to be
excluded from many of the community's activities. To be a
member of the community one must speak Chinese. Traditional
associations require that members speak Chinese. This is due
in part to the fact that mediation services are conducted in
Chinese. Thus, those second and third generation Chinese who
cannot speak the Chinese language automaticlly disqualify
themselves from membership and the use of the facilities and
services of the associations. The Kiu Ling also feel that

the second and third generation Chinese do not share with
them the Chinese values, the pro-Kuomintang ideology, the
ways of behaving, the criteria for judging performance.
Since most of the second and third generation Chinese have
been educated in the United States, speak English as their
native language, sympathize with the People's Republic of
China, and express their dissatisfaction of the leadership of
the community, it is natural for these Kiu Ling to take a
less-than-kind attitude toward these Chinese Americans. The
latter are labelled as "native savages" (To Fan) and "Bamboo
Sticks" (Juk Sing).

The hierarchical social order of Chinatown, mainly
patterned after the traditional peasant organizations in
China, is deliberately maintained by the Kiu Ling. According
to the Kiu Ling of the community, the following hierarchical
order of the community should be maintained. The CCBA is the
supreme authority of the community. Below it are the various
family, regional, and trade associations. At the bottom of these
are the village organizations called Fongs (cf. Chapter 3).
The leaders of the associations are the Kiu Ling-patrons.
There are horizontal ties between these patrons as well as a
hierarchy of patronage - phenomena recognized by
anthropologists who studied patronage elsewhere (Silverman
1965; Foster 1961, 1963). The Kiu Ling of the Fongs are
themselves the clients to more powerful, higher-status

patrons such as the Kiu Ling of the family, trade, regional
or merchant association. On the top of these patrons is the
super-patron who is the head of the CCBA, commonly known to
the American public as the unoffical mayor of Chinatown. An
ordinary Chinese, if he wants to ask for a favor from the
head of the CCBA, has to work through the patrons of the
fongs and the family associations.

The Kiu Ling still believe that Chinatown is a self-
sufficient community which can take care of its own welfare
problems, solve its own disputes, and police its own people.
Efforts are made to prevent intervention from the larger
society. One Kiu Ling, a senator of the Consolidated Chinese
Benevolent Association and president of a powerful Tong said
that only the leaders of Chinatown (Kiu Ling) can solve the
problems of the community:

> How could the Community Service Society, the Chinatown Planning
> Council, the Chinese Development Council help us? They are all
> outsiders. We know our problems, and we have the means to solve
> them.

Thus, the Kiu Ling themselves believe that they are the
legitimate resource personnel of the community.

All these Kiu Ling are present or former employers; most
of them are entrepreneurs in the typical Chinese business:
laundries, garment factories, restaurants, gift stores, and
groceries. Economically, they have succeeded. They
willingly donate thousands and thousands of dollars for

community activities and other worthy causes in order to
preserve Chinese culture, so long as they are properly
acknowledged. They are concerned that stories about their
generosity are published in the local Chinese newspapers
which are circulated not only within the United States but
also in the overseas Chinese communities throughout the
world. The Taiwan government, the Nationalist Chinese
Embassy, and the Chinese consulates also subscribe to these
local newspapers. Hence, patrons of the community are
identified and known. Whenever they visit Taiwan or other
overseas Chinese communities, they are often exalted, given
the VIP treatment, and even decorated by high-ranking
officials or Chang Kai Shek himself.

One of the most serious problems recognized by the Kiu
Ling-patrons of the community is Chinese education. As
mentioned earlier, Kiu Ling-patrons are self-appointed
saviors of Chinese culture. They are interested in having a
Chinese school in the community to serve their children as
well as the children of their clients. Furthermore,
education is valued highly by the Chinese, and being a donor
or patron for the community's education program will receive
the most publicity. The Chinese school is supported
financially by the Kiu Ling of the community. The most
powerful and richest Kiu Ling will sit on the Executive
Committee of the Board of Trustees. The leaders of the

various family regional, dialect and trade associations are trustees of the Chinese school. Presently, the President of the Board of Trustees is also the President of the Chinese Consolidated Benevolent Association. He said that the school has no intention of asking for help from the state or federal governments for reasons of autonomy. It is generally feared that once the Chinese school receives financial support from the government, the Kiu Ling can lose their control of the school. Thus, there is the isolationist policy enacted by the community's Kiu Ling-patrons to deliberately prevent the possible intervention by the dominant society. This phenomenon is not unique among Chinese ethnic groups. In The American Minority Community, Judith Kramer pointed out that most Jews and Catholics in America have not demanded the complete abolition of social distance and equality because they want to maintain their own communities (Kramer 1970: 64).

The Chinese school teaches not only Chinese language but also knowledge about Chinese culture. It teaches Chinese folk music, folk dance, and sponsors special programs to educate Chinese youngsters on "filial piety". The schedule of the school is specially designed so that the children who study in American public schools can attend the Chinese school. The Chinese grade school runs daily from 4:00-7:00 p.m.; it begins shortly after children are dismissed from

regular public schools. There are Chinese language programs
on Saturday and Sunday for high school age and adult Chinese.

The enrollment has been on the increase due to an
evergrowing population. According to statistics furnished by
the principal of the Chinese school the number of Chinese
students attending the school has increased from 200 in 1965
to 2,740 in 1973.

Not only do Kiu Ling-patrons refuse to seek financial
aid from the United States government for the Chinese school,
they are also hesitant to ask for assistance in other areas.
Nevertheless, they still think that they are the legitimate
channels through which the community's transactions with the
larger society must be conducted.

Strategies for Dealing with Outsiders

In addition to the ethnic symbols and adoption of
special rules governing internal interaction of members, the
Kiu Ling also select favorable strategies for the maintenance
of ethnic solidarity and Chinese culture. The favorable
strategies referred to here are strategies resorted to in
dealing with outsiders: the dominant society, the mother
country, and the overseas Chinese communities.

With the United States or Dominant Society: Numerous
students of ethnic boundaries have determined that the
various strategies selected by an ethnic group to deal with

the dominant society could have different effects on the maintenance of the ethnic boundary (Barth 1969: 33; Gordon 1964: 84-132; Hsu 1972: 129; R. Lee 1960: 405-414). A brief review of possible strategies which can be used by an ethnic group will be given first, and then the strategies resorted to by the traditional Kiu Ling-patrons will be discussed, followed by an examination of effects on the maintenance of the Chinese ethnic boundary caused by the adoption of these strategies.

In dealing with the dominant society, an ethnic group can resort to one or several of the following strategies: 1) attempt to pass and become incorporated into the larger society (Barth 1969: 33); 2) emphasize ethnic identity in the creation of new social positions and patterned activities in those sectors formerly not found in the larger society (Barth 1969: 33; Wirth 1945: 347-372; Lyman and Douglas 1973: 345); 3) seceding from the larger society to build a new state or enter into the plural structure of another state (Wirth 1945; Lyman and Douglas 1973: 345); 4) participating in some sectors of activities of the larger society while retaining significant aspects of its own culture identity (Barth 1969: 33; Lyman and Douglas 1973: 345) and 5) retaining confederational ties with the larger society while securing territorial and communal control for itself (Wirth 1945: 342-372; Lyman and Douglas 1973: 345). Among the five

alternatives listed above, the Kiu Ling-patrons of the
Chinese community have adopted the fourth and fifth
strategies.

Looking through the personal histories of the Kiu Ling,
it is not difficult to discover why they have excluded the
first three alternatives. As mentioned before, the Kiu Ling
are the older Chinese, mostly above fifty years old, who
have spent more than 20 years in the United States. When
they first came to the United States, they were laborers,
small merchants or employees. They witnessed the
discrimination waged by the dominant society against the
black and other minority groups including the Chinese. These
Kiu Ling-patrons realized that it was not realistic to
attempt "passing" to become incorporated into the dominant
white society. From interviews with these Kiu Ling, it was
learned that they are skeptical about the possibility for the
minority groups with racial distinctiveness to be integrated
into the dominant society. To prove their point, these
interviewees cited the example of the Japanese, Puerto
Ricans, and Blacks. "With our yellow skin and our Chinese
eyes, there is no chance for us to be part of the white
society." This is a common sentiment among the Kiu Ling.
Such an argument is not without justification. Gunnar Myrdal
(1949), Simpson and Yinger (1958) all seem to subscribe to
this view. The point here is not so much whether this view

is correct, but to reveal the reasonings behind the decision-making processes of these Kiu Lings. Suffice it to say that the Kiu Ling patrons in the community believe that physical characteristics prevent them from fully incorporating into the larger society.

Regarding the second alternative, i.e. the use of ethnic identity to create new social positions for the Chinese, the Kiu Ling generally feel that this is an individual decision. As a collective, the Kiu Ling think that the status quo is good enough. The Kiu Ling also feel that they do not have the political power to wage any campaigns for equal opportunity treatment. The third alternative, i.e. to secede from the larger society, is out of the question. "What do you think we are? We are just helpless strangers living under the fence of other people" - is a typical response to any suggestion about complete secession.

The path chosen by these Kiu Ling in dealing with the larger society is a combination of alternatives four and five; they will participate in some sectors of activities of the United States while retaining their cultural identity and securing communal control for themselves. The sectors which they participate in are restaurants, laundries, garment factories, Chinese groceries, and gift shop businesses. They are concerned with the steady increase of customers in the

Chinese restaurants, the image of the community as a safe place, the number of tourists visiting Chinatown, and parking and traffic problems which can affect the Chinese businesses. Any regulations and policies enacted by the government affecting these typical Chinese businesses will cause concern among the Kiu Ling. This is partly due to the fact that they are entrepreneurs in these fields and partly because the Kiu Ling represent mainly the interests of the Chinese business commnunity. In fact, all the associations are supported by rich businessmen. Hence, the Kiu Ling are concerned with the continued prosperity of the Chinese ethnic niche; they tend to identify their interests as the community's interests. Action is taken only if they are personally affected.

The leaders of the powerful Tongs and the Consolidated Chinese Benevolent Association are the most powerful Kiu Ling-patrons; they generally feel that a good "front" for Chinatown is good for Chinese business. They play host to many visiting dignitaries from the city, state, and federal governments. These Kiu Ling emphasize harmony and friendship; and they strongly oppose drastic methods such as protests, and demonstrations in dealing with the larger society. For the first time, the Kiu Ling of the Consolidated Chinese Benevolent Association were recently under pressure to organize a demonstration petitioning the police department for more protection for Chinatown in view

of the deteriorating safety standards in the streets there.
Again, it is because they are personally affected by the
presence of muggers and robbers in Chinatown that Kiu Ling
feel that they have to organize a peaceful petition to City
Hall.

As a rule, the Kiu Ling want to create a harmonious
relationship between the Chinese and the Whites. Peaceful
coexistence with other ethnic groups such as the Puerto
Ricans and Jews on the Lower East Side and the Italians in
Little Italy is emphasized. There is a harmonious
relationship between the Italians and the Chinese, partly
because they share many things in common. First, they
emphasize the value of the family. Second, they share the
use of many public facilities such as the configuration
Church in Chinatown which serves both Italians and Chinese.
Third, there is business interaction between the two groups.
There are Italian meat stores in the heart of Chinatown which
cater mainly to Chinese customers. There are also Chinese
pizza stores serving both Italians and Chinese. Fourth, both
have their own protective forces. The Italians have the
Mafia; the Chinese have the Tongs. Fifth, both Italians and
Chinese want to solve their disputes informally. Hence,
there is more communication between the two groups. During
my fieldwork, I have seen disputes involving Chinese and
Italians brought to the attention of the Consolidted Chinese

Benevolent Association. Both parties, at the end, accepted
the mediation decision of the CCBA, and the disputes were
settled satisfactorily.

Conflicts between the Chinese and the Puerto Ricans
occur mainly among the teenagers in public schools. Fist
fights between Chinese gangs and Puerto Rican gangs occur.
The Kiu Ling or patrons of the community feels that this is
not their problem and wash their hands of these teenagers.
They place the blame on the Chinese parents and their failure
to transmit family and Chinese values to these troubled
teenagers. Many Kiu Ling even use the exitence of teenage
gangs to prove the point that Chinese education emphasizes
how to become a "human being;" American education teaches
only technology and sciences. Hence, the Kiu Ling stress
that the parents should send their children to receive
Chinese education in the Chinese community school.

Likewise, harmony between the Jews and the Chinese is
emphasized, although there is only limited contact between
the two groups. Only owners of Chinese garment factories
deal with the Jewish garment manufacturers for the Chinese
garment factory owner usually contracts his materials and
orders from the Jewish garment manufacturer who controls the
garment industry in New York. Mutual gift givings and
invitations out to lunch are common among the Chinese garment
factory owners and some Jewish garment manufacturers.

To summarize briefly, then, the Kiu Ling-patrons have selected a strategy of peaceful co-existence with the dominant society and other ethnic groups as well. In dealing with the dominant society, they are careful to isolate its influence on the community. Only on matters affecting the ethnic niche and other unavoidable issues, will they take the initiative to transact and negotiate with the government. Effort is also made to police their own people and provide for welfare and dispute settlements in order to maintain the ethnic boundary of the Chinese.

Rules Governing Contact with the Republic of China and Other Overseas Chinese Communities: For the Kiu Ling, the legitimate government of China is the Republic of China. They perceive themselves as the bridges between the community and the Taiwan government, its representatives, consulates, and embassies. The Nationalist government (Republic of China) is glad to have the Kiu Ling as their middlemen and openly support them as the offical spokesmen for the community. Important notices, circulars, news releases, and economic opportunities in Taiwan are transmitted to the leaders of the consolidated Chinese Benevolent Association. The Nationalist government still requires the leaders (Kiu Ling) of the family, dialect, and regional associations as character references for the Chinese in the Chinese Community of New York. In order to get a visa, Chinese passport, export permit, etc., the applicant is required to produce a letter of recommendation from the Kiu Ling of his respective family or regional association and the CCBA.

Rules of propriety have to be followed when a member of the community wants to transact business with the Nationalist's Chinese consulate in New York. One has to approach the lower level association first before he approaches the higher level association such as the CCBA and ultimately the Chinese consulate. The Kiu Ling of the lower level association have to be coordinated by the Kiu Ling of the intermediate levels who in turn are coordinated by the Kiu Ling of the highest level. Recently, a Chinese went to the Chinese consulate to apply for a passport. He was told to get a recommendation from a Kiu Ling in the community. This Chinese went straight to the secretary of the CCBA. He was reprimanded by the secretary and told to approach his own family association or lower level association. Since he is not a Toysanese, he thought someone in the Lung Sing Association, an intermediate level association, could write such a letter for him. He was again refused any favor, since he was not recommended by the Kiu Ling of the lowest level association. Being a new immigrant, this Chinese was unfamiliar with the bureaucratic procedure and was shocked by the behavior of the Kiu Ling. However, what he did not know was that his behavior of bypassing the lower lever Kiu Ling

created the suspicion of the Kiu Ling on the upper level that
he was "undesirable."

The hierarchical order is shown also in the
communications of the Chinese community of New York with
overseas communities elsewhere. In the recent relief aid to
the Chinese earthquake victims in Managua, the New York
Chinese were asked to deliver relief materials to the
appropriate family associations first; from there they would
be forwarded to the CCBA which collected all the materials
and sent them to the equivalent organizations in the Chinese
community of Managua.

The various Chinese Associations in the United States
are coordinated by two major centers: the Chinatown of New
York and the Chinatown of San Francisco.

Thus, if a leader is accused of usurpation and is
subsequently kicked out of his association in New York City,
his name will be circulated immediately to the different
branches of the same association in the United States. The
associational network is not something new, it was
established during the Tong war days. News of Tong wars
travelled fast. If the On Leong Tong declared war on the Hip
Sing Tong in New York, the On Leong Tong and Hip Sing Tong in
Chicago and San Francisco immediately went to war with one
another.

Most of the major family, regional and merchant
associations have their headquarters in either New York City
or San Francisco. The leaders of the local association have
to confer with the leaders of the same associations on major
decisions. Thus, even within the same association, the
leaders of a branch association have to follow certain rules
on certain matters. For instance, if a Lee Association wants
to sell its old building to rebuild a new office, the leaders
of the associations are required to confer with the Lee
Association in New York. Similarly, if a member of the New
York Chan family association wants to use the dormitory
facility of the Chan Family Association in Chicago, it is
appropriate for him to have a letter of introduction from the
Kiu Ling of the Chan Family Association in New York. This
again points out the importance of patronage in all the
Chinese communities and that there is a hierarchical order in
the communication system even among the Kiu Ling patrons.

To sum up, then, the Kiu Ling perceive themselves as the
legitimate links between the Chinese community in New York,
the United States Government, and other Chinese communities
in the United States and the world. On the community's
official affairs or the associations' internal affairs, there
is a hierarchical channel for communication. The ordinary
Chinese have to work through the Kiu Ling patrons of
different gradations.

II. Brokers, Social Agencies and the Ethnic Boundary

There are patrons who do not associate with
associations. Similarly, there are brokers who do not
affiliate with any social agencies. However, since there are
a larger number of brokers concentrated in the social
agencies, a discussion of these agency-brokers' management of
ethnic identity, methods of consolidating the Chinese ethnic
group, concepts of the Chinese ethnic group, and the
strategies adapted in dealing with the larger society is
pertinent.

As mentioned earlier, the term "broker" is used to refer
to the middleman who has to do with "processing" information
and who recruits clients not by his powers to dispense
resources but by his ability to influence the person who
controls the resources (Meyer 1967: 168; Paine 1971: 21; Stuart
1972: 33). In the post-1965 era, such a group of brokers has
emerged. Within this group, however, there are several
subgroups which are distinguishable by age, occupation,
birthplace and place of education. Due to the similar
services that they perform for the community, similar views
about Chinese ethnic identity, and similar strategies adopted
in dealing with the larger society, a discussion on the
differences of these subgroupings will be short.

There are many different kinds of brokers: full time or
part time social workers, student volunteers, American born

Chinese and China born Chinese professionals. The similarities among these brokers are: 1) all have knowledge about the Chinese ethnic group and the United States society; 2) all have higher education; 3) all want to bridge the Chinese community with the larger society; 4) all are dissatisfied with the Kiu Ling patrons of the community; 5) all are relatively young (ranging between 20-40 years of age); 6) most are middle class Chinese-Americans living outside of Chinatown. In addition to the possession of these common social, educational and economic characteristics, their perception about the community and the strategies adopted in dealing with the larger society are also similar and will be shown in the following sections.

Perception of Ethnic Identity

Although the Kiu Ling assume three major identities -
Overseas Chinese, Chinese-Americans and real Chinese - the
brokers assume only one identity, Chinese-American. Every
American who has Chinese blood, irrespective of language
spoken and birth place, is a Chinese-American. Almost all of
these brokers are affiliated with social agencies such as the
Chinatown Foundation, the Chinese Community Service Society,
the Chinatown Advisory Council, Chinatown Planning Council,
Chinese Development Council and Basement Workshop, Inc.[1]
These brokers assist members of the community by adjusting
their visa status, helping to obtain social security benefits
for the old, helping secure funds for the operation of day
care centers for the young, finding jobs for the unemployed,
mediating disputes and providing free legal counsel. In
other words, they are the middlemen who help the Chinese to
participate in the resource distribution of the larger
society. Thus, in performing their bridging functions
between the community and American Society, these brokers are
also change agents in the sense that they are educating the

[1] The basement workshop is not exactly a social agency,
it is a non-profit organization performing services similar
to those of the social agencies. The operation of the basement
workshop is financed by donations and partially by the city
government.

Chinese on how to participate in the larger society and thus

purveying the values of the dominant society. That is why

Robert Paine (1971: 21) and Georg Henrikson (1971: 23) tend to

characterize brokers as change agents.

Since participating in the resource distribution of the

larger society needs cooperative effort, these brokers feel

that a united front among the Chinese is necessary. In

addition to the services they perform, they are eager to

awaken ethnic conciousness and create an action group with a

common culture as a base.

Symbols, Validation used for the Awakening of Chinese Consciouness

Like the Kiu Ling, the agency brokers also realize that
the continual expression and validation of Chinese culture
are necessary for ethnic solidarity. Symbols are used and
the memories of the tragic history of the early Chinese in
America are recalled. Chinese are encouraged to wear Chinese
clothes, especially during the parades and demonstrations.
Buttons like "Asian Power," "Yellow Power," and "Chinese
Power" are worn during demonstrations. Leaflets are
distributed by some social agencies to inform the Chinese
public on how to protect their human rights, how to perform
their civic duties, and how to file discrimination
complaints. the broker's vision of their role as "educators"
is clear in the words of one official of the Chinatown
Planning Council:

> The Chinese immigrants are generally apathetic about politics
> because they don't know the American political system. They don't
> know that the American government is supposed to exist for the
> benefit of the individuals. Many of them still hold the view of
> traditional Chinese peasant that it is good to stay away from the
> government, to live in a faraway place, to be separated from the
> influence of government by high mountains. The majority of the
> Chinese immigrants take for granted that because they are a
> minority group, they therefore have to swallow many grievances.
> don't know that they have to fight for their rights in this count
> This is America!

The brokers are aware of the fact that they have
solid following, it will be possible for them to secure more
funds and other resources for the community. In order to

build a sizable following among the Chinese, they proceed in a manner similar to many ethnic politicians, i.e. by way of "consciousness raising" (Novak 1972: 289).

While raising the ethnic consciousness of the Chinese, these brokers are at the same time, purveying the values of the larger society such as "government exists for the individual," and "equality for all." Thus, the efforts of the brokers aim at preparing the members of the Chinese ethnic group to participate in the larger society.

Concepts of the Chinese Community and Rules of Inter-action in the Community

The broker's concept of the Chinese community differs from that of the Kiu Ling's. The Chinese community, according to the Kiu Ling, should be reigned by the "real Chinese." For the brokers, every Chinese who is concerned with community affairs has the right to conduct community service, irrespective of their ability to speak the Chinese language. The Kiu Ling insist on the heirarchical communication channels for all Chinese and the use of different levels of associations. The brokers of social agencies consider associations obsolete vestiges, whose structures are good only for the retired and old Chinese. They believe the associations are inadequate in performing any service for the modern Chinese in Chinatown. The brokers

are particularly hostile to the Chinese Consolidated
Benevolent Association, a symbol of the stronghold for the
Kiu Ling patrons. Most of the social agencies neither
discourage nor encourage the Chinese to join the various
associations. However, the hostility between the
association and the social agencies is felt by most of the
Chinese. The latter has frequently attacked the ignorance of
the Kiu Ling on urban problems, United States politics, and
their concern for power and prestige. The brokers do not feel
the need for following the rules put down by the Kiu Ling for
the conduct of daily affairs among the Chinese.

On the other hand, all the Chinese are encouraged to use
the facilities and services of the social agencies. In fact,
several social agencies have made inventories of the various
types of services performed by the social agencies, Several
pamphlets have been published to inform the Chinese public on
how to use the social service agencies. In these
publications, they give particular emphasis to these items:
No fee, no favor, and no obligation. The public is
frequently reminded that no connection or bribery are needed
in the use of these social agencies. In fact, the welfare
functions which were once performed by the family and
regional associations have now been taken over by the social
agencies.

The Chinese are encouraged by the brokers to use the
resources of the larger society. They are told that they do
not have to depend on the Kiu Ling for gaining employment,
financing, or settling disputes. They were aided and
encouraged by the new brokers to gradually participate in the
activities of the larger society. As a result of the
activities of the brokers, the bond between the Kiu Ling and
Chinese public has weakened. Again, while the Kiu Ling's
effort has been in insulating the Chinese from the larger
society, the social agency brokers are interested in
assisting the Chinese to break away from this isolation. In
order to achieve such an end, some preparations have to be
made. Thus, while the Kiu Ling insists on founding the
Chinese school to preserve the Chinese culture in America,
the brokers are for the establishment of an English school or
center to teach English to the adults and new immigrants so
that they can take up employment in non-Chinese
establishments. In almost every major social agency, there
is an English program for the Chinese. Further, while the
Kiu Ling deliberately refuse to petition for the fundings
from the larger society for the Chinese school, the brokers
make deliberate efforts to secure funds from the larger
society for the establishment of English centers for adults.
Thus, the different emphases on the establishment of two

types of schools and different approaches in obtaining

fundings reflect the two opposing ideologies of the brokers

and Kiu Ling. The latter is for the community's autonomy and

for the preservation of Chinese culture; the former is

for the ethnic group's participation in the larger society.

While the Kiu Ling is for the preservation of the social

structure, the new brokers do not see the need for the

continued existence of these associations. While the Kiu

Ling insist that the public should follow the hierarchical

structure and work through the Kiu Ling of the family,

regional and other associations, the brokers feel that they

can provide better service with no strings attached. In a

word, the brokers intend to supplant the brokerage functions

of the Kiu Ling.

Strategies Adopted in Dealing with Outiders

While the Kiu Ling concieve themselves as the

indispensable link between the Chinese community and Chinese

culture, with China (Taiwan) and the United States, the

brokers see themselves as the important link between the

Chinese ethnic group and the larger society. Their goal is

the sharing of resources of the larger society by the Chinese

ethnic group. Their basic strategy is to use the Chinese

ethnicity to achieve equal opportunity and equal treatment

by the larger society. Under this basic strategy, two
devices are used: 1) emphasize ethnic identity to develop new
positions and patterns to organize activities in those
sectors formerly not found in the United States society
(Barth 1969: 33; Lyman and Douglas 1973: 345; Wirth 1945: 347-
372); and 2) form coalitions with other ethnic groups for the
obtainment of similar goals.

Dealing with dominant society: The traditional Kiu Ling
patrons are mainly entrepreneurs in the ethnic niche. Their
contact with the larger society is related to their own
ethnic niche. Protection of their economic interests from
the larger society is sought. The new brokers, on the other
hand, go beyond the activities in these sectors. Knowing the
Chinese restaurants, garment factories, laundries, groceries
and gift stores are still the important businesses of the
Chinese, the new brokers attempt to render services to people
in these areas. Thus, for instance, the Chinatown Planning
Council has been trying to get federal and city subsidies to
run day care centers for the Chinese seamstresses who have to
work out of economic necessity in garment factories thus
leaving young children unattended. They encourage Chinese
Americans to seek employment in all fields, from hospital
administration, civil service, construction, and commercial
positions to professional sectors. Notices on the

possibilities of employment with the police and F.B.I. are
posted in many social agencies. The agency brokers are
interested in placing qualified Chinese in positions in the
larger society where they were not found formerly, such as
New York Telephone, Con Edison, the U.S. Postal Service, city
government and the broadcasting industries. They also take
complaints concerning violations of human rights, Equal
Opportunity and Affirmative Action programs and send these
complaints on to the proper authorities. Since some of these
brokers for the community are volunteers who are from the
legal profession or related fields, they are relatively
familiar with procedures for obtaining attention of the
proper authorities.

The community's agency brokers are alert to available
resources which the Chinese ethnic group can tap. In order
to compete for these resources, American politicians are
enlisted to assist the Chinese. Moreover, brokers are
interested in enlisting community support for Chinese
candidates who are interested in running for government
offices in New York. However, due to the limited number of
registered voters, it is unlikely than any Chinese candidates
will have large support from the Chinese community in the
near future. However, the need to have Chinese politicians is
gradually being felt in the community. Due to the efforts of
these brokers, many Chinese have registered to vote. Some

years ago, there were hardly any Democrats in Chinatown.

Today, there are more than 200 registered democrats in

Chinatown. The number of registered republicans is said to

be about the same.

Not all the people come to Chinatown to perform the

brokerage functions for ideological purposes. Some come to

establish agencies because resources have been allocated for

community service by the Office of Economic Opportunity.

Full time social workers who perform the brokerage functions

in the federal or state funded social agencies can receive

competitive salaries. Other brokers come to help the Chinese

because of political ambitions, i.e. gaining possible votes

for future campaigns. The number of American-Chinese college

students who return to Chinatown to help community

development in recent years has been on the increase. They

are particularly zealous in assisting the Chinese to fight

for equal treatment and equal opportunity from the dominant

society. Thus, basically, the approach used by these brokers

is the conflict approach, not conflict in the sense of

physical force, but in the sense of social pressure and of

mental attitudes. This approach is sharply in contrast with

that of the Kiu Ling who insist on harmony, patience, and

inaction unless necessary. Having experienced prejudice and

discrimination in their early years, many of the Kiu Ling

simply think that publicity and high visibility will provoke jealousy among the larger society which will create unhappy

consequences and thus bring disaster to the community. The

brokers, on the other hand, feel that it is American to fight

for equality and freedom. These brokers are fond of using

methods commonly resorted to by many interest groups in

America such as protest, demonstration and strikes to obtain

their goals. The Kiu Ling normally think that these measures

are too drastic and do not approve such actions. Not only do

the brokers use these methods, they also want to form

coalitions with other ethnic groups to protest and to fight

for equal rights and create new social positions.

Coalitions with other Ethnic Groups: Frederik Barth

(1969) pointed out that the persuance of the strategy of

emphasizing ethnic identity in the creation of new social

positions and patterned activities not formerly found in the

larger society could generate many of the interesting

movements such as the nativistic movement and the creation of

new states (Barth 1969: 33). The emergence of the Chinese-

American movement and the alliance of the Chinese with

Japanese and other Asians are cases in point. All these

movements use ethnicity as a basis for organization. The

first uses the Chinese identity; the second, a larger ethnic

identity (Asia). The manipulation of regional ethnicity for

goal seeking activities is recognized by Lyman and Douglas

(1973: 344-365). There are situations which dictate an

appropriate ethnic choice. An individual has to respond by

assuming an appropriate ethnic identity:

> Thus, the American-born son of immigrant parents from Canton
> might find it advantageous to invoke his membership in the
> Sam Yup speech group when interacting with a speaker of Sze
> Yup dialect; in the Cantonese regional group, when
> encountering a fellow from Shanghai; in the Chinese "race,"
> when confronting whites; in the Asian peoples, when forming
> an ethnic studies program; and as an óriental, when
> discussing the influence of cultures on behavior. Moreover,
> he may find it to be fun or profitable to be "Japanese" when
> seeking a date with a nisei girl; to be "Hawaiian" when
> confronting people interested in peoples from exotic and
> tropical environments; and to be "just plain American" when
> seeking a job (Lyman and Douglas 1973: 355).

Although the Kiu Ling do assume several sub-ethnic

identities such as the real Chinese, the overseas Chinese,

the American Chinese or even Cantonese-Chinese, Toysanese-

Chinese, they never feel comfortable in assuming the Asian

identity. This is partly due to the fact that they prefer to

keep their distance from other ethnic groups and maintain the

autonomy of the Chinese ethnic group. In the case of the

organizers of the Chinese American movement, they understand

that if they want to make an impact on the larger society,

they need more participants. Thus it is advantageous to

incorporate with other Japanese and Koreans to form an Asian

movement to fight racism.

It is not just the need for more members that has

caused Chinese-Americans to cooperate with other Asians.

Common interests and destiny are also important bases for the

coalition. Japanese, Chinese, Koreans and other Asians are
frequently referred to in official legislation and documents
as Asians or Orientals. Thus, if one Asian group, say, the
Japanese, breaks a racist barrier, it is likely that the
Chinese and other Asians can also benefit from it. So far,
all Asian groups have cooperated in their struggle for equal
opportunity and human rights.

The Chinese American movement first showed its face in
Chinatown in 1970. A group of rather militant United States
born, college age, Chinese-Americans intended to awaken the
ethnic consciousness and ethnic power of the Chinese with
their publication of a bilingual newspaper, Getting Together.
They also organized anti-war and anti-tourist demonstrations
in Chinatown. However, very few Chinatown residents were
enthusiastic about the movement, and even fewer particpated
in the demonstration. The Kiu Ling are particularly hostile
to the organizers of the Chinese American movement because
the members of the movement are thought to be basically pro-
communist radicals who oppose the power structure of the
CCBA, and their activities are bad for the tourist business
in Chinatown. Because of the emergence of ethnic
consciousness, the Chinese American movement recently has
absorbed more members. Although some of the members of the
movement are critical about the work of social agencies such
as the Youth Mobilization and the Chinatown Planning Council

o render their free "brokerage" services to the Chinese and

elp them to participate in the resource distribution of the

arger society.

Many of these brokers, as mentioned earlier, do not

ive in Chinatown, They are middle class Chinese-Americans;

ome even live in the affluent suburbs or neighborhoods in

ew York City. Yet they still retain their ethnic identity.

his is an interesting phenomenon which deserves further

omment. Moving to an "American" neighborhood does not

ecessarily wipe out ethnic identity. It is possible for a

ember of an ethnic group to take up the American way of

peaking, dressing, and living, and at the same time, retain

is ethnicity. Milton Gordon (1964) distinguished

cculturation from assimilation by stating that acculturation

an take place without assimilation. Thus, a person can move

o the "American" suburbs, speak American English, and still

e a full-fledged member of an ethnic group. Michael Novak

1971), Andrew Greeley (1972), and Glazer and Moynihan (1963)

eem to agree that the indestructible character of ethnic

roups is a fact in American life. The reasons for the

ersistance of ethnic groups in America are: 1) early

hildhood socialization processes have passed unconsciously,

any ethnic traits and ethnic behavioral patterns onto the

hildren (Greeley 1972: 8); 2) ethnic groups are sometimes

eliberately maintained and used as carriers of cultural

traditions (Greeley 1972); 3) the persistence of ethnic
groups are advantageous and are used as interest groups for
social, political and economic activities (Glazer and
Moynihan 1963); 4) ethnic self-identification is a component
of personal identity for many members of ethnic groups
(Greeley 1972: 8); 5) it is more comfortable for individuals
to interact with people whose feelings, values, instincts,
and beliefs are similar (Novak 1972: 272). Members of an
ethnic group tend to share more similarities in these areas
mentioned. The increased ethnic consciousness among the
second and third generation Chinese-Americans is due mainly
to the five reasons just mentioned. In addition, however,
three more factors give impetus to the change: 1) the
emergence of the People's Republic of China as a world power
(Chinese Americans can therefore take more pride in their
Chinese heritage); 2) the failure of the old associations to
provide leadership in solving housing and social problems in
Chinatown and in assisting the participation of the Chinese
in the larger society; and 3) the examples of the Black and
Puerto Rican movements and their efforts in fighting for
equal economic opportunity.

To sum up, then, these new brokers from the social
agencies and youth organizations follow a strategy directly
opposed to the Kiu Ling. The former use ethnicity to
participate in the social, economic and political life in the
larger society. The latter want to limit contact with the
larger society and preserve the status quo of the community.
The Kiu Ling have been successful in protecting the Chinese
ethnic niche and in preserving the Chinese culture in
America. They are for the isolation of the community from
the larger society and maintenance of a closed community in
which the Kiu Ling are patrons or elites who can control the
community. This introversion is counter-balanced by the out-
reaching efforts of the brokers. The officials of the social
agencies as well as the youth organizations, in performing
their bridging functions between the Chinese community and
the larger society, are bringing the community into direct
contact with other ethnic groups and the larger society. As
a consequence of the new brokers' activities, the Chinese
community of New York has become more outwardly oriented, and
the ethnic boundary of the community has assumed a different
character from that of the pre-1965's Chinatown. Formerly
the Chinese ethnic boundary was almost impenetrable. Today,
the ethnic boundary of New York's Chinese community does not
prevent the social, economic and welfare assistance of the
larger society, or isolate the participation of the members

of the community in the social, economic, and political
resources distribution of the larger society. Due to the
activities of the new brokers, the community has become more
open to the larger society.

CHAPTER 8

CONCLUSION: PATRONAGE, BROKERAGE,
ENTREPRENEURSHIP AND ETHNICITY

This study has focused on the analysis of the formation and manipulation of the patronage and brokerage systems in the economic adaptation of the Chinese in New York.

The economic adaptive activities of the Chinese, as demonstrated earlier, have been undertaken under the reinforcement and constraint of the opportunity structure, the community's structure and the assets (capital, skills and social claims) available to the actors. From their immigration to New York in the 1870's, the Chinese have been making numerous economic adaptations. However, they have been made within relatively well-defined ethnic niches: Chinese restaurants, Chinese laundries, Chinese garment factories, groceries, and gift stores. The major adaptations within the ethnic niches include: 1) technical improvement; 2) internal adaptation through specialization; 3) formation of partnership firms to circumvent restrictive immigration laws; 4) creation of family firms; and 5) formation of self-protection societies or associations to protect the economic interests of the Chinese. As indicated earlier, patronage and brokerage have been formed and manipulated to launch economic adaptive activities within the Chinese ethnic niche. In particular, patronage and brokerage were and still are instrumental in the establishment of firms, obtaining of financing, obtaining of employment, business organization for production, settlement of disputes or conflicts, obtaining of business protection.

The manipulation of patronage and brokerage for economic activities
is significantly different in the eras both preceeding and following
1965. From 1870-1964, the kiu ling (patrons, employers, leaders)
were the indispensable actors in the Chinese community of New York.
In addition to assisting in employment, settling disputes, and financing,
these Kiu Ling mediated the interactions between the various segments
of the community organized on the basis of clanship, locality of origin,
or linguistic similarities. These kiu ling were the only bridges
between the Chinese community and the United States society, as
well as the Chinese government. The traditional patron-client
relationship still plays an important role in the economic activities
and community life of the Chinese at the present time (1965-1974).
However, other avenues are now opening for the Chinese to obtain
employment, financing, and relevant information for economic activities.
These new avenues are made available through social agencies,
employment agencies, accounting firms, law firms, and banking
institutions. Since these institutions are basically inter-systemic
between the Chinese community and the United States society, the
Chinese community has been able to have more contact with the larger
society. During the period 1870-1964, the kiu ling used either personal
resources or resources within the community to solve the economic
problems of the Chinese. Since 1965, the brokers from social agencies
and other brokerage institutions have been quite successful in
assisting the Chinese to participate in the resource distribution of

:he larger society. As a consequence, the Chinese community has
)ecome more open to the larger society.

The presence of the brokers does not imply the disappearance
)f the patron-client relationship or the Chinese ethnic boundary.
)n the contrary, the existence of the brokerage institutions, especially
:he social agencies and the activities of the brokers have posed a
:hallenge to the kiu ling of the community. They are in direct
:ompetition in the recruitment of clients. The kiu ling still hope
:hat with their extravagant use of money and generous donations to
:ultural preservation activities they will recruit a large following.
The brokers need a larger following to continue funding their projects
and their agencies. The kiu ling's efforts to preserve the Chinese
cultural identity is related to their desire to protect their personal
interests and the status quo of the community. However, the
brokers also use ethnicity as a resource to fight for more funding
for the community services and to increase the participation of the
Chinese in American life.

Thus, the present study of the formation and manipulation of
patronage and brokerage in the Chinese community of New York shows:
1) the continued use of patron-client relationships for economic
activities and the continued formation of patron-client relationships
within the Chinese institutions such as the various associations
and the Chinese family firms; 2) the gradual takeover by brokers in
the performance of functions traditionally within the province of
the kiu ling; and 3) patronage as a vehicle for the stability of

culture and the new brokerage as a vehicle for change.

Although the present study is concerned mainly with the descriptive
analysis of patronage and brokerage in the economic adaptation of
the Chinese in New York, its theoretical implication, however,
extends beyond the narrow confines of New York Chinatown. The
wider theoretical implications of the present study are related to
the following areas: patronage and brokerage, entrepreneurship,
and ethnicity.

SOCIO-ECONOMIC AMBIENCE AND THE OPERATION OF PATRONAGE AND BROKERAGE

On the Temporal Order of Patron-Client or Broker-Client Networks

The existence and operation of patronage and brokerage are
closely related to the formal structure or formal institutions.
Eric Wolf (1966:2) considers formal institutions as the fundamental
social systems of a society, while attributes of informal networks
such as kinship, friendship, patron-client networks were "supplementary
to the system." These informal networks are claimed to exist
and function by virtue of the formal system's existence (Wolf 1966).
Wolf further contends that formal systems logically, if not
temporally, precede informal networks such as patron-client relations.
This view of the place of network implies that society is rooted
in corporate groups (Dirks 1972:566). Perhaps it is with this assumption
that many anthropologists discuss the mediating or linking functions
of informal groups. Thus, for instance, Barnes (1968:109) showed
how the formal institutions are linked by informal networks. In one
of his essays, "Aspects of Group Relations in a Complex Society:

Mexico," Wolf (1956) specifically points out the important bridging function of patron-client and broker-client relations in linking the national level and local level institutions.

While there is little debate on the bridging functions of the patrons and brokers, there is substantial disagreement on the temporal order of informal network relations. Thus, Boissevain (1968:544) argues that informal networks are both _temporally_ and _logically_ prior to formal groups. With evidence obtained from the work of Metraux (1951:67-68) and of Gamble (1963:2-4) on Haitian work groups and the village government of China, Boissevain demonstrates that personal network is a general matrix out of which quasi-groups are formed. Thus, out of quasi-groups, corporate groups gradually emerge (Boissevain 1968:542-546).

The argument of whether patron-client networks precede formal groups in the temporal order is a non-productive one. The data of the present study suggest that actors can create patron-client contracts and enter business partnerships which lead to the formation of a corporate group such as work group or business firm (see Chapters 5 & 7). On the other hand, many patron-client networks are created within formal institutions and in the function of formal groups for existence (see Chapters 4 & 6). To argue that the temporal order of patron-client networks and formal groups is similar to the argument of the temporal order of "the chicken or the egg." Hence, it is a futile argument. A suitable question to ask concerning the existence of patron-client or broker-client networks is - "What causes the creation and formation of patronage and brokerage?" This will be dealt with in the following section.

Structural and Economic Conditions for the Emergence of Patronage and Brokerage

There are structural prerequisites for the existence and the operation of patron-client and broker-client networks. Sydel Silverman (1965) predicates the mediation role of the patrons to the early phase development of nation-state and associates the existence of patronage and brokerage with peasantry and the rural situation. Alex Weingrod (1968) hypothesized that patron-client ties usually arise in a state where considerable separation exists between the levels of village, community, society and state. Stuart (1972) argues that the existence of the patron-client system is related to loosely structure, non-integrated societies where derivational powers and hierarchical social strata exist. Mayer (1967) attributes the existence of patronage and brokerage in terms of a plural society and indirect rule. Bailey (1965; 1969) assigns the emergence of patronage and brokerage to encapsulated situations were the two co-existing structures need the mediation of middlemen. Common in these anthropological studies on the conditions of the emergence of patronage and brokerage are: 1) the existence of two systems; 2) a stratified society where some individuals have access to resources but others do not; 3) state organized societies where delegated power exists. What is missing in their discussion is the examination of the macro-economic structure's relevancy to the cultural system or community in question. While agreeing that the above three factors are important for the mergence of patronage and brokerage, I believe that the relevant resource structure and the rigidity and limitations imposed by the resource structure are conducive to the existence and operation of patron-client and broker-client networks.

The less control and participation an encapsulated community has over the resource distribution of the larger society, the more manipulation of patronage and brokerage is encouraged for decision-making activities. Examining the macro-economic environment or the opportunity structure available for the Chinese ethnic group throughout the past 100 years (Chapters 3, 4, and 6), I find that the economic activities of the Chinese have been confined to certain sectors of American society. They concentrate mainly on non-competitive service businesses. Attitudes, immigration policies, and discriminatory employment practices in the past have limited economic participation of the Chinese in the larger society. Even in ethnic businesses, few direct controls could be exerted by the Chinese on the market. Since the Chinese garment factory owners are the contractors who must receive materials and orders from American garment manufacturers, the former have little control over the buyer's market. Similarly, the Chinese restaurant businesses and tourist businesses have to depend a great deal on the attitudes of the Americans toward China. In an ethnic community where the actors have few direct accesses to economic domains and control over the markets and customers, networks seem to be best suited for goal-seeking activities. Thus, patron-client networks can be viewed

as adaptive strategies resorted to for the exploitation of resources

in certain situations. For instance, in a situation where a Chinese

may have no access to the legal system of the American society, it

is infinitely more advantageous for him to get his disputes settled

through go-betweens and the patrons within his own community.

Similarly, because of the limited employment opportunities available

to the Chinese (see Chapter 5), many have to work in family restaurant

or laundry firms. Thus, the macro-economic environment can play

a facilitative role for the existence and operation of patronage

and brokerage.

PATRONAGE, BROKERAGE, AND ENTREPRENEURSHIP

Family Firms and Entrepreneurship

It has recently been recognized that the family firm facilitates

entrepreneurial activities. Morton (1961) demonstrated how the Roth-

childs created a family banking empire which lasted over 150 years.

Reina and Cochran (1962) showed how the kinship network was utilized

by Italian-born industrialist Torcuato di Tella to build up a family-

based corporate empire in Argentina. Other authors which deal with

the advantages of familial and kinship network relationship for

entrepreneurial pursuit include Benedict (1968), Cohen (1967),

Timberg (1969), and Bailey (1962). The most eloquent thesis on

the contribution of familial and kinship network to entrepreneurship

is that of Burton Benedict (1968). Using transactional analysis as

a tool, Burton Benedict demonstrated the various adaptive advantages of family firms which include the maximal use of labor resources,

capital, business training for family members, and safeguarding business

secrets. In addition to these advantages, the present study shows

that Chinese family firms offer maximum flexibility which enables the

survival of businesses throughout both good and lean seasons. Chinese

family firms are suitable for risk taking too, since decisions

can be made quickly and action can be taken immediately with little

consultation. In the competition for customers and markets, it

is important for the entrepreneurs to have a " free hand" to take

quick action on unexpected economic opportunities. The authoritarian

power structure of Chinese family firms is thus suitable for

family heads to make quick decisions.

Patronage, Brokerage and the Family Firm

As mentioned in Chapter 6, patron-client and broker-client

relations are deliberately created and manipulated within the Chinese

family firms. In the Type 1 Chinese family firm which is run by

the family head and his immediate family members, the relationship

between the father or the eldest male and the rest of the family is

more than familial; it is an employer-employee, manager-trainee, and

protector-protegee relationship. In the Type 2 Chinese family firm

which has a core group of family members and employees not related

to the family, there is also the extensive patron-client relationship

between the employer and the personnel of the firm. In the Type 3

Chinese family firm, there are two systems of patronage; the employer

is the super-patron to all the employees of the firm, while the

labor boss is a patron to his personally hired staff. In all these
cases, the family heads are employers and patrons. They take care
of the needs of the employees in areas not directly related to the
firm, such as school and immigration problems of employees and their
relatives. One of the most important advantages obtained by the
manipulation of patron-client relationships is the retention of a
loyal labor force. In a situation where skillful labor is scarce
(in the Chinese community of New York there is a perrennial need for
chefs of the northern Chinese cuisines and a shortage of skillful
seamstresses), the retention of a loyal, skillful work force is of
paramount importance for the continued operation and production of
a firm or a factory.

An Open-minded Approach to the Study of Entrepreneurship

Different opinions and approaches to the study of entrepreneurship have been expressed by sociologists, economists, psychologists
and anthropologists.

Disagreements among social scientists over the study of entrepreneur
ship have centered on whether economic, social, cultural, or psychologic
factors are more important in the formation of entrepreneurship.
Schumpeter (1961) emphasized the creative response of some individuals.
Max Weber(1958) emphasized the Protestant ethic. He hypothesized
that elements in Calvinist theology which placed a high moral value
on a life of continual, honest, frugal, and rational application
of one's talents and property to a secular "calling," tends to
encourage the accumulation of wealth and entrepreneurial activities

(Weber 1958). Psychologists like Hagen (1962) attributed entrepreneurial formation to withdrawal of status respect. He believed that in many societies, child rearing practices produced generation after generation of "authoritarian" personalities. However, change will begin after some members of the society find themselves deprived of the social esteem or status respect which they believe to be their due. According to Hagen (1962), sons of these members internalized their anxieties and made a break through. Thus, Hagen thought that retreatism produced a generation of anxiety-ridden, creative personalities; and then, providing other conditions are favorable, the process of economic growth begins. Psychologists like McClelland (1961) attributed entrepreneurial success to achievement motivation. Sociologists such as Carroll (1965) thought that educational and occupational background were important to entrepreneurial formation. Thus, disagreement among the social scientists on the study of entrepreneurship is considerable.

Several years ago, Aubey (1969) and Glade (1967) attempted to make a programatic statement on the study of entrepreneurship. Both economists suggested a dual-level approach: examination of the macro and micro economic environments. Examination of the macro environment included the analysis of economic demands, political structure, and other environmental structures. The analysis of the micro economic environment was to uncover the socio-cultural traits, and the economic attributes of the actors. Thus, the approach of Aubey and Glade was mainly structural. How individuals manipulate their socio-economic assets to exploit the macro economic environment was, however, of no interest to Aubey or Glade. redrik Barth, on the other hand, emphasized the performance of the actors (Barth 1963). The Barthian approach accentuates the manipulation of assets such as capital, skills and social claims by the actors, under the relevant and specific reinforcement and constraints of the socio-economic environments, for gain seeking pursuit. In other words, the emphasis of the approach of Fredrik Barth is on the actor's strategic, manipulative activities. The stress of the approach of Glade (1967) and Aubey (969), on the other hand, is on the micro and macro economic structure. Thus, the three authors complement each other. The combined use of the two approaches, as demonstrated in this study, has yielded satisfactory results. For then, the available economic opportunity of the larger society, to which the Chinese made their economic adaptation, is revealed. The social and economic constraints of the Chinese, through the use of this model, are discovered. The process involved in the manipulation of internal structural features such as family, kinship, patronage, and community organizations in the exploitation of the ethnic niche is also brought to light.

The present study shows that the various adaptive strategies such as the preference for the partnership firm in the pre-1965 era, the process of "fusion and fission" involved in the establishment of family firm, and the formation of ethnic niche are related to the opportunity structure of the larger society and to the Chinese cultural "assets" of kinship, patronage and regionalism. Thus,

the economic activities of the Chinese could not be understood if
isolated from the larger society, but neither could knowledge of
the larger society alone have predicted the actions of the Chinese.
Hence, investigation of the economic adaptation of an encapsulated
community must be conducted within and without the social system
of the ethnic group, in relation to the socio-economic restraints
and reinforcement factors of the ethnic community and the larger
society.

Not only must the investigation be _intersystemic,_ but the use
of concepts, theories and procedures must be open-minded. The
present study suggests that the application of economists'
concepts and theories such as entrepreneurship, niche, assets,
maximization, and theories of entrepreneurial formation are
highly productive, for they serve as heuristic devices for the
analysis of the decision-making activities of the Chinese businessmen.
On the other hand, the cultural background, community organizations,
and social relationships of the Chinese community are important
for the understanding of the range of culturally acceptable alternatives
of economic actions (Keesing 1967:2). Thus, for instance, the
recruitment of region-mates and kinsmen for the formation of partnership
firms in pre-1965 Chinatown was a maximizing activity in a given
situation under the constraints of the United States immigration
law and the constraints of traditional kinship and regionalism.

An open-minded approach to entrepreneurship thus implies the
employment of the following: 1) examination of structural features;

2) investigation of the activity system of the actors; 3) delineation
of the economic relationship between the encapsulated social system
with the outside world.

PATRONAGE, BROKERAGE AND ETHNICITY

Entrepreneurs as Patrons, Innovators, and Culture Stabilizers

The combination of patrons, innovators and culture stabilizers
in one person is recognized by many anthropologists (Paine 1963;
Geertz 1963; Strickon 1973). The findings of the present study
indicate that the kiu ling of the community are patrons, brokers,
innovators, and culture stabilizers. This is not contradictory
since the performance of these functions is conducive to goal-
seeking activities. Briefly, then, being a patron, one can have
more power and prestige which can be converted to economic
activities. Performing brokerage functions will enhance the
authority of the kiu ling and add more prestige. Innovation in
technology will aid production. Participation in cultural preservation
activities will help to preserve the power of the kiu ling and
status quo of the community.

Paine (1963:52) also found that the entrepreneurs in a community
often seek political influence on members. Although they are
innovators in the economic field, they are not revolutionary. On the
contrary, they are the active opponents to externally imposed
change (Paine 1963). This phenomenon is also found elsewhere.
Geertz (1963:150) noticed that the aristocratic entrepreneurs in
both Modjukuto and Tabanana, Indonesia, perceive themselves as culture

preservers; they are strong defenders of cultural traditions (Geertz

1963:150-151). Similarly, the kiu ling of the Chinese community

of New York perceive themselves as vehicles for Chinese culture

maintenance in Chinatown, New York.

Patrons as Brokers

In the pre-1965 era, the patrons of the Chinese community were

usually the entrepreneurs who had more connections within and without

the community. Paine (1963) also pointed out the capability of the

entrepreneurs in the community to perform the bridging role because

of their connections. Likewise, Geertz (1963) showed the connections

of the aristocratic entrepreneurs in Taban, Indonesia.   These

connections not only facilitated entrepreneurial activities but also

enabled them to link the local community with the outside world.

Thus, entrepreneurs in general are the potential brokers for members

of the community.

The entrepreneur-patron (kiu ling) of the Chinese community has

been shown as fond of performing the brokerage functions. This

has also been noted by Henriksen (1971). Not only do the patrons

have the resources and facilities to perform brokerage functions,

they are also eager to assume the role of broker to enhance

their prestige and buttress their positions as patrons (Henricksen

1971:23-33). The present study on the kiu ling reveals this technique

of assuming the role of broker to strengthen their positions as

308

patrons of the community. The power and prestige connected with the
position of patron, in turn, enhances gain pursuit by attracting
more customers and more invitations to participate in different
economic activities.

Non-Patron-Brokers and Ethnic Identity

In the post-1965 era, non-patron-brokers emerge and affiliate
themselves with social agencies, brokerage firms and youth
organizations which assist the members of the community to use
the resources of the larger society and to participate in the public,
political, and social life of America. These brokers differ from
the kiu ling - patrons in many respects. One is that the former's
rendering of mediating and bridging functions does not necessarily
require an immediate return from the client. The patron, however,
did. Second, these brokers are change agents, who have made
the Chinese community more outwardly oriented (see Chapter 7).
The patrons are interested in maintaining the status quo. Both
the patron - kiu ling and the brokers of the social agencies
have one thing in common; both use ethnicity. In their efforts to
make the Chinese community more outwardly oriented by wider
participation in American life, the brokers of the agencies use
Chinese ethnicity as a resource to facilitate their bridging
activities. This raises the interesting question about the the
persistence of ethnic identity in the United States.

It has been recognized that "melting pot" did not actually
take place in America (Glazer and Moynihan 1963). Further, despite

acculturation and assimilation, ethnic differences still persist
in America. Among Chinese-Americans who have returned to Chinatown
to perform their bridging functions are professionals who reside
in affluent neighborhoods and have adopted the American life style.
Rose Hum Lee (1960) and Beaudry (1966) both presented evidence on
the assimilation and acculturation among the Chinese in New York
and other parts of the United States. Why do these people still
maintain their ethnic identity? From findings of this study,
several explanations can be offerred on the use of ethnicity in
general and the ethnic identification of the Chinese in particular.

First, discrimination is a fact of American life (Yin 1973:xvii;
Hsu 1971:114-130; Glazer 1971:51-58; Knowles and Previtt 1969), and
continued discrimination by the larger society against the ethnic
group serves as a unifying force among the members of the ethnic
groups (Simmel 1955; R. Lee 1960). In the face of discrimination
by the dominant group, minority groups which possess physical
characteristics which differ from its, find it particularly
difficult to pass (Lyman and Douglas 1973). They therefore feel
more vulnerable unless they are unified in a group. This feeling
of insecurity is succinctly stated by Rose Lee:

> Incidents of prejudice and discrimination may be infrequent
> for some but when they arise, they evoke feelings of
> marginality and resentment and dormant fears. On such occasions,
> they are made conscious of their ancestry and physical
> characteristics, traits which they have not power to eradicate
> (R. Lee 1960:406).

Second, ethnicity is used as a resource for political, economic
and other goal-seeking activities (Greeley 1971; 1972; Novak 1971;

Ianni 1973; Glazer and Moynihan 1963). The findings of the present
study indicate that brokers are using ethnicity to develop new
positions and pattern activities in the larger society for the
Chinese and themselves as well. Further, in view of the newly created
Equal Opportunity and Affirmative Action programs, these brokers
are conscious of the advantage of having a strong, unified group which
bargains and negotiates with the larger society. Thus, it seems
to me that the workings of a plural society and the obtainment of
goals in the United States require the manipulation of ethnicity.

Third, it is likely that the improved Sino-U.S. relations and
the emergence of China as a world power have had consequential effects
on ethnic identification of the Chinese in America. Within the
scope of this study, the extent to which the rise of ethnic
pride is related to the emergence of China and the Sino-U.S.
relations has not been determined.

Thus, the use of Chinese ethnicity and strong Chinese identification among brokers are adaptive strategies for goal-seeking
activities and are related to the opportunity structure of the
larger society. Therefore, both brokers of agencies and kiu ling-
patrons use ethnicity, but for different institutional goals.
This should not be taken as a suggestion that there is perfect
harmony in the groups of kiu ling-patrons or brokers (see Chapter
7).

Although the brokers of social agencies and newly established
brokerage institutions such as the labor unions share in the general

pursuance of the strategy which uses ethnic identity to develop new
positions and patterns and to organize activities in those areas
formerly not found in the larger society, there are different approaches
or sub-strategies within this general strategy. Thus, some are
for working within the system, through peaceful means and proper
channels to obtain equitable treatment in employment and housing
from the larger society. The methods used include complaints to
the Human Rights Commissioners or other civil rights organizations
and petitions for government subsidies through government agencies.
Some brokers are interested in creating community action, i.e.,
encouraging members of the community to protest and participate
in demonstrations and strikes to get funds, to obtain legal aid,
and to exert community pressure on legislation and implementation
of Affirmative Action and Equal Opportunity programs. The
third group of brokers aims at directing their efforts in co-
ordinating all the factions of the community to achieve greater
solidarity for a common cause of the Chinese ethnic group. The
fourth group of brokers is composed mainly of college-age, second
and third generation Chinese-Americans who elect to use more
radical methods to fight for the dignity of the Chinese. As mentioned
in Chapter 7, many members of this group are in the so-called
"Chinese-American movement" which professes ideological affiliations
with the People's Republic of China. Many of them see all the
social problems in Chinatown stemming from discrimination of the
larger society. This group of brokers is consciencious, however,
in obtaining medical equipment and supplies from the larger society

to run a free health clinic for the Chinese in the community. They are quite concerned that the Chinese get their 'fair share' legally and economically and advocate the use of protest, demonstration, and strike to bargain with the larger society.

The last group of brokers' activities deserve more comment. First, it indicates that brokers are more than information processors (Paine 1971:21). In purveying values of the larger society and in educating the Chinese to the working of the American system (see Chapter 7), these brokers purposely change the emphasis and content of the values and information purveyed. Second, the technique which uses ethnic identity to fight "discrimination" and the "establishment" has produced an effect which Fredrik Barth observed as ethnic and nativistic movements (Barth 1969:33). The anti-establishment's and the anti-outsiders' activities (such as the anti-tourist demonstrations) of this group of people are cases in point.

The four different approaches of the four groups of brokers cited earlier also indicate that sub-strategies can exist within the general strategy which uses ethnic identity as a resource. Not only did Fredrik Barth (1969) neglect to mention these sub-strategies, but the different consequences of the pursuance of these sub-strategies as well. The diversified use of ethnic identity in creating new positions and opportunities for the Chinese by different groups of brokers has produced the following results. These include: 1) making the traditionally closed community become more open to the larger

society; 2) inspiring separatist movements among some members of
the ethnic group; 3) enabling the ethnic group to have wider
participation in the social, political and economic life of the
larger society; 4) altering the nature of dependence of members
on the traditional patrons or elite; 5) the continued existence of
the ethnic group and the ethnic boundary.

As a consequence of the activities of the brokers, Chinatown
today has more interaction with the American society. It has
gradually learned to use the legal, financial, recreational,
welfare, judicial facilities of the larger society. People of the
community have become more active in exercising the rights of
citizenship such as competing for offices and voting. Their
social and economic activities have transcended the Chinese ethnic
niche and the geographic boundary of Chinatown. Instead of
limiting their economic activities within the confines of Chinatown
and the traditional Chinese restaurant and laundry businesses,
they have gradually taken up the less stereotypical jobs such as
civil service, repairmen in the electric and telephone companies,
in the mass media, in the various U.S. commercial establishments, and
in the trade unions. The Chinese also gradually extend their economic
activities to the real estate, transportation and movie businesses.
In the area of employment, capital formation, legal disputes, they
do not have to depend on the favor of the traditional patrons alone.
The new brokers can also help the Chinese to alleviate the problems
they encounter in their daily life. Because of the constant use

of ethnicity by the brokers, the community is gradually educated in the values and techniques of using Chinese ethnic identity for collective bargaining for the well being of the Chinese in New York. It is likely that Chinese ethnicity will be put into further use, collectively and individually, in the near future for the various decision-making activities of the Chinese.

List of Chinese Associations in New York City (1974)*

Name	Nature
China Buddhist Association	Religious
Chinese Laundry Association	Trade
Chinese Laundry Social Athletic Club	Recreational & mutual aid
Chang Yuen Club	Recreational
Chee Tuck Sam Tuck Association	Multi-family names
Chee Yue Community Association	Civic
Chew Lun Association	Multi-family names
Chin Shou Kai Association	Village-cum-family name
Chin Wing Chuen Tong	Family name
China Photo Society	Professional
China Institute in America	Educational
China Democratic Club	Political club
Chinese American Elks Club	Charitable
Chinese American Restaurant Association	Trade
Chinese Baptist Mission	Religious
Chinese Chamber of Commerce	Business
Chinese Christian Women Fellowship	Religious
Chinese Community Club	Civic
Chinese Consolidated Benevolent Association	Over-all community association
Chinese Dramatic & Benevolent Association	Recreational & mutual aid
Chinese Evangel Mission	Religious
Chinese Grace Faith Mission	Religious
Chinese Mason Youth Athletic Club	Recreational & mutual aid
Chinese Merchant's Association	Businessmen & mutual aid
Chinese Musical & Theatrical Association	Recreational
Chinese Women's Benevolent Association	Civic
Chung San Association	Regional
Cuban Chinese Refugee Association	Regional
Dep Fook Fong	Village
Dragon Lodge No. 1413	Charitable
Eastern States Buddhist Temple of America	Religious
Eng Lun Hing Society	Family name
Eng Suey Sun Association	Family name
Fay Chow Merchant's Association	Regional-cum-businessmen
First Baptist Chinese Church	Religious
The First Chinese Presbyterian Church	Religious

---

*Only the more active associations are listed and their nature
briefly indicated.

List of Chinese Associations in New York City (1974) (continued)

Name	Nature
Fonn Lun Benevolent Association	Multi-family names
Four Seas Association	Mutual aid
Fow Sak Association	Village
Fukien Association	Regional
G.H. Oak Tin Association	Multi-family names
Gee How Hing Association	Family name
Gee Poy Kuo Association	Family name
Hainan Association	Regional
Hing Wah Alumnus Association	Alumni
Hip Sing Association	Mutual Aid
Hok San Society	Regional
Honk Kwong Fong	Village
Hoy Ping Association	Regional
Hoy Shom Company	Club
Hoy Sung Ning Yeung Benevolent Association	Regional
Hoy Yin Association	Regional
Hurricanses Association	Recreational
Kang Jai Wu Joy Association	Regional
Kuo Ming Tang, Eastern Regional Offices	Political
Kuo Ming Tang, N.Y. Branch Office	Political
Kwangtung Kou-Ming University Alumni Assoication	Alumni
Kwong Hoy Association	Regional
Kyew Ching Musical Association	Professional
Lan Yee Bat Suey	Family name
Lee's Family Association	Family name
Lee King Shue Club	Family name
Leung Chung How Tong	Family name
Li Ka Athletic Association	Recreational
Lingnam University Alumnus Association	Alumni
Lion's Club of Chinatown	Businessmen & charitable
Ling Sing Association	Mutual aid
Lingnam Benevolent Association	Mutual aid
Lt. B.R. Kimlau Chinese Memorial Post 1291, The American Legion	Veteran
Lum Sai Ho Association	Family name
Lung Hing Association	Multi-family names
Lun Wo	Village
Lun Yee Association	Political club
Lung Kong Tin Yee Association	Multi-family names
Min Chih Tang (Chinese Freemasons Democratic Party)	Political
Min Yee Club	Recreational
Ming Sum Club	Recreational
Nam Shun Association	Regional
National Chinese Seamen's Union	Occupational

List of Chinese Associations in New York City (1974) (continued)

Name	Nature
N.Y. Chinese Christian Missionary	Religious
Num Young Association	Multi-family names
Num Yuen Brothers	Recreational
On Tin Club	Family name
Overseas Chinese Mission	Religious
Republican Club of Chinatown	Political club
Sam Yick Association	Multi-family names
Sam Jo Kong Fong	Regional
San Kiang Charitable Association	Regional
San Min Club	Recreational
Sing Lee Social Club	Recreational
Soo Yuen Tong	Multi-family names
Sun Yet-San University Alumnus Association	Alumni
Sun Wei Association	Regional
Sze Kong Mutual Benevolent Association	Mutual Aid
Tai Che Chuan Association	Recreational
Tai Look Merchant's Association	Businessmen-cum-regional
Tai Pun Association	Charitable
Tai Wan University Alumnus Association	Alumni
Tien Sang Club	Recreational
Toon Luock Club	Recreational
Tseng Sum Sing Association	Family name
Tsung Tsin Association	For the Hakka Speaking Chinese
Tung Goon Association	Regional
Tung On Association	Regional
V.F.W. Chinatown Post 6532	Veteran
Victory in Christ Church	Religious
Wah Hong Club	Recreational
Wah Pei Association	Regional
Whyte Home Association	Multi-family names
Wong Wan Sun Association	Family name
Wong Shee Bat Suey	Family name
Yan Ping Gong Yee	Regional
Woo On Ding Tong	Family name
Yee Benevolent Association	Family name
Yee Gai Association	Trade
Yee Moo Kai	Family name
Yee Shan Benevolent Society	Regional
Yook Dong Bat Suey	Multi-family names
Yuen's Association	Family name

GLOSSARY[1]

Bun Chu Kwang Hei[2] 賣主關係

        Literally, it means guest-host relation. It is used
by members of the community to indicate a relationship similar to that of patron-client as used by
anthropologists. The Mandarin Pronunciation is
Bin Chu Kuang Hsi.

Cantonese 廣卅話

        The dialect spoken in the city of Canton. The
Mandarin pronunciation is Kuang Chou Hua.

Chan Ching 親情

        Literally, it means the warmth of kinship. Close
kinsmen are expected to display their affections
or concerns (Chan Ching) for each other. The Mandarin pronunciation is Chin Ching.

Chu Hak Kwang Hei 主客關係

        Literally, it is host-guest relation. It can be
translated as patron-client relation in many con-
texts. In Mandarin it is pronounced as Chu Ka
Kuang Hsi.

Chu Ku Kwang Hei 主顧關係

        Literally, it is host-client relation. It is used
inter-changeably by informants with Bun Chue Kwang
Hei or Chue Hak Kwang Hei to indicate patron-client
relation. The Mandarin pronunciation is Bin Chu
Kuang Hsi.

Chuen Moon Yan Choy 專門人材

        This is a term used to refer to specially trained
people or professionals. In Mandarin it is pronounced as Chuang Men Jen Tsai.

---

[1]This ia a glossary of the frequently used terms appearing in this
dissertation.

[2]The system of Romanization is strictly my own. All the terms
appearing on the left column are Romanized Cantonese words.

Chung Shing Yup Sig 中成入息

Middle income people. In Mandarin, it is pronounced as Ching Cheng Ju Hsi.

Chung Wah Kung So 中華公所

Literally, it means the Chinese Public Assembly Hall. This is a supreme organization of the Chinese community. The English name for it is the Consolidated Chinese Benevolent Association, known to the American public as the unofficial city hall of Chinatown. In Mandarin, Chung Wah Kung So is pronounced as Chung Hua Kung So.

Da Kung 打工

To be employed is call Da Kung. It is frequently referred to employees of general stores or unskilled laborers.

Dai Yup Sig 底入息

It is a term referring to the low income people. In Mandarin, it is pronounced as Ti Ju Hsi.

Dai Lo Pan 大老板

Big boss or rich employer. The Mandarin pronunciation is Ta Lao Pan.

Fong 房

Literally, it means room. A subdivision of a clan. That is to say, a clan can have several fongs. In Mandarin, it is called fang.

Hoi Yin 海員

Literally, it means sailor. In the community, it refers to those sailors who jump-shipped. The Mandarin pronunciation is Hai Yuan.

Heung Ching 鄉情

Literally, it means warmth of village-mates. This term is used by the local Chinese newspapers and members of the community to indicate the bond between people who share the same locality of origin, In Mandarin, it is pronounced as Hsiang Ching.

Hui 會

> Literally, it means meeting. In the Chinese community, it is used to refer to the informal credit clubs.

Kam Ching 感情

> Literally, it means sentimental warmth. It indicates the mutual liking and trust between individuals. In Mandarin, it is pronounced as <u>Kan Ching</u>.

Kiu Ling 僑領

> Literally, it is the leader of the overseas Chinese. The term, as used by members of the community, is applied to individuals who have power and connections. These individuals play the role of protectors for their followers. In addition, the former are expected to finance generously the community's welfare projects. The Mandarin pronunciation of the term is <u>Chiao Ling</u>.

Lo Wah Kiu 老華僑

> Old overseas Chinese. In the Chinese community of New York, the term is used to refer to Chinese immigrants who came to New York before the 1960's.

Lay Yau 理由

> Reason. In Mandarin, it is pronounced as <u>Li Yu</u>.

Lo Pan 老板

> Boss or employer. In Mandarin, it is pronounced as <u>Lao Pan</u>.

Mien Tsi 面子

> One's face or honour. <u>Mien Tsu</u> is the Mandarin pronunciation of the term.

Po Tai 舖底

> Literally, it means the foundation fee of a shop. In the pre-1965 era, the Consolidated Chinese Benevolent Association required that an owner of a Chinese business establishment pay a fee before he used the property to initiate any profit-making activity. In Mandarin, it is pronounced as <u>Pu Ti</u>.

ai Lo Pan 細老板

> Petty employer or boss. Hsiao Loa Pan is the Mandarin pronunciation of the term.

un Yee Man 新移民

> Literally, it means new immigrants. In the community, it is used to refer to those immigrants who came to the United States after the 1960's. In Mandarin, the term is pronounced as Hsin I Min.

heung Shing Yup Sig 中成入息

> This is a term used to refer to people who have high income. In Mandarin, it is pronounced as Sheng Cheng Ju Hsi.

oen Yung 信用

> Reliability or trust. The Mandarin pronunciation is Hsin Yung.

i Hing Dai 師兄弟

> It is a term referring to individuals sharing the same master in a trade. Literally, it means siblings sharing the same master. In Mandarin, it is pronounced as Shih Hsiung Ti.

oysanese 台山話

> The dialect spoken in the district of Toysan. Taisanhus is the Mandarin pronunciation of the term.

ah Yoey 華裔

> Literally, children of the overseas Chinese. In the community, the term is used to refer to Chinese born in the United States or Chinese-Americans. Hua I is the Mandarin pronunciation of the term.

ee Hey 義氣

> Trusting righteousness. It is pronounced as I Chi in Mandarin.

an Ching 人情

> Human feelings. In Mandarin, it is called Jen Ching.

BIBLIOGRAPHY

Abbott, Grace
    1917   The Immigrant and the Community. New York: The
            Century Co..

Amyot, Jacques
    1960   The Chinese Community of Manila: A Study of
            Adaptation of Chinese Familism to the Philippine
            Environment. Research Series Monographs, No. 2,
            Philippine Study Program, University of Chicago.

Anderson, Charles W.
    1967   Politics and Economic Change in Latin America. Princeton:
            D. Van Nostrand Company, Inc..

Aubey, Robert T.
    1969   Entrepreneurial Formation in El Salvador.
            Explorations in Entrepreneurial History 6 (3):268-285.

Aubey, Robert, John Kyle and Arnold Strickon
    1974   Investment Behavior and Elite Social Structures in
            Latin America. Journal of Interamerican Studies
            and World Affairs 19 (1):73-96.

Bailey, F. G.
    1962   The Scope of Social Anthropology in the Study of
            Indian Society. In Indian Anthropology Essays in
            Honor of D.N. Majumdar. T. N. Madan and Gopala
            Sarana, Eds. Bombay/New York: Asia Publishing House.

    1967   Strategems and Spoils: A Social Anthropology of
            Politics. New York: Schocken.

Banton, M.
    1957   West African City. London: Oxford University Press for
            International African Institute.

Barnes, J. A.
    1954   Class and Committees in a Norwegian Island Parish.
            Human Relations 7:39-58.

    1969   Networks and Political Process. In Social Network in
            Urban Situations. Clyde Mitchell, Ed. Manchester:
            Manchester University Press. pp. 51-74.

Barnett, Milton J.
1955   Alcoholism in the Cantonese of New York City.
        In Etiology of Chronic Alcoholism. O. Diethlen, Ed.
        Madison: University of Wisconsin Press. pp. 179-227.

1960   Kinship as a Factor Affecting Cantonese Economic
        Adaptation in the United States. Human
        Organization XIX:40-60.
Barth, Fredrik
1963   The Role of the Entrepreneur in Social Change
        in Northern Norway. Bergen: Arbok for Universiteteti
        Bergen 3.

1966   Models of Social Organization. Royal Anthropological
        Institute Occasional Paper No. 23. Glasgow:
        University Press.

1967   On the Study of Social Change. American Anthropologist
        69:661-669.

1969   Ethnic Groups and Boundaries. Oslo: Universitetesforlaget.

Barth, Gunther Paul
1964   Bitter Strength: A History of the Chinese in the
        United States, 1850-1870. Cambridge: Harvard
        University Press.

Beaudry, J. A.
1966   Acculturation and Assimilation: Chinese Professionals
        in Upstate New York. Ph. D Dissertation. Ann Arbor:
        University Microfilms.

Beck, L.
1898   New York's Chinatown. New York: Bohemia Publishing Co..

Belshaw, Cyril S.
1955   The Cultural Milieu of the Entrepreneur: a Critical
        Essay. Explorations in Entrepreneurial History
        7 (3): 146-163.

1967   Theoretical Problems in Economic Anthropology. In
        Social Organization. Maurice Freedman, Ed.
        Chicago: Aldine Publishing Co. pp. 25-42.

Bennedict, Burton
1968   Family Firms and Economic Development. Southwestern
        Journal of Anthropology 24 (1): 1-19.

Bennett, John W.
    1969   Northern Plainsmen. Chicago: Aldine Publishing Co..

Bennett, John W. and Iwao Ishino
    1963   Paternalism in the Japanese Economy. Minneapolis:
            University of Minnesota Press.

Berger, Mike
    1957   New York Chinatown. Fiftieth Anniversary.
            New York: Chinese Chamber of Commerce.

Boissevain, Jeremy
    1966   Patronage in Sicily. Man 1 (1): 18-23.

    1969   Patrons as Brokers. Sociologische Gids XVI (6):
            379-386.

Boonsanong, Punyodyana
    1971   Chinese-Thai Differential Assimilation in Bangkok.
            Ithaca: Coernell University.

Boswell, D. M.
    1969   Personal Crises and the Mobilization of the Social
            Network. In Social Networks in Urban Situations.
            Clyde Mitchell, Ed. Manchester: Manchester
            University Press. pp. 245-287.

Briggs, Jean
    1971   Strategies of Perception: The Management of
            Ethnic Identity. In Patrons and Brokers in the
            East Artic. Robert Paine, Ed. Newfoundland:
            Institute of Social and Economic Research.
            pp. 56-73.

Broom, Leonard and John Kitsuse
    1953   The Validation of Acculturation: A Condition of
            Ethnic Assimilation. American Anthropologist
            LVII: 44-48.

Campbell, J. K.
    1964   Honour, Family and Patronage. Oxford: Clarendon Press.

Cattell, Stuart H.
    1962   Health, Welfare and Social Organization in
            Chinatown, New York City. New York: Community Service
            Society.

arroll, John
1965   The Philippine Manufacturing Entrepreneur:
        Agent and Product of Change. Ithaca: Cornell University
        Press.

hen, Ta
1923   Chinese Migration with Special Reference to Labour
        Conditions. United States Bureau of Labour
        Statistics, No.340.

1940   Emigrant Communities in South China. New York:
        Institute of Pacific Relations.

heng, David Te-Chao
1948   Acculturation of the Chinese in the U.S.: A
        Philadelphia Study. Foochow, China.

hinatown Health Project
1970   Chinatown Health Project Report, (Manuscript).
        New York: Basement Workshop Inc..

hinatown Study Group
1969   Chinatown Study Group Report, (Manuscript).
        New York: Basement Workshop Inc..

The China Times
1972-4 The China Times (a Daily Newspaper). Vols. 9-11.
        New York: The Mei Kuo Publishing Co..

hinese American Restaurant Association of Greater New York
1963   30th Anniversary Journal of the Chinese American
        Restaurant Association of Greater New York.
        New York.

1965   32nd Anniversary Journal of the Chinese American
        Restaurant Association of Greater New York. New York.

1969   By-Laws of the Chinese American Restaurant Association
        of Greater New York, Inc. (Amended and Revised).
        New York.

1973   60th Anniversary Journal of the Chinese American
        Restaurant Association of Greater New York. New York.

Chinese Cahmber of Commerce
1970   Chamber News. New York.

1966   The 60th Annieversay Journal of the Chinese Chamber
        of Commerce of New York, Inc.. New York.

Chinese Garment Makers Association
    1969   Fifth Anniversary. New York.

Chinese Laundry Association
    1970   37th Anniversary of the Chinese Laundry Association.
            New York.

Chu, H.
    1973   The History of the Associations and Societies
            of the Chinese in the United States, (Manuscripts).
            New York.

Chung, Wen-hui
    1952   Changing Social-Cultural Patterns of the Chinese
            Community in Los Angeles. Los Angeles: University
            of Southern California.

Chrisman, Noel
    1970   Situation and Social Network in Cities.
            The Canadian Review of Sociology and
            Anthropology 7 (4): 245-257.

Cochran, Thomas and Rubene Reina
    1962   Entrepreneurship in Argentine Culture. Philadelphia:
            University of Pennsylvania Press.

Coughlin, Richard J.
    1955   The Chinese in Bangkok: A Commercial Oriented Minority.
            American Sociological Review XX (June): 311-316.

Consolidated Chinese Benevolent Association
    1948   By-Laws of the Consolidated Chinese Benevolent
            Association, (Revised Edition). New York.

Coolidge, Mary Roberts
    1969   Chinese Immigration. New York: Arno Press and the
            New York Times.

Coombs, Gary
    1973   Networks and Exchange: The Role of Social Relationships
            in a Small Voluntary Association. Journal of
            Anthropological Research 29 (2): 96-112.

Comber, Leon
    1957   An Intorudction to Chinese Secret Societies in
            Malaya. Singapore: D. Moore.

327

Crissman, Lawrence W.
    1967   The Segmentary Structure of Urban Overseas Chinese
            Communities. Man 2: 185-204.

Culin, Stewart
    1890   Customs of the Chinese in America. Journal of
            American Folklore III (10): 191-200.

    1891   Social Organization of the Chinese in America.
            American Anthropologist, October, pp. 347-352.

    1970   The I Hing or Patriotic Rising. San Francisco: R and
            E Research Associates.

Danton, George H.
    1931   The Culture Contacts of the United States and
            China. New York: Columbia University Press.

Davenport, W.
    1960   Jamaica Fishing: A Game Theory Analysis.
            Yale University Publications in Anthropology 59.
            New Haven: Yale University Press.

Desai, R. H.
    1965   The Family and Business Enterpise among the
            Asians in East Africa. In East African Institute of
            Social Research Papers, January, 1965. Section C -
            Sociology and Anthropology. pp. 1-6. Kampala.

Dirks, Robert
    1972   Networks, Groups, and Adaptation in an Afro-Caribean
            Community. Man 7 (4): 565-585.

Eng Ying Gong and Bruce Grant
    1930   Tong War. New York: Nicholas L. Brown.

Epstein, A. L.
    1969   The Network and Urban Social Organization. In Social
            Networks in Urban Situations. Clyde Mitchell, Ed.
            Manchester: Manchester University Press. pp. 51-74.

Fallers, L.A. (Ed.)
    1967   Immigrants and Associations. The Hague: Mouton.

Farrar, Nancy
    1972   The Chinese in El Paso. El Paso: Texas Western Press.

Farwell, Willard B.
    1970   The Chinese at Home and Abroad. San Francisco: R and E
            Research Associates.

Feng, Han-yi
    1937   The Chinese Kinship System. Cambridge: Harvard
            University Press.

Firth, Raymond (Ed.)
    1967   Themes in Economic Anthropology. London: Tavistock.

Firth, Raymond and B. S. Yamey (Ed.)
    1964   Capital, Saving and Credit in Peasant Societies.
            Chicago: Aldine Publishing Co..

Fong, Stanley L. M.
    1965   Assimilation of Chinese in America: Changes in
            Orientation and Social Perception. American Journal
            of Sociology 71 (November): 265-273.

Foster, George
    1961   Interpersonal Relations in Peasant Society.
            Human Organization XIX: 174-175.

    1963a   The Dyadic Contract: A Model for the Social
            Structure of a Mexican Peasant Village. American
            Anthropologist 63: 1173-1192.

    1963b   The Dyadic Contract in Tzintzuntzan, II: Patron-Client
            Relationship. American Anthropologist 65: 1280-1294.

    1967   Tzintzuntzan: Mexican Peasants in a Changing World.
            Boston: Little, Brown and Co.

Frankel, M.
    1964   Tribe and Class in Monrovia. London: Oxford University
            Press.

Freedman, Maurice
    1957   Chinese Family and Marriage in Singapore. London: Her
            Majesty's Stationary Office.

    1958   Lineage Organization in Southeastern China. London: The
            Athlone Press.

    1960   Immigrants and Associations: Chinese in Nineteenth
            Century Singapore. Comparative Studies in Society and
            History III: 25-48.

    1963   A Chinese Phase in Social Anthropology. British Journal
            of Sociology 14: 1-9.

1964 What Social Science Can Do For Chinese Studies.
Journal of Asian Studies XXIII (4): 523-529.

Freedman, Maurice (Ed.)
1970 Family and Kinship in Chinese Society.
Stanford: Stanford University Press.

Freeman, Maurice and William Willmott
1961 Southeast Asia, with Special Reference to the
Chinese. International Social Science Journal XIII (2):
245-270.

Fried, Morton
1956 Fabric of Chinese Society. London: Atlantic Press.

_____ (Ed.)
1958 Colloquium on Overseas Chinese. New York: Institute
of Pacific Relations.

Geertz, Clifford
1960 The Javanese Kijaji: The Changing Role of a Cultural
Broker. Comparative Studies in Sociology and History
2 (2): 228-249.

1963 The Integrative Revolution. In Old Societies and
New States. Clifford Geertz, Ed. New York:
Free Press. pp. 105-157.

Glade, William
1967 Approaches to a Theory of Entrepreneurial
Formation. Exploration in Entrepreneurial History
4 (3): 245-259.

Glazer, Nathan
1954 Ethnic Groups in America: From National Culture to
Ideology. In Freedom and Control in Modern Society.
Morrow Berge, Theodore Abel and Charles H. Page,
Eds. New York: Octagon Books Inc.. pp. 158-173.

1971 The Limits of Social Policy. Commentary 1971
(September):51-58.

Glick, Carl
1941 Shake Hands with the Dragon. New York: Whittlesey House.

1945 Double Ten, Captain O'Banion's Story of the Chinese
Revolution. New York: Whittlesey House.

Gluckman, Max (Ed.)
    1964   Closed Systems and Open Minds: The Limits of
            Naivety in Social Anthropology. London: Oliver and
            Boyd.

Gordon, Milton M.
    1964   Assimilation in American Life. New York: Oxford
            University Press.

Gould, Peter R.
    1969   Man Against his Environment: A Game Theoretic Framwork. In
            Environment and Cultural Behavior. Andres P. Vayda, Ed.
            Garden City: The Natural History Press. pp. 234-251.

Greeley, Andrew M.
    1971   Why Can't They be Like Us? New York: E. P. Dutton & Co..

    1972   That Most Distressful Nation. Chicago: Quadrangle Books.

Gulliver, P. H.
    1971   Neighbours and Networks. Berkeley: University of
            California Press.

Hager, Everett
    1962   On the Theory of Social Change. Homewood: Dorsey Press.

Handlin, Oscar
    1953   Uprooted. Boston: Little, Brown and Co..

Hart, Robert, Adam Krivsty and William Stubee
    1968   Chinatown New York: A Report on the Conditions and
            Needs of a Unique Community. New York.

Henriksen, Georg
    1971   The Transactional Basis of Influence: White Men
            Among Naskapi Indians. In Patrons and Brokers
            in the East Arctic. Robert Paine, Ed. Newfoundland:
            Institute of Social and Economic Research.

Heyer, Virginia
    1953   Patterns of Social Organization in New York's
            Chinatown. Ph. D.Dissertation. Ann Arbor:
            University Microfilms.

Ho Ming Chung
    1959   Overseas Chinese Enterprises in South America.
            Taipei: Chung Kuo Chiu Chin She Hui.

Ho Ming Chung
    1967   Manual de la Colonia China. Lima: Man Shing Po Press.

Horowitz, Michael M.
    1967   A Decision Making Model of Conjugal Pattern in
            Martinique. Man 2:245-453.

Hoselitz, Bert F.
    1963   Entreprenuership and Traditional Elites.
            Explorations in Entrepreneurial History 1: 36-49.

Howard, A.
    1963   Land Activity and Decision-Making Models in
            Rotuna. Ethnology 2:407-440.

Hoy, William
    1942   The Chinese Six Companies. San Francisco.

Hu, Shien-chin
    1944   The Chinese Concept of Face. American Anthropologist
            46: 45-64.

    1948   The Common Descent Group in China. New York: Viking
            Fund Publications.

Huck, Arthur
    1968   The Chinese in Australia. Melbourne: Longmans.

    1971   The Assimilation of the Chinese in Australia.
            Canberra: Australian National University Press.

Hsu, Francis L. K.
    1971   The Challenge of the American Dream. Belmont:
            Wadsworth Publishing Co.

Ianni, Francis A.
    1972   A Family Business. New York: Russell Sage Foundation.

Immigration and Naturalization Service
    1930   Annual Report. Washington D.C.: U. S. Department of
            Justice.

    1972   Annural Report. Washington D.C.: U. S. Department of
            Justice.

Kapferer, B.
    1969   Norms and the Manipulation of Relationships in a
            Work Context. In Social Networks in Urban
            Situations. Clyde Mitchell, Ed. Manchester:
            Manchester University Press. pp. 184-240.

Keesing, R.
1967   Statistical Models and Decision Models of Social
        Structure: A Kwaio Case. Ethnology 6: 1-6.

Kenny, Michael
1960   Patterns of Patronage in Spain. Anthropological
        Quarterly 33 (1): 14-23.

Khuri, F.
1965   Kinship, Emigration and Trade Partnership Among the
        Lebanese of West Africa. Africa 35 (4): 285-295.

Knowles, Louis and Kenneth Presitt (Eds.)
1969   Institutional Racism in America. Englewood Cliffs:
        Prentice-Hall Inc.

Kramer, Judith R.
1970   The American Minority Community. New York: Thomas
        Y. Crowell Co.

Kung, S. W.
1962   Chinese in American Life: Some Aspects of Their
        History, Status, Problems and Contributions.
        Seattle: University of Washington Press.

Lai, Vivien
1971   The New Chinese Immigrants in Toronto. In
        Immigrant Groups. Jean Leonard Elliot, Ed.
        Scarborough, Ontario: Prentice-Hall of Canada.
        pp. 120-140.

Lande, Carl
1965   Leaders, Factions and Parties - the Structure of
        Philippine Politics. New Haven: Yale University
        Southeast Asian Studies Monograph No. 6.

Lang, Olga
1946   The Chinese Family and Society. New Haven: Yale
        University Press.

Lee, Calvin B.
1965   Chinatown, U.S.A. Garden City: Doubleday.

Lee, David T.
1967   A History of Chinese in Canada. Vancouver: Ka Na Dai
        Chi Yau Press.

333

Lee, James
   1972a   The Story of the New York Chinese Consolidated
          Benevolent Association. Bridge Magazine 1 (5): 15-18.

   1972b   The Chinese Benevolent Association: An Assessment,
          Part II. Bridge Magazine 1 (6): 15-47.

Lee, Rose Hum
   1949a   Chinese Dilemma. Phylon (Second Quarter 1949): 195-202.

   1949b   Research on Chinese Family. American Journal of
          Sociology 54(May): 497-504.

   1956   The Chinese Abroad. Phylon (Third Quarter 1956):
          257-270.

   1960   The Chinese in the United States of America.
          Hong Kong: Hong Kong University Press.

Leeds, Anthony
   1964   Brazilian Careers and Social Structure: An
          Evolutionary Model and Case History. American
          Anthropologist 66: 1321-1347.

Leong, Gor Yun
   1936   Chinatown Inside Out. New York: Barrows Mussey.

Levy, Marion J.
   1949   The Rise of the Modern Chinese Business Class.
          New York: Institute of Pacific Relations.

Levi-Strauss, Claude
   1953   Social Structure. In Anthropology Today.
          A. L. Kroeber, Ed. Chicago: University of Chicago Press.

Lewis, Herbert S.
   1974   Neighbors, Friends, and Kinsmen: Principles of Social
          Organization Among the Cushitic-speaking Peoples
          of Ethiopia. Ethnology XIII (2): 145-157.

Liang, Yuan
   1951   The Chinese Family in Chicago. Unpublished
          Master's Thesis. Chicago: University of Chicago.

Light, Ivan H.
   1972   Ethnic Enterprise in America. Berkeley: University
          of California Press.

334

Little, Kenneth
    1957   The Role of Voluntary Associations in West African
            Urbanization. American Anthropologist 59(4): 576-596.

Loewen, James W.
    1971   The Mississippi Chinese. Cambridge: Harvard
            University Press.

Lowe, Chuan-hua
    1972   The Chinese in Hawaii: A Bibliographic Survey.
            Taipei.

Lui, Garding
    1948   Inside Los Angeles Chinatown. Los Angeles.

Lyman, Stanford M.
    1961   The Structure of Chinese Society in Nineteenth-century
            America. Ph. D. Dissertation. Berkeley: Library
            Photographic Service, University of California.

    1964   Chinese Secret Societies in the Occident.
            The Canadian Review of Sociology and Anthropology
            1(2): 79-102.

    1968   Contrast in the Community Organization of Chinese
            and Japanese in North America. The Canadian
            Review of Sociology and Anthropology 5(2): 1-17.

Lyman, Stanford and William Douglas
    1973   Ethnicity: Strategies of Collective and Individual
            Impression Management. Social Research 40(2): 345-365.

Mangin, William
    1965   The Role of Regional Associations in the Adaptation
            of Rural Migrants to Cities in Peru. In Contemporary
            Cultures and Societies of Latin America. Dwight B.
            Health and Richard N. Adams, Eds. New York: Random
            House.

Mayer, Adrian C.
    1966   The Significance of Quasi-groups in the Study of
            Complex Societies. In The Social Anthropology of
            Complex Societies. Michael Banton, Ed. London:
            Tavistock. pp. 97-122.

    1967   Patrons and Brokers: Rural Leadership in Four
            Overseas Indian Communities. Social Organization.
            Maurice Freedman, Ed. Chicago: Aldine Publishing
            Co. pp. 167-188.

Mayer, Philip
    1961   Townsmen or Tribesmen. Cape Town: Oxford University
            Press.

McCleland, David
    1961   Achieving Society. New Jersey: D. Van Nostrand.

McCarthy, Charles
    1971   Philippine-Chinese Integration. Manila: Pagkakaisa
            Pagunlad.

Miller, Stuart Creighton
    1969   The Unwelcome Immigrant. Berkeley and Los Angeles:
            University of California Press.

Mintz, Sidney W. and Eric R. Wolf
    1950   An Analysis of Ritual Co-Parenthood (Compadrazgo).
            Southwestern Journal of Anthropology 6: 341-368.

Mitchell, Clyde (Ed.)
    1969   Social Networks in Urban Situations. Manchester:
            Manchester University Press.

Morris, H. S.
    1956   Indians in East Africa. British Journal of Sociology
            1956: 144-211.

    1968   The Indians in Urganda. Chicago: University of Chicago
            Press.

Morse, Hosea B.
    1918   The International Relations of the Chinese
            Empire. London: Longman, Green and Co..

Myrdal, Gunnar
    1944   The American Dilemma. New York: Harper Bros..

New York Magazine
    1971   New York Magazine 4(39): 35-59.

Ng, Kwee Choo
    1968   The Chinese in London. London: Oxford University
            Press.

Novak, Michael
    1972   The Rise of the Unmeltable Ethnics. New York:
            Macmillan Co.

Ohnuki, Emiko
    1964   The Detroit Chinese: A Study of Socio-cultural
             Changes in the Detroit Chinese Community from
             1872-1963. Master Thesis. Madison: University of
             Wisconsin.

Overseas Chinese Economy Year Books of 1969, 1970, 1971, 1972,
1973. Taipei: Overseas Chinese Economy Year Book Editorial
Committee.

Owens, Raymond
    1972   The Anthropological Study of Entrepreneurship. In
             Anthropological Approaches to the Study of a
             Complex Society. Agrawal, Ed. New Delhi: Indian
             Academy of Social Sciences. pp. 75-95.

Paine, Robert
    1967   What is Gossip About? Man 2: 278-285

—————— (Ed.)
    1971   Patrons and Brokers in the East Arctic.
             Newfoundland: Institute of Social and Economic
             Research, Memorial University of Newfoundland.

Park, R. E.
    1926   Behind Our Masks. Survey Graphic 56: 135-139.

Plotinicov, Leonard
    1967   Strangers to the City: Urban Man in Jos, Nigeria.
             Pittsburgh: University of Pittsburgh Press.

Purcell, Victor
    1965   The Chinese in Southeast Asia. London: Oxford
             University Press.

Rausbenbush, Winifred
    1926a   Their Place in the Sun. The Survey Graphic
             LVI (3): 141-145.

    1926b   The Great Wall of Chinatown. The Survey
             Graphic LVI (3): 154-158.

Rowell, Chester
    1909   Chinese and Japanese Immigrants - a Comparison.
             Annals of the American Academy of Political and
             Social Science XXIV (2): 233-260.

Sahlins, Marschall
1965   On the Sociology of Primitive Exchange.
         In The Relevance of Models for Social Anthropology.
         Michael Banton, Ed. London: Tavistock. pp. 139-236.

Sandmeyer, Elmer Clarence
1939   The Anti-Chinese Movement in California.
         Urbana: The University of Illinois Press.

Scharfstein, Ben-Ami
1974   The Mind of China. New York: Basic Books.

Schumpeter, Joseph
1961   The Theory of Economic Development. London:
         Oxford University Press.

Schwartz, Shepherd
1948   Chinese Population in New York City. Unpublished
         documents, Columbia University Research in
         Contemporary Cultures. New York: Columbia University.

Scott, James C.
1972   The Erosion of Patron-Client Bonds and Social Change
         in Rural Southeast Asia. Journal of Asian Studies
         XXXII (2): 5-37.

Seward, George F.
1881   Chinese Immigration. New York: Charles Scribner's
         Sons.

Silverman, Sydel F.
1965   Patronage and Community-Nation Relationships in
         Central Italy. Ethnology 4: 172-189.

Simmel, George
1955   The Web of Group Affiliations. New York: The Free Press.

Simpson, George E. and Milton Singer
1958   Racial and Cultural Minorities: An Analysis of
         Prejudice and Discrimination. New York: Harper
         Bros.

Siu, Paul
1952   The Sojourner. American Journal of Sociology
         VIII (July): 32-44.

1944   The Isolation of the Chinese Laundryman. In
         Contributions to Urban Sociology. Ernest W. Burgess
         and Donald Bogue, Eds. Chicago: University of Chicago
         Press. pp. 429-440.

Skinner, George
    1957   Chinese Society in Thailand: An Analytical History.
            Ithaca: Cornell University Press.

    1958   Leadership and Power in the Chinese Community
            of Thailand. Ithaca: Cornell University Press.

Smith, William C.
    1925   Changing Personality Traits of Second Generation
            Orientals in America. American Journal of Sociology
            33 (May): 922-929.

    1928   The Second Generation Oriental American. Journal
            of Applied Sociology 10: 160-168.

Strickon, Arnold
    1967   Folk Models of Stratification, Political Ideology,
            and Socio-Cultural Systems. Sociological Review
            Monograph 11: 93-117.

    1969   Traditional and Modern Systems of Stratification
            in Argentina. Paper read at the Wenner-Gren
            Symposium on Traditional Systems of Stratification,
            June 16-20, 1969.

    1972   Carols Felipe: Kinsman, Patron, and Friend. In
            Structure and Process in. Latin America. Arnold
            Strickon and Sidney Greenfield, Eds. Albuquerque:
            University of New Mexico Press. pp. 43-69.

Strickon, Arnold and Sidney Greenfield, (Eds.)
    1972   Structure and Process in Latin America.
            Albuquerque: University of New Mexico Press.

Stuart, William T.
    1972   The Explanation of Patron-Client Systems: Some
            Structural And Ecological Perspectives. In
            Structure and Process in Latin America.
            Arnold Strickon and Sidney Greenfield, Eds.
            Albuquerque: University of New Mexico Press. pp. 19-42.

Sung, Betty Lee
    1967   Mountain of Gold. New York: Macmillan.

Tien, Ju-kang
    1953   The Chinese of Sarawak. London: London School of
            Economics and Political Science.

Timberg, Thomas A.
1969   Industrial Entrepreneurship Among Trading
        Communities of India. Paper presented at the
        Fifth Annual Bengali Studies Conference, Urbana,
        Illinois, May 15-17, 1969.

Topley, M.
1964   Capital, Saving and Credit Among Indigeneous
        Rice Farmers and Immigrant Vegetable Farmers in
        Hong Kong's New Territories. In Capital, Saving
        and Credit in Peasant Societies. Raymond Firth and
        B.S. Yamey, Eds. Chicago: Aldine Publishing
        Co. pp. 157-186.

1967   The Emergence and Social Functions of Chinese
        Religious Associations in Singapore. In
        Immigrants and Associations. L.A. Fallers, Ed.
        The Hague: Mouton. pp. 49-82.

Tsien Tche-hao
1967   The Social Life of the Chinese in Madagascar.
        In Immigrants and Associations. L.A. Fallers, Ed.
        The Hague: Mouton. pp. 87-102.

United States Census of Population
1940   Characteristics of the Non-White Population by
        Race. U.S. Department of Commerce.

1950   Characteristics of the Non-White Population by
        Race. U.S. Department of Commerce.

1957   Special Census of New York City. U.S. Department
        of Commerce.

1960   General Social and Economic Characteristics of
        New York. U.S. Department of Commerce.

1970   General Social and Economic Characteristics of
        New York. U.S. Department of Commerce.

1970   Japanese, Chinese and Filipinos in the United States.
        U.S. Department of Commerce.

Van Norden, Warner M.
1918   Who's Who of the Chinese in New York. New York.

Weber, Max
1958   The Protestant Ethic and the Spirit of Capitalism.
        New York: Charles Scribner's Sons.

340

Weingrod, Alex
  1968   Patrons, Patronage, and Political Parties.
          Comparative Studies in Society and History 10: 1142-1158.

Willmott, Donald Earl
  1960   The Chinese of Semarang: A Changing Minority Community
          in Indonesia. Ithaca: Cornell University Press.

Willmott, William E.
  1964   Chinese Clan Associations in Vancouver.
          Man LXIV (49): 33-37.

  1967   The Chinese in Cambodia. Vancourver: Publications
          Centre, University of British Columbia.

  1970   The Political Structure of the Chinese Community
          in Cambodia. London: Athlone Press.

Wirth, Louis
  1945   The Problems of Minority Groups. In The Science of
          Man in the World Crises. Ralph Linton, Ed.
          New York: Columbia University Press. pp. 347-372.

Wheeldon, P. D.
  1969   The Operation of Voluntary Associations and Personal
          Networks in the Political Processes of an Inter-Ethnic
          Community. In Social Networks in Urban Situations.
          Clyde Mitchell, Ed. Manchester: Manchester University
          Press. pp. 128-174.

Wolf, Eric
  1951   Closed Corporate Peasant Communities in Mesoamerica and
          Central Java. Southwestern Journal of Anthropology
          13: 1-8.

  1956   Aspects of Group Relations in a Complex Society: Mexico.
          American Anthropologist 58: 1065-1078.

  1966   Kinship, Friendship, and Patron-Client Relations
          in Complex Societies. In The Social Anthropology of
          Complex Societies. Michael Banton, Ed. London:
          Tavistock. pp. 1-35.

Wolfe, Alvin W.
  1970   On Structural Comparisons of Networks. The Canadian
          Review of Sociology and Anthropology 7 (4): 226-244.

341

Wong, Bernard
    1971   Chinese in Lima. Manuscript. Fieldwork Report
            Submitted to Ibero-American Studies Program.
            University of Wisconsin-Madison.

    1972   Social Stratification in the Chinese Community of
            Lima. Manuscript. Madison.

Wong, Jade Snow
    1950   Fifth Chinese Daughter. New York: Harper Bros.

Ward, Barbara E.
    1965   Varieties of the Conscious Model: The Fisherman of
            South China. In The Relevance of Models for Social
            Anthropology. Michael Banton, Ed. London: Tavistock.
            pp. 113-137.

Wu, Cheng-tsu
    1958   Chinese and Chinatown in New York City. Ph. D.
            Dissertation. Ann Arbor: University Microfilms.

    _____ (Ed.)
    1972   "Chink!" - A Documentary History of Anti-Chinese
            Prejudice in America. New York: World Publications.

Wu, Shang-ying
    1954   Mei-kuo Hua Chau Pai Nien Chi Shih (One Hundred
            Years of Chinese in the United States and
            Canada). Hong Kong.

Wynne, Robert E.
    1964   Reaction to the Chinese in the Pacific Northwest
            and British Columbia, 1850-1910. Ph.D Dissertation.
            Ann Arbor: University Microfilms.

Yin, Robert K. (Ed.)
    1973   Race, Creed, Color or National Origin.
            Ithaca, Illinois: F. E. Peacock Publishers Inc..

Yuan, D. Y.
    1963   Voluntary Segregation: A Study of New York Chinatown.
            Phylon XXIV (3): 255-268.

    1966   Chinatown and Beyond: The Chinese Population in
            Metropolitan New York. Phylon XXVII (4): 321-332.

Instrumental goals, 229

International Ladies Garment Workers Union, 187

Jang, 139

Juk sing, 67

Juvenile delinquent, 38, 47

Kam ching (Sentimental warmth), 12, 115, 139, 191, 202

Kiu ling (Leaders of the overseas Chinese), 8, 68, 75, 111-112, 133, 136, 142, 146, 149-152, 160, 199, 204-205
    as patrons, 307

Kuomintang, 101, 109, 180

Labor unions, 187-188

Laundry Alliance, 89, 103-105

Lee, Ah-bow, 30, 31

Legal proof, 247

Lingual franca, 41

Lion's Club of Chinatown, 184

Lo wah kiu (Old overseas Chinese), 67, 68, 75

Lo pan (owners), 72

Low income, 172, 173

Mahjong, 235

Mid-Autumn Festival, 68

Middle income, 172-7

Min Chih Tang, 110

Nakama system, 216

National Origins Act, 157

New immigrants, 193-196

Nixon's visit to China, 167

Office of Economic Opportunity, 162

On Leong Association, 109, 140

Partnership firm, 122-123

Patron, 148
    definition, 10

Patron-client relations, 8, 9, 10
    changed nature of, 189, 190

Patronage, 198

People's Republic of China, 70, 259

Personal set, 198

Population increase, 159

Prestation, 11, 12, 207

Quota Act of 1924, 156

Refugee Act of 1953, 156

Regional Associations, 97-101

Ritual-parenthood, 233

Role system set, 198

Rules of propriety, 271